THE GIFT OF TRUTH

THE GIFT OF TRUTH

GATHERING THE GOOD

STEPHEN DAVID ROSS

STATE UNIVERSITY OF NEW YORK PRESS

Published by
State University of New York Press, Albany

© 1997 State University of New York

Printed in the United States of America

For information, address State University of New York Press,
State University Plaza, Albany, N.Y., 12246

Production by Marilyn Semerad
Marketing by Bernadette LaManna

Library of Congress Cataloging-in-Publication Data

Ross, Stephen David.
    The gift of truth : gathering the good / Stephen David Ross.
        p.   cm.
    Includes bibliographical references and index.
    ISBN 0-7914-3267-X (alk. paper). — ISBN 0-7914-3268-8 (pbk. :
alk. paper)
    1. Truth. 2. Ontology. 3. Knowledge, Theory of. I. Title.
BD171.R69   1997
111'.84—dc20   96-38789
                                                              CIP

10 9 8 7 6 5 4 3 2 1

Contents

respond without limit. Touch, exposure, interruption. Aristotle, desire to know beyond any limit. Nietzsche, will to truth. Anaximander, restitution for injustice. Truth as restitution; responsiveness and responsibility. Something beyond knowledge and truth calls us to truth, endless questioning of truth. Habermas, normativity and validity claims. The good in trust, exceeding norms and measures.

Plato and the good. Diotima's speech on love describing "nature of wondrous beauty." Beyond all binary oppositions. Nature's abundance. Love intermediary figure interrupting gathering of being. Interruption with Irigaray; angels intermediary figures, engendered figures of crossings. Mucus embodied, threshold figure. Socrates' denial that he knows, possesses truth. Knowing what one does not know; obligation to know. Truth's authority. Divine gifts in Plato. Madness in *Phaedrus*. *Poiēsis, mimēsis* interrupting rule of *technē*. Socrates' unlimited desire for wisdom.

Theaetetus and definition of knowledge. Socrates and mother, Phaenarete, midwives, barren themselves. Infinite regress of knowledge, being. Midwife's art given from gods. Figures of women as midwives, intermediary figures. Irigaray and angels always on the move. Socrates as stinging fly, as stingray. Always on the move. Meno's paralysis by Socrates, obligation to restore movement. Birth, generation, *poiēsis*, gifts and giving. Being's abundance, heterogeneity, beyond measure. Inexhaustible movement of truth and knowledge, resisting closure. Knowledge as perception, memory. *Anamnēsis*, recollection, endless pursuit. Living memory. Truth and *mimēsis*. Memory as possession, repetition; memory as *anamnēsis*, circulation and interruption, wound of forgetting, disaster, loss. Truth not possession but endless movement toward abundance.

Aristotle and desire for truth. Deleuze and Guattari and schizoanalysis. Desire turns back on itself, beyond itself, in intermediary movement. Aristotle's bat. Aristotle and use of animals by human beings. Unmoved mover. Carlo Sini and truth. Sini on Aristotle. Truth and saying. Bats and

and *involvit* material, embodied, figures. Truth and bodies, embodied truth. Nature one individual made up of infinite parts varying in infinite ways, all bodies. Nature's abundance. *Conatus, potentia,* striving and power throughout nature. Hatred of strangers, nation and class. Hate destroyed by love. External causes overpower us with contingency, free in relation to God. Use of animals. Exclusion of women from ethics. Inadequate ideas and adequate ideas. Relation to bodies. Eternity of mind, eternity of bodies. Double register of truth.

Hobbes, Locke, and Hume: truth in words not things. Swift and Lagado. Wittgenstein and the totality of facts. Truth and authority. Two kinds of philosophy. Reason's war against superstition. Adversarial view of truth. Mill and pluralistic truth. Truth and ethical|political authority. Repetition in Hume. Iterability. Repetition of repetition. Memory and experience. Memory and loss. Regularity of experience. Custom and habit. Liberty and necessity.

Hume and miracles. Rational authority and repetition. Political figures of epistemic authority. Human differences and repetitions. Communication and shared experience. Liberty and necessity. Whitehead and freedom. Hume and human universality. Singular events. Truth's authority. Bataille and miracles. Hume's skepticism. Darker side of experience. Truth without authority in Dewey and Whitehead.

Kant, truth as accordance. Impossibility of universal test of truth. Ethical|political figures of reason. Tower to heaven. Authority of ethics and religion. Safety and land of truth. Kant's ethical|political| architectural| territorial project. Transcendental use *(Gebrauch)* of a concept ethical| political. Hegel and truth. Sini's reading of Hegel on truth. Truth as the whole. Truth as development. Hegel and animals. Universality. Death. Individuals and kinds. Hegel and the Good. Identity and difference of identity and difference. The good as interruption. Circles of circles. Repetition, memory, and loss. Authority and the good.

Heidegger and *alētheia,* essence of truth. Truth as untruth. Truth as agreement. Sini's reading of Heidegger. Sovereignty in name of truth, over animals and plants. Truth as freedom. Comportment *(Verhalten).* Letting-be *(sein lassen). Brauch,* usage, ethical|political. The good as ek-stasis, otherwise. Freedom as exposure. Truth as mystery of being as whole. Being and the gift, the gift and giving. Errancy and error. Sheltering. Unconcealment and concealment. *Dasein* and guilt, recalling the good. Sini and enchantment, enchantment and the Same. Anarchy of music and song. Ari does not see but hears. Penelope waiting. Ari short for Ariadne, women and touch. Letting-be resists authority of being. Interrupted by Irigaray and woman without a place. Angels and intermediary figures. Supposing truth is a woman.

Nietzsche supposes truth is a woman. Truth and life are women. Women wear the veil, truth unveils. Nietzsche says hateful things of women. Man creates image of woman. Interruption by Irigaray, under water, Nietzsche's marine lover. Another interruption, Kristeva's "foreigner." Truth and strangeness. Truth and strangers. Together with women. Women and music. *Stabat Mater.* Man—or woman—without qualities. Music, woman, and the Dionysian. Woman is castration, wound. Women and Jews. Truth is woman is artist is Jew is lie is love. Suppose truth were bat or spider or frog. Suppose truth were never what we take it to be. Woman, truth, and animals fluid and indeterminate figures. Truth and masks. Shallowness and depth. Capitalism and commodities; women as possessions. Life as woman, remembering Jews, Europe's oppressed. Remembering and forgetting disaster. Woman and forgetting of truth. Staying on top with truth. Women's pudendum, shame. Women ornament themselves; Jews are actors. Suppose truth were nomadic, of the earth, not human. Truth and woman cannot be possessed, though they may be coerced. Sea as figure of fluidity and abundance. Woman and abundance.

Truth gathered in *legein.* Singularity unreachable, beyond the gathering of being. Levinas. Subjectivity and singularity. Subjectivity and animality. Irigaray and air. Mucus. Exposure and fecundity. Foucault and prose of world. Signatures as interruptions. Levinas and responsibility for the other.

Subjectivity. Glory of infinite. Witness and betrayal. Touch, abundance, and fecundity. Bataille and general economy. Bataille and the curse, mark of the good. Irigaray and sexual difference as heterogeneity.

What truth is. Gathering of being and saying. Memory of the good, *anamnēsis,* interrupting gathering. Plenishment, abundance, resisting and giving of cultural authority. Cherishment, sacrifice, plenishment. Cherishment as exposure, desire. Truth as plenishment. Authority and debt. Cherishment as ideality of truth and being. Cherishment as general economy, movement of desire. Western science given by and responsive to earth's abundance and truth's ideality. Science as general and restricted economy. Ideality and evil. Habermas, normative grounds of normative judgments. Something interrupts the norms of being. Gathering of being in abundance as truth. Derrida and gathering of truth in painting rather than language. Gathering in representation. Gathering as curse. Representation as interruption. Whitehead and prehension, gathering and interruption. Guidelines to plenished truth, given from the good. Plenishment as general economy and restricted economy. Truth as restitution, gathered within gifts from the good, circulating in abundance of the earth.

General Preface to the Project: The Gift of the Good*

This volume is the second of several devoted to the good,[1] understanding human and natural worlds to be filled with gifts,[2] calling us and others to respond in turn with endless movements in every place, exposing us everywhere to others. The works we know, their priceless ingredients, all human works and natural kinds, come as gifts in the name of something other than themselves, unlike any thing, touching the limits of places and worlds. I speak of these gifts as given in the name of the good everywhere in nature, understanding nature as the general economy of the good, the circulation of goods beyond expense, the earth's abundance, interrupting measure.[3]

I speak of the good in memory of Plato, who recalled Socrates' death as a disaster.[4] I read every word he wrote in memory of that and other ruins, memories of the good. Yet we do not find it congenial today to speak of the good. We prefer to speak of value, or virtue, or the good life; and God. We pursue being as if it bore no ethical exposure. I hope to rehabilitate the thought of the good in relation to each of these and more, as what calls us to them and what disturbs our relation to them, what impels them in circulation. But the good is not any of them, is not a thing, or event, or being; does not belong to us, to human beings; and is not God—though many have spoken of the good in terms of the divine. It is neither in this world nor out, inhabits no immanent or transcendent place, but is the

---

*This general preface, with minor changes, begins every volume of the project, reaching out to those who may not have prior knowledge of the undertaking, to introduce them to the good. The first volume of the project is *The Gift of Beauty: The Good as Art*. I hope to trace the good here in another place, with minimal repetition.

Each volume may be read independently, in its terms. Each may benefit from the preceding volumes. I discuss much of truth, related to art, in *GB*, not repeated here. I am concerned here with the gathering of being as truth.

unlimiting of every limit and the displacement of every place, exposes each creature and thing to others, moves then incessantly to respond. The good of which I speak is not a category, does not oppose the bad or beautiful, does not war with evil; it interrupts the authority of choice and judgment, gives us responsibility for making and unmaking categories, opposing evil, struggling to make things better, or worse. The good is not good opposed to bad, right opposed to wrong, justice opposed to injustice.[5] It expresses what is priceless, irreplaceable, in things, worth cherishing, in human beings and their works, and other creatures, throughout nature, all born in immeasurable exposure to others, imposing a debt to foster them and to pursue the ideal. It haunts the limits of individual things in their identities and relations and of the kinds and collectives of the earth, belongs to nature everywhere, composing the circulation of goods beyond measure.

To speak of the good is to speak of an exposure given as a gift that comes from no place or thing, which circulates everywhere, in every place, a giving without a giver, without a receiver, given everywhere. In this sense, it is impossible to speak of the good, impossible to fix its limits, not because the good is something we cannot know but because speaking of it is endless interruption. My efforts here are endeavors in an ongoing struggle to understand and to participate in working to make things better where every such effort is a betrayal. The struggle is to interrupt the flow of continuities and identities that do the work of the good in nature. It is a struggle to keep the gifts moving, not to let them stop in a better that denies its own betrayal.

I call exposure to the good everywhere "cherishment"; I call the impossibility of fulfilling conflicting demands everywhere "sacrifice"; I call work in response to the good, the coupling of cherisment and sacrifice, "plenishment," inexhaustible exposure to the good. These make it possible to undertake and to resist binary divisions between good and bad, true and false, high and low, make it possible to place goods in circulation, unlimiting every limit, dwelling in and crossing every threshold, in the endless responsiveness in which we do ethical work, calling us to work for justice and to resist injustice by struggling against the authority of every category and identity.

This thought pursues Socrates' suggestion that the good grants authority to knowledge and truth, perhaps grants the possibility of being to all things and kinds: "This reality, then, that gives their truth to the objects of knowledge and the power of knowing to the knower, you must say is the idea of the good, and you mush conceive it as being the cause *[aitian]* of knowledge, and of truth in so far as known" (Plato, *Republic,* 508e), described by Glaucon as "[a]n inconceivable beauty" (Plato, *Republic,* 509a). This beautiful idea of the good, giving knowledge and truth, and more, meets and surpasses the idea of the sacred as nature's sonance, radiance, glory.[6] Plato speaks of it in Diotima's voice as a "nature of wondrous beauty *[phusin kalon]*" (Plato, *Symposium,* 211). The sacred here touches the mundane with beauty, disturbs the hold of categories and distinctions, bears little echo of the profane. The good touches the sacred with an unending call to resist injustice, including endless injustices perpetrated in the name of the good, and God. For the good resists every authority, including the rule of the gods. In the institution of authority, it resists authority.

Socrates' words evoke Anaximander, who understands all things together to bear the mark of the good, demanding restitution for endless injustices.[7] All things. The idea of the good is the "cause" *(aitian)* of knowledge and truth, and perhaps thereby of the being of all things, imposing a burden on them, accusing them of injustice. All things are "charged" by the good with their truth and being, charged, accused, and blamed, the most prominent meanings of *aitia* and *aitios:* responsible for who and what they are, in the extreme, guilty of injustice no matter what and who they are. The sense of "cause" here is "for the sake of," exposed to heterogeneity, where knowledge and truth are for the sake of, demanded by, the good, bearing an unlimited responsiveness everywhere and always. The gift of the good is that which within each thing, everywhere, for the sake of which it is and for which it moves, gives it ideality.

This ideality, as I understand it in Plato, does not measure up the goal for which things strive, but undercuts the inescapable wound of measure, reaches to measure's limits. The interpretation guiding my project follows Levinas's thought that the good does not rule over being, does not reassemble being in its place together with the authority of identity and difference, but interrupts the order of being, disrupts the totality of identities and truths, displaces every place, in immeasurable exposure. The gift of the good interrupts the rule of identity, undermines the domination of being and law, challenges the authority of every rule, brings us face to face with heterogeneity, with other beings and other kinds, touches everywhere with strangeness. The good is less an encounter with the face of the other, something that only humans may know, than touching another, exposure to others in skin and flesh, reaching beyond one's limits to others, something known to every thing, in every place. The good does not rule over knowledge and truth, does not govern them with its authority, but undermines every authority, including its own, following Anaximander's thought of injustice. For all things, he says, including knowledge and truth, "make reparation to one another for their injustice according to the ordinance of time."[8] This debt incurred by being is a remembrance of the good, lacking forever any possibility of an instituted justice, of inaugurating the good without injustice. Everything is done for the sake of the good, bearing endless responsiveness toward injustice.

I believe that the forms of thought around which philosophy has traditionally coalesced, even understood as Western, Greek, have been sites of interruption, not of work, where the good displaces the hold of work upon us, interposes ideality. The work of human life, the promulgation of rules, the coercion of political powers, all institute excessive authorities against which we struggle to recapture a freedom we never had. This mobilization against the claims of authority, legitimate and otherwise, fills the world of disciplines, including philosophy, themselves filled with clashes of authority, with coercion and exclusion. The possibility that an authority might claim legitimacy, or that it might be resisted, both draw sustenance from the good, not a good with overarching authority, preempting this clash of power and resistance, but a good that resists authority, that takes authority always to be questioned, always to be questionable, and yet a good that demands authority to do its work. The space of this ceaseless struggle with authority presupposes the call of the good, demands from us endless responses to the injustices of every authority.

Any project of this magnitude will undergo transformations in its realization. The first volume of the project is *The Gift of Beauty*. At the time of this second volume, the other volumes projected in this series, in the order of their production, are *The Gift of Touch, The Gift of Nature, The Gift of Work, The Gift of Place, The Gift of Law, The Gift of Authority, The Gift of Property, The Gift of Community, The Gift of History, The Gift of Self, The Gift of Desire, The Gift of Love, The Gift of Sacredness, The Gift of Earth, The Gift of Air, the Gift of Fire, The Gift of Water, The Gift of Peace, The Gift of Life: The Good as Death*, and finally, perhaps, in retrospection, *The Gift of the Good*. There may be others. More likely, more than one of these gifts will be examined together, to avoid repetition. And I may not find myself with time enough to fulfill the promise offered at the beginning.

Why do I begin with beauty and art, followed with truth, embodiment, and work? Why not speak at once, in general, of the gift of the good, throughout nature, specifying beauty and truth in their places? That will take more than one volume to answer, perhaps the entire project, in relation to the good, but I respond that truth and beauty have no proper places, but come from the good, as gifts, displaced, unplaced, in Heidegger's words, *ek-static*: out of place. The good places things outside themselves, interrupts the hold of being on all things, not just us, everywhere in nature, everywhere in every kind. The forms of displacement are inexhaustible.

I begin with art to address Nietzsche's challenge to the authority of the good, undertaken in the name of art. Yet Nietzsche interrupted the authority of truth in the name of the good. With this thought a radical possibility emerged that Nietzsche himself did not explore in its extremity, nor did Heidegger, who accepted Nietzsche's challenge in the name of Being. The thought of Being, however forgotten, remained gathered in Being's truth. I understand Nietzsche to pose another possibility, that the challenge posed to truth by the will to power cuts to the heart of being and being's authority. What if the Western philosophic tradition, from the beginning and nearly always, gave precedence to being and truth, precedence to gathering and assembling being; and what if that privilege gestured toward something that was neither truth nor being, but gave them forth as gifts, interrupting the gathering? The provocation I undertake in this volume is to explore the dismantling of the privilege of truth and being—not to destroy being and truth, if that were possible, possible even to think it, but to resist their inordinate authority.

If the Western tradition, from its beginning with the Greeks, followed the trajectory I have described, instituting the rule of truth within the gathering of being, and if this sovereignty and rule are to be understood as I have suggested, as ethical|political, in memory of the good, where the work of the good is always inseparably ethical and political,[9] then this volume undertakes the most radical and critical movement of the project, the one most incongruous with traditional philosophy. Yet I hope to show that this great departure can be understood from within that same tradition, that the most fervent defenders of the privilege of truth and being, in their ardor, gesture toward the good. And I hope as well to show that this great departure is something entirely understandable to us even as we understand it to challenge the limits of intelligibility.

This book is shorter than the topic of truth demands, which could be as long as the Western tradition. I have said much in framing this discussion here of gifts and goods in other places, beginning with *The Ring of Representation* through *Injustice and Restitution: The Ordinance of Time* and *Plenishment in the Earth: An Ethic of Inclusion*. My project of gifts pursues this ethic of inclusion. All these different works come together in the name of the good, remembering countless injustices, sorrows and joys.

I begin my task each time in the same movement, beginning with traditional Western philosophers to interrupt the hold of their authority and that of the tradition that has fixed their reading, to open them and others to abundance, fecundity.[10] I understand the call of the good, our endless responsiveness, to release the authority of every category, including the categories of tradition, but ask us to read traditional works in different ways, and to read nontraditional works, both interrupting authority.

With this immeasurability before us, I undertake the impossible project of working toward the good without impeding its circulation.

Introduction: The Good in Truth

Some say that Aristotle's words on truth—"To say of what is that it is not, or of what is not that it is, is false, while to say of what is that it is, and of what is not that it is not, is true" (Aristotle, *Metaphysics*, 1011)— is a correspondence theory of truth, the first such theory (Kirkham, *TT*, 119). Or if it is not the first, then perhaps the first may be found in the Eleatic Stranger's words to Theaetetus:

> . . . the true one [statement] states about you the things that are as they are. . . .
>
> . . . Whereas the false statement states about you things *different* from the things that are. . . .
>
> . . . And accordingly states *things that are not* as being. (Plato, *Sophist*, 263b)

Perhaps it is true—what is instead of what is not—that these words of Aristotle and Plato express a correspondence theory of truth—not, for example, a coherence or other theory of truth. Perhaps.

Some say that what truth is is different from knowledge of what is true, that they are to be distinguished (Kirkham, *TT*, 27–28). We must (truly) understand what truth is as distinguished from knowing what is true.[1] Perhaps. In both cases, truth and what is true belong to being, and we may hope to say what they are, still under the rule of being. This link of truth with being, joined with saying, marks something persistent in Western philosophy, interrupted repeatedly by something other, something that repeatedly interrupts this triangle in unexpected ways.

I do not propose to re-traverse the matrix of theories of truth, reduced in the end to saying the truth of what is against what is not. I am concerned instead to explore how Aristotle's words, perhaps together with the Eleatic Stranger's, bring truth together with saying what is, falsehood together

1

with saying what is not, joining truth with being and saying, gathering being in saying as truth. I read these words, whether correspondence or some other theory of truth, read virtually every Western theory of truth, as placing truth under the rule of being and saying, subordinating truth to being. I understand this abject movement to pervade Western reason to the point that even reason's critique repeats the giving of truth over to the *logos*, founding the logic of truth. I read Heidegger's return to *alētheia*, against correspondence theories of truth, and others, as repeating this rule of being and saying, repeating the assignation of truth to being in the form of saying, within resistance to the *logos*. Truth gathers in the space of being and saying, gathers up the world into its opening between language and being, a gathering called *legein*. That is what he says, I believe, though I also believe that he touches something very different, something that resists the dominion of being over truth.

Legein is the gathering of things into their *parousia*, their "presence" *("Anwesenheit")*, in the now, the "present" *("Gegenwart")*, of the *logos*, where language gathers up things in their truth (Heidegger, *BT*, 47).

> *Legein* is the clue for arriving at those structures of Being which belong to the entities we encounter in addressing ourselves to anything or speaking about it. (p. 47)

> The "Being-true" of the logos as *alēthemein* means that in *legein* as *apophainesthai* the entities *of which* one is talking must be taken out of their hiddenness; one must let them be seen as something unhidden *(alēthes);* that is, they must be *discovered [entdeckt].* (pp. 56–57)

> In the ontology of the ancients, the entities we encounter within the world are taken as the basic examples for the interpretation of Being. . . . Entities are encountered therein. But the Being of these entities must be something which can be grasped in a distinctive kind of *legein* (letting something be seen), so that this Being becomes intelligible in advance as that which it is—and as that which it is already in every entity. (p. 70)

The truth which is inseparable from untruth, which "in its nature, is untruth" (Heidegger, *OWA*, 54), assembles within the Being which is already gathered in every thing and place. The gathering takes place in the House of Being, where language collects Being into its presence, into presentness, presents the hiddenness of Being as something to be seen, and grasped, gathered into *legein*. *Legein* marks a gathering of being and saying in a truth given as the dominion of Being. For *Dasein*. For Us. The structures of the Being we encounter.

Why does Heidegger fail to sense that within the gathering and assembling of *legein*, including *alētheia*, something of what he calls *Bestand* (Heidegger, *QT*, 298) collects between being and knowing: the stockpiling of truth, held in reserve for us. The holding of things as standing-reserve gathers in the space of *legein* together with *technē*. The mastery of modern technology goes back to the Greeks, perhaps, beyond *technē* to the idea of a gathering in saying of truth as the dominion of Being. However mobile, whatever untruth remains in truth, the oblivion of Being, its entire frame is an assembling, gathered or ungathered in its human place. Yet that which calls upon truth to move, to come forth, to respond, the wonder that beckons for Being to show itself in thought, in truth, in representation, does not belong to truth or to humanity; it interrupts the gathering of being into representation, not as untruth or ungathering, but as an interruption from elsewhere, from the sacred beauty of the good.

The *logos* is a wonderful thing: language, thought, reason, and truth all share the wonder *(thauma)* of which Plato speaks as the beginning of disclosure. At the heart of truth lies a wonder, a sacred mystery, which Heidegger asks us to encounter again, repeatedly, the uncovering of things in their hiddenness, all gathered into language, as truth. The truth that can emerge only as untruth remains in this gathering, offers itself in wonder. This wonder, given as a gift, comes from the good, responds to the good. For it demands, and calls, and touches us with awe. And it is given as a gift, not demanded or possessed. We find ourselves in wonder at the goodness of the earth to which we respond in truth. This goodness is not compared with badness or evil, not a good gathered in opposition with the bad, but a good that calls and beckons and entreats, asks us to respond. The wonder is a beauty that calls for endless response. Plato speaks of this in another place, read in a different way, in relation to truth.

> those who are already wise are no longer friends to wisdom, be they gods, or be they men, nor, again, are those friends to wisdom who are so possessed of foolishness as to be evil, for no evil and ignorant man is a friend to wisdom. There remain then those who possess indeed this evil, the evil of foolishness, but who are not, as yet, in consequence of it, foolish or ignorant, but still understand that they do not know the things they do not know. And thus, you see, it is those who are neither good nor evil, as yet, that are friends to wisdom [philosophers], but those who are evil are not friends, nor again are the good. (Plato, *Lysis*, 218ab)

Something which is neither good or evil is a friend to truth, allows truth to come forth, something that remains touched with wonder. Something which is neither this nor that, which is in Diotima's words "a nature of wondrous beauty" neither good nor evil, fair or foul, "but beauty absolute, separate, simple, and everlasting, which without diminution and without increase, or any change, is imparted to the ever-growing and perishing beauties of all other things" (Plato, *Symposium*, 210e–211a).[2] What is gathered in the truth of being looks in wonder at something otherwise. If truth is to be encountered and renewed in its wonder, it must go beyond and behind the gathering of *legein* to that which gives the wonder of truth, which has been taken in another gathering to be the dominion of Being. The authority of truth, and being, as showing or saying, gathered up into *legein*, comes as a gift in memory of that to which we are responsible in virtue of its wonder and mystery. *Legein* touches something immeasurable and sacred far beyond its gathering.

I hope to resist the dominion of being over truth, repeated in the impossible mediation of language, the violence of *legein*. I understand this dominion to be resisted almost nowhere in the Western tradition despite the upheaval of Western thought under the pressure of those who have read Nietzsche and Heidegger, and under the critique of those who have suffered under this dominion, women and other strangers to Western ontology. I understand the question of truth—if there be such a question, rather than endless questions of representation and work—as one of authority, endless questions of the good. One place where this understanding can be heard is in Foucault, who tells us that "[t]he political question . . . is truth itself" (Foucault, *TP*, 133). I take this thought to the extreme, understanding the question of truth, truth itself—if there be such—to be ethical and political.[3] In the name of the good, I resist the dominion of being and saying over truth. I understand the good, after Plato, to give birth to truth, calling it to respond, charging it with responsibility, touching it with gifts. This gift of truth echoes Heidegger's words on the gift of Being, resisting its dominion. The *es gibt* gives truth to Being. I understand the gift to come not from being, but from the good. I hope to de-ontologize deontology, releasing the bonds tying ethics to being.

Heidegger speaks of the gift as giving, always in terms of Being, joined with a thought of something other.

> We say of beings: they are. With regard to the matter "Being" and with regard to the matter "time," we remain cautious. We do not say: Being is, time is, but rather: there is Being and there is time. Instead of saying "it is," we say "there is," "It gives *[es gibt]*."
>
> In order to get beyond the idiom and back to the matter, we must show how this "there is" can be experienced and seen. The appropriate way to get there is to explain what is given in the "it gives," what "Being" means, which—It gives; what "time" means, which—It gives. Accordingly, we try to look ahead to the It which—gives Being and time. Thus looking ahead, we become foresighted in still another sense. We try to bring the It and its giving into view, and capitalize the "It." (Heidegger, *TB*, 5)

I might spend some precious time exploring how this remarkable attention devoted to the It remains joined with Being in virtually all of Heidegger's writing, except perhaps for this essay in which something else emerges, something of the giving and the good. Even here, however, Heidegger does not think of the It in relation to the good.

> Being, by which all beings as such are marked, Being means presencing.... To let presence means: to unconceal, to bring to openness. In unconcealing prevails a giving, the giving that gives presencing, that is, Being, in letting-presence. (Heidegger, *TB*, 5)

He thinks away from Being in order to think Being as presencing.

> To think Being explicitly requires us to relinquish Being as the ground of beings in favor of the giving which prevails concealed in unconcealment, that is, in favor of the It gives. As the gift of this It gives, Being belongs to giving.... There is, It gives Being as the unconcealing; as the gift of unconcealing it is retained in the giving. Being is not. There is, It gives Being as the unconcealing of presencing. (Heidegger, *TB*, 6)

Even so, to think away from Being is to think of the It in terms of unconcealing and concealing, in terms of presencing, that is, in terms of truth and being and saying. It is to think in terms of language, for the gift calls us back to language in a supremely contaminated way, a way that returns us to the good.

> In the common view, the hand is part of our bodily organism. But the hand's essence can never be determined, or explained, by its being an organ which can grasp. Apes, too, have organs that can grasp, but they do not have hands. The hand is infinitely different from all the grasping organs—paws, claws, or fangs—different by an abyss of essence. Only a being who can speak, that is, think can have hands and can handily achieve works of handicraft....
> ...To be capable we must before all else incline toward what addresses itself to thought—and that is that which of itself gives food for thought. What gives us this gift, the gift of what must properly be thought about, is what we call most thought-provoking. (Heidegger, *WCT*, 357)

In Derrida's words, speaking of the sentence beginning "The hand is infinitely different from all the grasping organs ...": "This sentence in sum comes down to distinguishing the human *Geschlecht*, our *Geschlecht*, and the animal *Geschlecht*, called 'animal'" (Derrida, *G2*, 173). The abyss of essence marks our *Geschlecht*. The Human stands upright within the gathering.

I have spoken elsewhere of *Geschlecht*, and especially of the sexual difference, gender, it embodies, so that this gift, given to us, separating humanity from animals, also divides men from women, explicitly repeating the logic of sexual domination.[4] Heidegger distinguishes human beings from animals in a gesture that repeats the historically oppressive distinction between men and women. In Derrida's reading, the distinction at the heart of *Geschlecht*, between men and women, the distinction of gender, is in the very same movement a distinction between humans and animals, differences of domination and subordination. I have spoken of these themes elsewhere, so I will not repeat them here, but will instead traverse them along a different trajectory, arriving at an adjacent place. Yet I would add that the good of which I speak recalls the binary oppositions of man and woman, and human and animal, as modes of being and as categories of domination and exclusion, recalls them to displace them. The gift of language, which seems to know nothing of sexual and animal difference, in *Dasein*'s neutrality, knows them to exclude them. Sexual and animal difference express the gift of the good, from the beginning, if there be a beginning. The wonder in which thought begins, of language, truth, and being, is given from something beyond any of them, a nature beautiful beyond compare whose giving calls to us for endless response. An inexhaustible responsiveness beckons in the responsibility given from the truth.

I have spoken elsewhere of *Geschlecht* and the contamination of the gift of thought and language that returns us to the good. I find myself repeating these passages from Heidegger's account of the gift of the hand and language in every introduction to the works of this project to call attention, at least for a moment, both to the debt I owe to Heidegger for the gift and to its betrayal. I do not wish to speak at length of Heidegger's betrayal of German people and others, of his relation to National Socialism and concentration camps, though I believe it something we must recognize. I wish rather to exhibit through Heidegger's words the impossibility of speaking of the gift except in ethical terms. Lyotard says much the same. "The forgetting of Being becomes constitutive of Western philosophy" (Lyotard, *"HJ,"* 146); "But remaining anchored in the thought of Being, the 'Western' prejudice that the Other is Being, it has nothing to say about a thought in which the Other is the Law" (Lyotard, *HJ*, 89). The Other, from which gifts are given, including the gifts of Being and truth, is ethical. We receive a gift that calls us, indebts us, touches us with a demand to respond. Another name for this touch is desire. No truth can touch us except within a desire beyond any limits, in memory of the good.

Except for his almost unbroken silence on concentration camps and the murder of Jewish people, there is nothing on which Heidegger exhibits a comparable refusal except ethics and politics, memories of the good, repeatedly refused, though we may wonder how he could write, could think, could pursue the gift except in memory of a good, driven by desire for something better. Yet within this almost total refusal, he comes close to what I hope to say of the good, in this endless project to give another truth to the Western domination of the good by truth. For he continues his reading of the gift and the It with two additions. He tells us to think not of the gift, of Being, but of the giving. "In the beginning of Western thinking, Being is thought, but not the 'It gives' as such. The latter withdraws in favor of the gift which It gives. That gift is thought and conceptualized from then on exclusively as Being with regard to beings" (Heidegger, *TB*, 8). He has already spoken in the same essay of Being's abundance *(Fülle)* (p. 8). I would characterize my entire project as the attempt to join this abundance of being and nature with the good, understanding the giving and its abundance to circulate from the good, indebted to it, but a good that knows no measure, whose abundance unmeasures every measure, interrupts every gathering. I believe it a project impossible to undertake within Heidegger's understanding of the gift, within any ontology, however fundamental or primordial, without memory of the good, of debt and obligation and desire. This is Levinas's critique of Heidegger, expressed in different terms by Lyotard above, a critique I take to bear some truth, some ethical gravity, though I withdraw from Levinas in his characterization of the gift as given only in subjectivity. I think that Levinas knows too little of nature's abundance. I hope to join heterogeneity with abundance, in relation to the kinds of the earth. I join desire with heterogeneity in the abundance of giving.

The gift of which I speak in this volume is the gift of truth, given endlessly as exposure, circulating beyond limits, interrupting every limit. It echoes something of what Heidegger says of truth, and I will explore his words in some detail in chapter 10. His characterization of the gift, however, because it remains "anchored in the thought of Being" rather than the good, never touches its own exposure to the debts that permeate it, never touches a desire that reaches elsewhere. Why think of Being except as called, as desired? Why does Being open under the gaze of human questioning except as responding to a yearning beyond limits, except as human beings, and other beings, are exposed to each other, touched by each other, called together by endless desire? Put more directly, the opening of Being to questioning, the opening of the earth to world, institutes events and works, but never terminates. The temporality of the opening is an endless giving, an endless deferral. The giving is endless. The endless possibility of thinking emerges from an endless desire for something more than any truth, any being, any thought might express, from inexhaustible, endless exposure. It is repeatedly spoken of by Plato.

In the beginning of Western thought, and elsewhere, and always, being shows itself to others, beings touch each other everywhere. It is a touch, at least for human beings, that institutes an infinite debt. It is a giving that calls for endless response. And I would say, will say as I pursue the giving of the gift, that it gives to everything in the earth a call to respond, an endless touch and yearning met by responses, not by fulfillments, always in the name of something beyond any event, or moment, or revelation of being. Being always goes beyond itself, exposes itself to others inexhaustibly, called to respond beyond the measures and limits of its places. We know this exposure beyond any limit as desire, though we tend to think of it acquisitively rather than as movement and response. The good cannot be acquired or owned, is not a thing. In this sense, the It of which Heidegger speaks is nothing, and everything. In this sense, the It dissolves not into the gift of Being, into any gift, but into endless giving, endless circulation, endless abundance, endless desire, where the abundance of being calls forth endless relations to the Other, to others, to heterogeneity. Heterogeneity is abundance, impossible without Being. But Being is always touched by something beyond, *au delà*, otherwise than Being, but not Being's Other, its repetition. At least, that is Levinas's language. I speak of desire and the good, excess, general economy.[5]

As I think of gifts from the good I find myself repeatedly returning to Plato and Aristotle, and before, where the most vivid and compelling understanding of giving I know can be found, in memory of the good. I have spoken of Anaximander, who understands the ordinance of time, of being and truth, and more, as restitution for injustice, the injustice of things to one another. To be is to be unjust, to commit violence, to destroy, and harm, and nurture, and tend. Being and truth, and saying, work in this memory of injustice, joined in justice. I think of it instead as the good, resisting the image of fallenness as original sin. It is fallen indeed, but more, and it cannot be told as injustice, nor as justice, but as endless exposure and interruption, calling us to respond in truth, called in our desire for truth, and more. Truth is a response called forth from infinite desire.

I have begun here with Aristotle and Plato to think of the gift of truth as joined with the gifts of being and saying. I will continue my discussion in chapters 1 and 2. Yet the act of resistance in which I hope to participate, against the rule of being over truth, through language, leads me away from Plato and Aristotle to begin with the opening of modernity upon a new scientific truth, breaking the hold of one truth—God's truth—with another God, still in the light of Being. I take my discussion of Descartes in chapter 4 to open the possibility of understanding science in an ethical way, given from the good.

I would recall that in the same tradition in which Aristotle's words are understood as a theory of truth, one among other contestants, the relation of truth to being, to what is, becomes taken for granted, first, in relation to God, then in relation to science. Yet in both cases, within this rule of Being—Heidegger calls it "ontotheology," the rule of being joined with God and *logos*—we can see the imposition of rule in an ethical frame. In Aristotle, for example, the relation of human beings, *anthrōpoi*, to knowledge and truth is one of desire, perhaps an excessive, uncontrollable desire. "All human beings by nature desire to know" (Aristotle, *Metaphysics*, 980a). Desire, I insist, relates to knowledge and truth by force, imposing authority. Desire, I insist, imposes this authority in an act that goes beyond, exceeds, any act of imposition, far surpasses any possibility of letting truth be in being.

Aristotle's words may be read as establishing a standard of desire, met by truth. They may also be read as overwhelming every standard. The desire to know exceeds any standard, exceeds truth. In both cases, we may order and categorize the world so that it comes under our mastery, driven by insatiable desire to rule. On the second reading, however, the excessiveness of desire, beyond every limit, points to what I mean by the good. The desire for knowledge is a desire for standards but is given by something beyond all standards, without limits, known to us as infinite desire, the immeasurability of the good, perhaps what Bataille calls general economy. The goods and truths we know, within the ordinance of time, respond to something beyond time, immeasurable. Desire is the name for this excess, giving itself excessively everywhere, instituting a circulation beyond any restricted economy.[6] Whatever desire touches goes to excess. Desire is memory of the good.

Nietzsche speaks of the will to truth and power. I hope to take this thought as far as possible to understand this will as desire and to understand desire as given from the good. On this reading, we find desire divided by finite ends for which we strive, finite things and finite kinds, with stable identities, and longings beyond any identity or place, for strange and remarkable things, a desire that produces and is produced, beyond any limits and places. The will to truth is a desire—Nietzsche calls it Apollinian—beyond any limits. Apollo promotes a madness, a frenzy to know, for truth. The madness and frenzy are covered over by this same frenzy, so that the excessive desire for truth does not know its own truth, its own excessiveness, its own desire. This excessiveness of desire, this longing, is the giving I speak of, from the good. For the good here is no measure or standard, but the giving, the yearning, the call and exposure. If we madly yearn, we madly yearn not for the good, as if it were a thing, but from the good, called by it to respond, where responsiveness is our responsibility.

Truth, here, is what Anaximander calls restitution; I call it responsibility, understood as unlimited responsiveness and exposure. We strive for truth through our exposure to the things around us and insofar as they are exposed to each other and us, and respond. We reach for truth by our responses and the responses of other things. But truth is not something at which we arrive, on which we stand, but dwells in endless questioning, endless critique, infinite interruption and exposure. This is how I understand the arrival of modernity, despite its betrayals: as the institution of endless uncertainty as the world of truth. This endless uncertainty, endless questioning, constitutes reason as exposure and responsiveness. I add interruption to mark heterogeneity, the abundance of things. The flow of truth without interruption, even endless, does not face the endless others in their surprising abundance and heterogeneity. Endless questioning is endless surprise. The desire that strives for truth exceeds every stable arrival of truth. The good exceeds every stable measure and identity. The good destabilizes every stability, called by us desire, sometimes called error. In this sense, if truth responds to the good through desire, error is the kindred response. Truth and error belong together, given from the good.

I close this introduction with a claim upon the good that appears throughout the Western tradition, within its call to being. It appears in Plato, who I believe knows more of the gift of the good than anyone, who suggests that being comes from the good in the form of desire. The claim is that to know what is good, to divide the good from bad, we must already know the good, must already know in order to tell. Meno asks how we can know, how we can tell what we do not know, unless we already know. The answer in terms of truth is that we do and do not know, that being and truth are indeterminate. The answer in terms of the good is that it is nothing to know but calls forth the desire to know, love of truth, without which we will never know.

A similar claim appears in Descartes, who asks, "how could I understand that I doubted or desired—that is, lacked something—and that I was not wholly perfect, unless there were in me some idea of a more perfect being which enabled me to recognize my own defects by comparison?" (Descartes, M, 3, 31), a being such that "whatever I clearly and distinctly perceive as being real and true, and implying any perfection, is wholly contained in it" (p. 31). I can think of any perfection or imperfection only in the light of an idea of total perfection, the complete and ultimate standard of the good.

In my time, this argument has been given powerful voice by Habermas and his followers, for whom to speak of ethics is to speak of something that grounds, however fluidly, something that sets standards, norms. We are drawn to standards. This movement links truth and the good in terms of the task of communication. I take Habermas's claim to go much further, to the very possibility of truth.

> Speaker and hearer can reciprocally motivate one another to recognize validity claims because the content of the speaker's engagement is determined by a specific reference to a thematically stressed validity claim, whereby the speaker, in a cognitively testable way, assumes
>> with a truth claim, obligations to provide grounds,
>> with a righteous claim, obligations to provide justification, and
>> with a truthfulness claim, obligations to prove trustworthy. (Habermas, *CES*, 70)

In every case I might offer qualifications concerning grounds, justification, and truth, not in refutation but in supplementation. All are more ambiguous than Habermas allows. My concern in this moment is to offer a sympathetic examination of Habermas's assumption that the good that allows communication is a ground, a proof, a trust. Or rather, I resist the grounding of truth with the example of trust—though I would hate to forget the splendor of the great liar. I think of trust as resistant to every standard. Nothing can ground trust, no framework or edifice. It comes from the good as immeasurable debt.

The idea of the good in Plato has been interpreted in terms of standards, that is, the being whose form determines, grounds, makes intelligible, all other forms. Yet many who read Plato become aware of intermediary figures, love and desire, that always move, as if the good that gives birth to goods, to knowledge and truth, always calls, sets in motion, by being no being itself, having no form. Something similar appears in Aristotle's unmoved mover, again traditionally interpreted under the rule of being, but which I hope to reinterpret under the giving of the gift, where motion, desire, and truth are the gifts but the giving comes from the good, something never given, never identical, not a being at all, therefore not a standard. The good demands that it never freeze into being, supplements being with endless movements of desire.

This movement is what I hear lacking in Habermas's otherwise striking recognition of the place of the good. Wherever and whoever we are, we are moved by standards, decisions, choices, ethically moved by something that makes that movement possible. Yet against the reading of this possibility that what makes choice possible is a being that stands upright, with its identity, grounded on trust and proof, or anything else, something with authority, for all, I worry that that upright being is another God, beyond critique, stopping the mobility. The critique is endless, I respond, given from the good, circulating in every place. The proofs always call for further proof; the trust must be restored again and again; the grounds recede. The endless movement is the general economy of desire, always exceeding every ground, always drawing us beyond, always given from the good, interrupting every limit. The good that gives knowledge and truth gives the possibility of endless work and endless critique. Wherever the circulation of goods halts, there critique halts as well.

Plato famously ascribes all desire to the good, puzzling those who know of evil, of hateful people who desire to harm others, and of endless failures to pursue the most accessible goods. We all desire the good, and if we knew the good we would achieve it. I add the qualification that the good is no being and nothing to be known, but always to pursue. Desire exceeds any and every object, drawn by the sense of something wondrous, beautiful, abundant, different from what is here, so different as to be no something, but endless pursuit. We can engage in critique, pursue truth and rightness, only in the abundance of a gift that gives endless movement. The giving of the good is endless intermediary movements around the truth and other gifts.

CHAPTER 1

Soul Wings

Of Western philosophers, Plato is perhaps the one who beyond all others represents the ethical soul of truth, the procreation of truth by the good. And this despite the historical role he has been assigned, at least since Nietzsche, of establishing the authority of reason's truth. I have marked Socrates' extraordinary claim in Plato's *Republic* that the good oversees knowledge and truth, gives them their authority.[1] Even here, if the good is understood as a standard, a measure, then the claim it makes on truth belongs to truth, to being, despite Socrates' explicit denial.

> This reality, then, that gives their truth to the objects of knowledge and the power of knowing to the knower, you must say is the idea of good, and you must conceive it as being the cause of knowledge, and of truth in so far as known. Yet fair as they both are, knowledge and truth, in supposing it to be something fairer still than these you will think rightly of it. But as for knowledge and truth, even as in our illustration it is right to deem light and vision sunlike, but never to think that they are the sun, so here it is right to consider these two their counterparts, as being like the good or boniform, but to think that either of them is the good is not right. Still higher honor belongs to the possession and habit of the good. (Plato, *Republic*, 509a)

Truth is not the sun, is not sunlike; the light of truth comes from the good, from what is fair and beautiful. It is no minor matter, perhaps the most important matter, that this light of truth reflects something beautiful as well as honorable, beautiful beyond compare.[2] "An inconceivable beauty you speak of, he said, if it is the source of knowledge and truth, and yet itself surpasses them in beauty. For you surely cannot mean that it is pleasure" (Plato, *Republic*, 509bc). The good that entrusts truth and knowledge with their authority, and their responsibility, is a beauty beyond compare, perhaps that of which Diotima speaks to Socrates in *Symposium*,

13

speaking of nature's abundance and of love. For one who has learned the lessons of love:

> when he comes toward the end will suddenly perceive a nature of won-
> drous beauty *[phusin kalon]* (and this, Socrates, is the final cause of all
> our former toils)—a nature which in the first place is everlasting, not
> growing and decaying, or waxing and waning; secondly, not fair in one
> point of view and foul in another, or at one time or in one relation or at
> one place fair, at another time or in another relation or in another place
> foul, as if fair to some and foul to others, or in the likeness of a face or
> hands or any other part of the bodily frame, or in any form of speech or
> knowledge, or existing in any other being, as for example in an animal, or
> in heaven, or in earth, or in any other place; but beauty absolute, separate,
> simple, and everlasting, which without diminution and without increase,
> or any change, is imparted to the ever-growing and perishing beauties of
> all other things. (Plato, *Symposium*, 210e–211a)[3]

The good, nature's abundance, is understood in terms of beauty and love, beyond all limits and distinctions, beyond the gathering of being. With love and beauty I will return to the way in which truth and being cannot stand alone in the majesty of their authority, but present themselves in the light of something beyond authority, at least that authority which excludes, divides into binary oppositions. All things, including truth and being, are included in the good, an inclusion quite different from gathering them into totality.

> In like manner, then, you are to say that the objects of knowledge not only
> receive from the presence of the good their being known, but their very
> existence and essence is derived to them from it, though the good itself
> is not essence but still transcends essence in dignity and surpassing power.
> (Plato, *Republic*, 517ac)

This surpassing power, in a tradition that gives precedence to being, to truth and reason, evokes the idea of force, of mastery and rule over beings. Dignity is another matter, together with beauty and love. The thought I hope to pursue is of a love and beauty, a dignity and fecundity, that belong to the good beyond any being, therefore beyond any nonbeing, reason, or truth. This "beyond," an impossible thought or condition, calls beyond all oppositions, all exclusions, to a good beyond measure, present everywhere as interruption, immeasure. Yet nothing seems more obvious in Plato, including the passages I have quoted, that the good is a supreme measure. If it seems obvious, still I resist it.

For to be a measure is to be, and is to be truly a measure. Measures belong to the world in which to be is to cut, divide, to separate beings from each other, individual beings and kinds of beings. Everlasting measures, measures grounded in eternity, are no less measures, filled with authority, dividing finite from infinite, temporal from atemporal. Yet Diotima speaks of a nature of wondrous beauty whose everlastingness knows nothing of measure and authority, dividing one from the other, which cannot then be identified with the totality of beings, but is closer to the *apeiron*, except for its beauty and love. In some places, Christianity says that God is love where God and the earth belong to different realms of being. I follow a thought of love as messenger between earth and heaven, finite and infinite, expressed by Diotima in *Symposium*, but interrupt this movement with a thought from Irigaray, suggesting that angels are messengers without a message or a place, crossing boundaries, thresholds, displacing places, liminal, intermediary figures of the "intermediary-interval" (Irigaray, *ESD*, 8), interrupting the gathering of truth in *legein*. Irigaray's figure of identity and place is the envelope, wrapping indeterminate figures of the good, always in motion, with material, engendered identities.

> *angels* . . . circulate as mediators of that which has not yet happened, of what is still going to happen, of what is on the horizon. Endlessly reopening the enclosure of the universe, of universes, identities, the unfolding of actions, of history.
>
> The angel is that which unceasingly *passes through the envelope(s)* or *container(s)*, goes from one side to the other, reworking every deadline, changing every decision, thwarting all repetition. Angels destroy the monstrous, that which hampers the possibility of a new age; they come to herald the arrival of a new birth, a new morning. (Irigaray, *ESD*, 15)

This thought of the unceasing traversal of borders and judgments, intermediary movements, is given by Irigaray as an ethical thought, a thought that insists on sexual difference, material crossings from one envelope to another, heterogeneous movements. The ethical thought of the good faces up to heterogeneity by resisting, crossing, boundaries, still heterogeneous, for example, between men and women, divided by sexual difference—and, I add, between humans and animals, humanity and nature, living and dead, and more, the world divided into heterogeneous and multiple kinds. I will return to Irigaray and sexual difference, return to intermediary figures and truths of natural kinds in the name of the good. I think that no thought of the good in our time, perhaps ever, can be undertaken without confronting sexual difference in its complexity, a heterogeneous multiplicity closely related to nature's abundance. I understand abundance as an intermediary figure, expressed in nature's species and kinds.

I return to Diotima's nature as the abundance of the good. The nature of wondrous beauty of which she speaks is either the totality of the world without borders or a general economy in which messengers cross cease-lessly from one envelope to another, traverse boundaries and thresholds—material and other thresholds, including that which Irigaray describes as "A remaking of immanence and transcendence, notably through this *threshold* which has never been examined as such: the female sex. The threshold that gives access to the *mucous*. Beyond classical oppositions of love and hate, liquid and ice—a threshold that is always *half-open*" (Irigaray, *ESD*, 18). Like Diotima, another woman, Irigaray speaks beyond oppositions and di-visions, thereby speaking of the good, or nature, or love—but not love divided from hate. The good takes us on a journey beyond knowledge and truth, beyond truth and falsity, beyond good and evil. The nature of won-drous beauty of which Diotima speaks takes us beyond the being of iden-tities and essences, beyond good and bad, high and low, to a good which includes rather than excludes. Or if this beyond imposes infinite transcen-dence on us, we may think of angels and love, intermediary figures, a different beyond, in endless circulation.

This thought of the gift of the good to truth and being is so different from the idea of the good ascribed traditionally to Plato that I must pursue it a bit further throughout the dialogues, though I believe I have traced it sufficiently for my purposes here. The good of which I speak is this nature of wondrous beauty quite unlike any other thing—unlike any thing and like all things, no figure of the same—but where the likeness is as indetermi-nate, as beautiful, as what it resists: envelopes and identities, intermediary movements. To measure, to know, to cut what we know from what we do not know, to know truth as a measure, something must call us to that task, something from the good that does not exclude, named desire, interrupting the gathering of things under truth and measure, intermediary figures of thresholds and crossings. We must be exposed to things beyond measure to know their truth, for them to open to us in truth, and they must be exposed to us, liminal crossings. But crossing requires desire, a love of wondrous beauty, and more, a love belonging to the earth in abundance, in hetero-geneity. I hold this thought in abeyance for a while.

Socrates incessantly repeats that he does not know, representing his superiority to other people, who think that they know.

> I am certainly wiser than this man. It is only too likely that neither of us has any knowledge to boast of, but he thinks that he knows something which he does not know, whereas I am quite conscious of my ignorance. At any rate it seems that I am wiser than he is to this small extent, that I do not think that I know what I do not know. (Plato, *Apology*, 21d)

For truth belongs to God.

whenever I succeed in disproving another person's claim to wisdom in a given subject, the bystanders assume that I know everything about that subject myself. But the truth of the matter, gentlemen, is pretty certainly this, that real wisdom is the property of God, and this oracle is his way of telling us that human wisdom has little or no value. It seems to me that he is not referring literally to Socrates, but has merely taken my name as an example, as if he would say to us, The wisest of you men is he who has realized, like Socrates, that in respect of wisdom he is really worthless. (Plato, *Apology*, 23ab)

In particular, he denies knowledge of good and bad. "I share the poverty of my fellow countrymen in this respect, and confess to my shame that I have no knowledge about virtue at all" (Plato, *Meno*, 71b). Reason, truth, are gifts of the gods, come from the good, and bear that debt within themselves, a debt betrayed by granting them authority, especially self-legitimating authority.

Against such an understanding, we must consider the possibility that he claims to know virtue in *Republic* and rejects skepticism in *Theaetetus*, together with another refusal of knowledge. I briefly anticipate my extended discussion of *Theaetetus* in the next chapter with a few selected passages to which I shall return.

the highest point of my art is the power to prove by every test whether the offspring of a young man's thought is a false phantom or instinct with life and truth. I am so far like the midwife that I cannot myself give birth to wisdom, and the common reproach is true, that, though I question others, I can myself bring nothing to light because there is no wisdom in me. (Plato, *Theaetetus*, 150bd)

I know nothing of such matters and cannot claim to be producing any offspring of my own. I am only trying to deliver yours, and to that end uttering charms over you and tempting your appetite with a variety of delicacies from the table of wisdom, until by my aid your own belief shall be brought to light. (157cd)

If what every man believes as a result of perception is indeed to be true for him; . . . then, my friend, where is the wisdom of Protagoras, to justify his setting up to teach others and to be handsomely paid for it, and where is our comparative ignorance or the need for us to go and sit at his feet, when each of us is himself the measure of his own wisdom? (162de)

I offer two observations at this time. One is that this denial of the relativity of measure concerns the possession of truth and knowledge while at no time does Socrates repudiate his passionate desire for truth and the good. If he does not know the good, if he does not possess knowledge, still he is called by it, yearns for it. What he denies is a knowledge of virtue, the good, or anything else, closed to criticism, as if owned. The second observation is that his criticism of Protagoras has traditionally been read to suggest that if knowledge is a measure, it must cut, divide, what is known from what is not; and, moreover, we must be able to know the difference between what we know and what we do not. It follows that one cannot deny the existence of knowledge as if one knows that knowledge does not exist. Nevertheless, Socrates repeatedly claims to be wiser—closer to the gods and the good—in denying that he knows, denying that there is wisdom in him. Perhaps even here he would prefer to claim that he does not know but cannot know that he does not know. He says in his *Apology* that "I do not think I know what I do not know" (21d), not that he knows that he does not know it.

Can one think (or know) that one does not know what one does not know without self-contradiction? Several answers may be given, but at least one must be that if one does not know something then one ought to be able to think, even to say, that one does not know it. I do not know, and I know that I do not know, how to read or speak Chinese. Yet perhaps we may identify a difficulty here that bears upon the good, which cannot be considered in relation to being and truth alone. Can one think of what is not?—a famous Sophistic question, to which Socrates himself devotes considerable attention. What if we were to rephrase the question away from being, so that it did not belong to the gathering of being and saying, did not concern whether one can speak of what is not, but responded to being and saying as given from the good? What good is given when we speak of what is not, when we think that we ought to speak of what is and not of what is not? Heidegger offers a powerful answer, despite his refusal to relate it to the good. We have forgotten nothing, have transformed nothing into nonbeing. We must think again of nothing in order to think Being, in order to approach the It that gives. In order, I suggest, to respond to the good as giving. The good is nothing, NOTHING.[4]

To say "I know that I do not know" is to say something difficult and strange from the standpoint of being and language gathered together; it runs afoul of the logical structure of ontology. Heidegger speaks of ontotheology, the movement toward a God who resolves the nonbeing in the heart of being by a movement toward the infinite. This movement toward the infinite, however, traditionally involves the good, in Plato the debt the good levies on being and truth, the good that comes before being, truth, and saying; in Descartes, the perfection of the world, from God, allowing error. Truth and knowledge concerning what is not, concerning falsity and error, lead to the good, away from truth. "[I]s it better, then, that I should be capable of being deceived than that I should not?" (Descartes,

M, 4, 146). I suggest that error and deception are intermediary figures of the intermediary movements of knowledge and truth, movements that do not come to rest in gathering, but circulate in memory of the good.

We may read Descartes's movement from the truth of error to its goodness as bearing on free will and God. If we are free we must be free to err, though God is not. Even here, we can see that Descartes does not think that the question of error is a question of truth alone, perhaps not a question of knowledge and truth at all. Error is an imperfection in a perfect universe; the will that causes error is a mark of God. Whatever we think of divine perfection, we face an ethical demand in facing error. And if we believe, as I believe, that truth and error are profoundly intermixed, then truth and knowledge also bear an intimate and profound relation to the good, carry ethical weight.

To say "I know that I do not know," whatever its ontological and epistemological shortcomings, reflects something it must be possible to say and do, however liminally, speaking here in ethical terms. If I do not know, I must, I am obligated, indebted, to refrain from acting as if I know; the task is given from the good to avoid falsehood. This is true—I speak in an ethical voice—no matter how difficult it might be to know what I do not know, however impossible. I bear this debt toward truth within its impossibility despite an ethical tradition that denies impossible obligations.

The infinite debt of which I speak is described by Levinas, not a responsibility relieved by impossibility, by any calculation, but a debt that grows beyond measure. "[I]n the measure that responsibilities are taken on they multiply. . . . The debt increases in the measures that it is paid" (Levinas, *OB,* 12). Even if it is impossible, I am still obligated beyond all limits to avoid error, to know that I do not know, exposed to the things around me within an infinite responsibility for pursuing truth and avoiding error. Even if there is no truth unmixed with error, no complete and total or purified truth, no knowing without not-knowing, so that we cannot avoid error no matter what we do, even so, the truth as given from the good, together with error, calls upon us beyond measure to seek the truth and to avoid error. And this is so even as we also know that where the truth is given from the good, it is always given in error, together with error, and error also comes from the good. A lie, deception, error, is not always wrong, is sometimes a wonderful accomplishment. This is how I understand Socrates' suggestion in *Phaedrus* that "just" and "good" are "disputed terms": "we diverge, and dispute not only with one another but with our own selves" (Plato, *Phaedrus,* 263ad); we also dispute love and, I am arguing, truth. We dispute endlessly with ourselves and others about what is deeply and profoundly disputable, intrinsically disputable, everything involving justice and the good and truth, everything ethical and political. Some seem to believe that truth and knowledge, bound to being, can be indisputable. In Plato, I believe, we find the understanding that truth and knowledge are fundamentally disputable in relation to the good, bear responsibility to the good, making them disputable. Disputability is given from the good as endless exposure.

All this bears on the authority of knowledge and truth, an authority I understand as given from the good. All authority is ethical|political authority. That is what we hear in Descartes's transition from error to imperfection, ethical imperfection, bearing upon God's goodness and human free will. And it is what we hear in Plato, whose Socrates speaks endlessly of his ignorance, driven as gadfly toward the good, obsessed by the good. Whatever his failings—and I believe he has many—Socrates is portrayed by Plato as obsessed beyond all obsessions by the good, to the point of dying for it, too obsessed perhaps, we might say, though only in terms of an analogous obsession toward the good. Socrates claims that his ignorance is better than others' claims to knowledge; not truer but better. It is a better, I believe, that knows no best, knows no measure. Truth is not quantitatively better than falsity but responsive to a call to which falsity fails frequently to respond—not always.

Plato speaks incessantly of the good, and speaks as well of gifts. Socrates describes himself as a divine gift, another expression of his obsession for the good.

> If you doubt whether I am really the sort of person who would have been sent to this city as a gift from God, you can convince yourselves by looking at it in this way. Does it seem natural that I should have neglected my own affairs and endured the humiliation of allowing my family to be neglected for all these years, while I busied myself all the time on your behalf, going like a father or an elder brother to see each one of you privately, and urging you to set your thoughts on goodness? ... The witness that I can offer to prove the truth of my statement is, I think, a convincing one— my poverty. (Plato, *Apology*, 31bc)

It is an extraordinary claim to truth that Socrates was poor, so obsessed by goodness as to neglect his daily life. I take it to be a response, an exposure, to the good. Socrates' obsession is a divine gift, bearing memory of the good, driven by insatiable desire—for the good beyond any attainment. His quest for knowledge—more aptly, I would say, his pursuit of ignorance— belongs to the same obsession. He himself is victim of the madness he describes in *Phaedrus*, another gift of the gods, including *poiēsis*.

> in reality, the greatest blessings come by way of madness, indeed of madness that is heaven-sent. (Plato, *Phaedrus*, 244c)

it was because they held madness to be a valuable gift, when due to divine dispensation, that they named that art as they did. . . . Corresponding to the superior perfection and value of the prophecy of inspiration over that of omen reading, both in name and in fact, is the superiority of heaven-sent madness over man-made sanity. (244d–245a)

when grievous maladies and afflictions have beset certain families by reason of some ancient sin, madness has appeared among them, and breaking out into prophecy has secured relief by finding the means thereto, namely by recourse to prayer and worship . . . (245ab)

if any man come to the gates of poetry without the madness of the Muses, persuaded that skill alone will make him a good poet, then shall he and his works of sanity with him be brought to nought by the poetry of madness, and behold, their place is nowhere to be found. (245bc)

I have spoken elsewhere of *poiēsis* together with *mimēsis* as divine gifts, anarchic interruptions of the rule of *technē*.[5] Truth without madness is lifeless, lacks the divine spark given from the good. Here I wish to speak of the good whose gift is the madness that obsesses Socrates and Descartes, overwhelms philosophy with passion for the truth, an insatiable passion given from the gods as madness, mad desire for the good.

Recall that "real wisdom is the property of God . . . human wisdom has little or no value." This remark can be read as skeptical, and much of the Western tradition has been directed against its skepticism, within the rule of being. Socrates' claim has another side, however, given from the good. For it is not that human wisdom is false but that it has no value, that whatever value it has is ethical—and you and I may disagree with Socrates, believe that truth and wisdom are very good, bear memory of the good, understood here as a gift from the gods. We who are obsessed with the good are obsessed with its sacredness and divinity. Yet we have given ourselves over to that obsession as if we were prepared to give up the gods in the name of truth. Instead, we need to remember the madness for the good that drives our obsession, remember that every madness is a sacred gift from the good, remember the madness of truth.

One of the themes of Western reason, closely tied to knowledge and truth, is that emotion stands in the way of truth. Socrates speaks of this in *Phaedo*; Descartes famously speaks of it in his *Meditations*. I leave Descartes aside for later, noting that his obsession for certainty may be the greatest obsession known to philosophy. But Socrates' desire for the good is quite unlimited.

In fact, it is wisdom that makes possible courage and self-control and integrity or, in a word, true goodness, and the presence or absence of pleasures and fears and other such feelings makes no difference at all, whereas a system of morality which is based on relative emotional values is a mere illusion, a thoroughly vulgar conception which has nothing sound in it and nothing true. The true moral ideal, whether self-control or integrity or courage, is really a kind of purgation from all these emotions, and wisdom itself is a sort of purification. (Plato, *Phaedo*, 69bc)

I leave aside for another time reading *Phaedo* in the light of death, so that consolation and resolution are called for in the face of fear. Wisdom's strength belongs to goodness; Socrates' words are designed to call forth emotion, passion, obsession, for wisdom rather than other emotions, courage or integrity, even self-control. These may respond to the good but they do not touch it, bear its force directly. Only obsession for the goodness of wisdom, purified of every other emotion, can respond to the gift of the good. The purification of which Socrates speaks, the purification of wisdom, is described as philosophy, obsession with truth in the name of the good. "Well, in my opinion these devotees are simply those who have lived the philosophical life in the right way—a company which, all through my life, I have done my best in every way to join, leaving nothing undone which I could do to attain this end" (76a).

One of *Phaedo*'s most important thoughts concerns recollection, repeated in *Meno*. It is described as remembrance of a knowledge before our birth, but it works throughout our lives, always knowing.

Then if we obtained it before our birth, and possessed it when we were born, we had knowledge, both before and at the moment of birth, not only of equality and relative magnitudes, but of all absolute standards. . . . So we must have obtained knowledge of all these characteristics before our birth. . . . And unless we invariably forget it after obtaining it we must always be born knowing and continue to know all through our lives, because 'to know' means simply to retain the knowledge which one has acquired, and not to lose it. . . . Either we are all born with knowledge of these standards, and retain it throughout our lives, or else, when we speak of people learning, they are simply recollecting what they knew before. In other words, learning is recollection. (Plato, *Phaedo*, 75c–76a)

Thus the soul, since it is immortal and has been born many times, and has seen all things both here and in the other world, has learned everything that is. So we need not be surprised if it can recall the knowledge of virtue or anything else which, as we see, it once possessed. All nature is akin, and the soul has learned everything, so that when a man has recalled a single piece of knowledge—learned it, in ordinary language—there is no reason why he should not find out all the rest, if he keeps a stout heart and does not grow weary of the search, for seeking and learning are in fact nothing but recollection. (Plato, *Meno*, 81cd)

This always knowing seems an extraordinary, indefensible claim if we are to know standards, concepts, the specific determinations, truths, of empirical experience and good and bad. The truth of the good rules over the good itself, holding it in its grip. But if we are always to know something that makes it possible to seek and find truth, including the truth of good and bad, it is a gift that must come without standards, cannot itself be the standard, a truth without truth so to speak, without being, bearing ethical gravity. We recollect not what is good and bad, but bear an immeasurable vision of the ideal from which good and bad may be judged. That is how I read Anaximander's injustice.[6]

I could continue speaking of Plato without end. But I wish to consider other places in which the good emerges in the Western tradition in the name of truth. I will devote the next chapter to *Theaetetus*, where we may imagine another view of truth can be found, closer to its ontology. Perhaps. After that I will leave Plato to himself.

CHAPTER 2

Bird Flight

Theaetetus begins with a story describing how Theaetetus the soldier was wounded in battle, admirable and brave (Plato, *Theaetetus*, 142b), ethical moments. The dialogue takes place predominantly between Socrates and a much younger Theaetetus, described as possessing "[t]he combination of a rare quickness of intelligence with exceptional gentleness and of an incomparably virile spirit with both" (144a). Theaetetus is an exceptional youth, intelligent and courageous, modest and noble, perhaps the perfect pupil to learn what Socrates may teach him, all ethical qualities. After a brief discussion of different subject matters that Theaetetus is studying with Theodorus (145e–146d), subjects Socrates does not teach, Socrates opens the question of what knowledge is, again expressing ignorance. "I cannot make out to my own satisfaction what knowledge is. Can we answer that question?" (146a). The dialogue ends with several telling remarks, one by Theaetetus: "for my part I have already, thanks to you, given utterance to more than I had in me" (Plato, Theaetetus, 210b); he has learned from Socrates something that may be valuable for the rest of his life. Socrates replies that such knowledge is more likely to be useless—"All of which our midwife's skill pronounces to be mere wind eggs and not worth the rearing?" (210b)—concluding with a striking account of the goodness of what Theaetetus has learned, although from the standpoint of knowledge he has learned nothing.

> Then supposing you should ever henceforth try to conceive afresh, Theaetetus, if you succeed, your embryo thoughts will be the better as a consequence of today's scrutiny, and if you remain barren, you will be gentler and more agreeable to your companions, having the good sense not to fancy you know what you do not know. For that, and no more, is all that my art can effect; nor have I any of that knowledge possessed by all the great and admirable men of our own day or of the past. But this

midwife's art is a gift from heaven; my mother had it for women, and I for
young men of a generous spirit and for all in whom beauty dwells. (210bd)

The dialogue concludes in memory of Socrates' trial and death.

I take this account to sum up the dialogue. And perhaps we need go
no further than this summary in our reading. The definition of knowledge
with which Socrates and Theaetetus begin is fulfilled with a definition
familiar to Western epistemology: knowledge is true belief together with an
account, an explanation or justification. Of this, Socrates remarks: "to the
question, 'What is knowledge?' our definition will reply, 'Correct belief
together with knowledge of a differentness,' for, according to it, 'adding an
account' will come to that" (Plato, *Theaetetus*, 210a). Yet "nothing could be
sillier than to say that it is correct belief together with a *knowledge* of
differentness or of anything whatever" (210b).

One way to read this conclusion is that knowledge is situated within
an infinite regress, that to know is always to know that one knows, and that
nothing can break the regress. Knowledge, science, philosophy, whatever,
none can know itself to be true. Later, Cartesian, accounts of methods for
guaranteeing certainty, or claims to truth that contain their own assurances, or knowledge as completion of a journey through territories of
finiteness and ignorance, all fail to break this regress. The modern project
to show that reason legitimates itself remains within this project of breaking the endless regress.

The regress belongs to being. The truth of truth is left to thought, or
reason, or language, showing the being of truth within the gathering of
being. Yet Plato departs from this gathering repeatedly in the dialogue, first
by presenting Theaetetus's nobility, not traits of being or truth at all, but
given from the good. He is intelligent and quick but also noble and brave.
Then, concluding the dialogue, Socrates denies the truth and usefulness of
their investigation, but claims that Theaetetus will be better for the inquiry,
better for not believing that he knows what he does not know. If he follows
Socrates, he will never claim to know anything whatever. But the denial
that he knows neither halts the movement of thought nor interferes with
the work of the good. To the contrary. Ignorance interrupts the gathering
of truth in being in the name of the good. The gift of the good works toward
the good as interruption, interrupting being and being's truth. The midwife's
art is a gift from heaven, from the gods and the good, given to men and
women. Socrates' mother had it. No doubt, Diotima also.

This neglected line more than any other, I believe, represents Plato's
understanding of women and the good, of issues of gender and sexual difference. Greek women did not know geometry, astronomy, calculation, music,
and the liberal arts (Plato, *Theaetetus*, 145a) because they were not taught,

were denied the right to study. And women today, in many countries, are denied the right to education, understood as subject learning. But where Descartes claims that "the power of judging aright and of distinguishing truth from error" (Descartes, *DM*, 39) belongs to all human beings, most likely including women, though certainly not to brutes, a gift from heaven, the gift of which Socrates speaks, and which his mother possesses, is the midwife's art of bringing out knowledge of the limits, the inadequacies, of knowledge, in the name of the good. Plato names the gift as ethical, belonging to the good, where Descartes fails to name it as ethical—though he shows quite clearly that it is so. I will discuss Descartes in detail in chapter 4.

Here I will consider a few additional moments in *Theaetetus* that contribute to this reading, resisting the authority of truth in being in the name of the good, given as a gift from the gods. For in this dialogue Socrates extends the image of midwife, given from heaven to his mother and himself, perhaps to others, extends it as far as he ever does. His mother is a midwife named Phaenarete (Plato, *Theaetetus*, 149a), where *phainō* means to bring to light, to make appear, to shine, and *aretē* means goodness, excellence. Socrates' mother is a midwife who brings the good to light, or brings truth and being to light from the good, or both. The midwife figure expresses the gift of the good, given from the gods.

This gift of the gods, from the good, whether of truth or knowledge or being or virtue or whatever, is brought forth from those who do not have them.

> Consider, then, how it is with all midwives; that will help you to understand what I mean. I dare say you know that they never attend other women in childbirth so long as they themselves can conceive and bear children, but only when they are too old for that. . . .
>
> They say that is because Artemis, the patroness of childbirth, is herself childless, and so, while she did not allow barren women to be midwives, because it is beyond the power of human nature to achieve skill without any experience, she assigned the privilege to women who were past childbearing, out of respect to their likeness to herself. . . .
>
> Moreover, with the drugs and incantations they administer, midwives can either bring on the pains of travail or allay them at their will, make a difficult labor easy, and at an early stage cause a miscarriage if they so decide. (Plato, *Theaetetus*, 149bc)

Midwives are too old to bear,[1] barren themselves, full of experience, close to the gods, working with drugs *(pharmaka)* and incantations. We may read *Theaetetus* as an extended figure of the midwife in relation to the gathering of knowledge and truth, closing the figure with the goodness of knowing that we do not know, a figure of unclosure in relation to disclosure.

Midwives are women; Socrates is the son of a midwife who brings the good into being as truth. These figures of age, experience, barrenness, proximity to the gods, magic and *pharmakeia*, all are intermediary figures of mobility. Including women. Diotima, Pharmakeia, and Phaenarete are all powerful women midway to the gods, strong intermediary figures, brought before us by Socrates who repeatedly denies that he possesses knowledge, repeatedly takes on for himself the mobility, ambiguity, and magical powers of more powerful women, whose power lies not in possessing the good, something that cannot be possessed, nor possessing the truth, which likewise cannot be possessed, but in the gifts they set into motion and keep in circulation.

Irigaray tells us, if we had forgotten, that women as women (or Woman) inhabit intermediary intervals, have no place of their own, understanding place in terms of bounded identities, fixed in place, lacking mobility. In return, she speaks of angels that always move, crossing thresholds. Plato speaks of Socrates, himself always on the move, crossing boundaries, who always refuses to be fixed in place. But Socrates is the son of woman, as are all men, a woman whose task is to move, always to move, to bring forth, to bring beauty and truth forth from the good. Socrates' task is inherited from a woman, from Phaenarete, another Pharmakeia, an intermediary figure of the crossing of the good into being. Like his mother, Socrates always moves, continues to move, resisting the fixing of truth and goodness into being. That is how I understand the other figure with which Socrates describes himself, that of stinging fly.

> God has specially appointed me to this city, as though it were a large thoroughbred horse which because of its great size is inclined to be lazy and needs the stimulation of some stinging fly. It seems to me that God has attached me to this city to perform the office of such a fly, and all day long I never cease to settle here, there, and everywhere, rousing, persuading, reproving every one of you. (Plato, *Apology*, 30e–31a)

I read this figure of the gadfly as a figure of mobility, an intermediary figure that moves in memory of the good, understanding all the figures of remembrance to circulate, never to fix in place, moved by desire of the good, beyond all limit and measure. The state tends to fix in place, fix its laws, to take the truth as ready to hand, as if it either knows the truth and the good or does not need to know them, where the knowing recalls the unsettled movements of the good.

I recall that other famous figure of Socrates, who paralyzes and brings to rest his interlocutors, the utmost extreme against which he must deploy his witch's powers.

Socrates, even before I met you they told me that in plain truth you are a perplexed man yourself and reduce others to perplexity. At this moment I feel you are exercising magic and witchcraft upon me and positively laying me under your spell until I am just a mass of helplessness. If I may be flippant, I think that not only in outward appearance but in other respects as well you are exactly like the flat sting ray that one meets in the sea. Whenever anyone comes into contact with it, it numbs him, and that is the sort of thing that you seem to be doing to me now. My mind and my lips are literally numb, and I have nothing to reply to you. Yet I have spoken about virtue hundreds of times, held forth often on the subject in front of large audiences, and very well too, or so I thought. Now I can't even say what it is. In my opinion you are well advised not to leave Athens and live abroad. If you behaved like this as a foreigner in another country, you would most likely be arrested as a wizard. (Plato, *Meno*, 79e–80b)

Within a repeated figure of magic and witchcraft, Pharmakeia again, and recalling Socrates' trial and death, Meno tells Socrates that he has paralyzed him. This may be the most disastrous condemnation of Socrates in the dialogues, far worse than corrupting the youth. For the stinging fly and midwife Socrates must keep his interlocutors moving, keep the city from coming to rest in complacency and ignorance. The good demands ceaseless motion, ceaseless bringing forth, resists the closure of truth. Socrates, then, cannot leave matters as they stand with Meno, must bring Meno back into circulation. Socrates is forced to claim that he is paralyzed himself, but that he is ready to continue a joint pursuit of truth and virtue, framed by another figure of movement, that of infection.

It isn't that, knowing the answers myself, I perplex other people. The truth is rather that I infect them also with the perplexity I feel myself. So with virtue now. I don't know what it is. . . . Nevertheless I am ready to carry out, together with you, a joint investigation and inquiry into what it is. (Plato, *Meno*, 80d)

Socrates infects others with his own disease, desire for the good.

We may return to the figure of the midwife in *Theaetetus*, reading the dialogue as an account of Socrates as midwife to truth in service to the good, understanding truth as brought to light and motion by Socratic questioning, remembering that he is the son of a powerful woman who brings others to birth. For Socrates continues that "the genuine midwife is the only successful matchmaker" (Plato, *Theaetetus*, 150a), knowing how to bring parents together to "produce the best children" (149d), with "skill in tending and harvesting the fruits of the earth" (149e). Such a midwife brings forth real children (150b), whose "highest and noblest task . . . would be to discern the real from the unreal" (150b), given over entirely to the gathering of being. By comparison, Socrates gives birth to nothing real, does not perform a task given over to being.

> the highest point of my art is the power to prove by every test whether the offspring of a young man's thought is a false phantom or instinct with life and truth. I am so far like the midwife that I cannot myself give birth to wisdom, and the common reproach is true, that, though I question others, I can myself bring nothing to light because there is no wisdom in me. The reason is this. Heaven constrains me to serve as a midwife, but has debarred me from giving birth. So of myself I have no sort of wisdom, nor has any discovery ever been born to me as the child of my soul. Those who frequent my company at first appear, some of them, quite unintelligent, but, as we go further with our discussions, all who are favored by heaven make progress at a rate that seems surprising to others as well as to themselves, although it is clear that they have never learned anything from me. The many admirable truths they bring to birth have been discovered by themselves from within. But the delivery is heaven's work and mine. (150bd)

The art comes from heaven; the progress Socrates' pupils make is to acquire wisdom, except that the wisdom acquired by Theaetetus, in the name of the good, is, like Socrates', barren. The barrenness is its virtue: "if you remain barren, you will be gentler and more agreeable to your companions, having the good sense not to fancy you know what you do not know. For that, and no more, is all that my art can effect" (210c).

It is crucial to remember Meno's attack on Socrates, the one attack, I claim, that Socrates must be able to resist in the name of the good. The critique is that Socrates paralyzes Meno, and might paralyze Theaetetus, that instead of keeping inquiry in circulation, understanding barrenness as a goad, a sting, to keep the city from freezing in place, Socrates' midwifery might bring forth nothing, close off the inquiry, destroy any possibility of knowledge or truth, fail its intermediary movements around the good. That is how I read the rest of *Theaetetus*, as struggling with this possibility of closure. Socrates himself describes his work as a struggle, as the labor of birth—another figure of women—recalling once more that he does not bring anything forth in Theaetetus and Meno, despite tremendous struggle and pain, but the experience of the struggle. We must understand the bringing forth as the only thing brought forth. "[T]hose who seek my company have the same experience as a woman with child; they suffer the pains of labor and, by night and day, are full of distress far greater than a woman's, and my art has power to bring on these pangs or to allay them" (Plato, *Theaetetus*, 151ab). We might hesitate at just one thought: we may hope that women will bring forth capable and caring children. Socrates is barren and brings forth barrenness himself. Yet this barrenness, Socrates' ignorance, is not an ignorance that stops the circulation. We return to Irigaray's figure of the subject, the child, the angel, as intermediary figure. Women's goal is the same as Socrates', to give birth to intermediary movements that never cease, in memory of the good.

For Socrates concludes his description of himself as midwife with a figure of the movement of the truth in memory of the good. Those who feel that Socrates deprives them of a truth they take themselves to possess have been

> positively ready to bite me for taking away some foolish notion they have conceived. They do not see that I am doing them a kindness. They have not learned that no divinity is ever ill-disposed toward man, nor is such action on my part due to unkindness; it is only that I am not permitted to acquiesce in falsehood and suppress the truth. (Plato, *Theaetetus*, 150cd)

Yet Socrates begins his dialogue again with Theaetetus with a complete and total rejection of skepticism and epistemic despair. "[T]ry to explain what knowledge is. Never say it is beyond your power; it will not be so, if heaven wills and you take courage" (151d). Nothing in this endless barren movement results in giving up the pursuit of knowledge. That stops the movement. Heaven gives forth knowledge, truth, and being from the good in endless circulation. We must have the courage to continue the pursuit. Truth belongs to nature's abundance, circulating in the general economy of desire.

The themes of birth and barrenness are organized in *Theaetetus* around the figure of the midwife who, barren herself, brings new beings into being. Socrates' emphasis is not on what is brought into being, the birth, but the giving, the gift given to the figure of midwife, who does not possess things of this world, is not tied by possession to being. The gift, spoken of in Plato repeatedly in relation to the gods and heavens, comes to pass as a gift. But the importance of the gift is to remain in giving, endlessly. At least, that is what gadflies like Socrates do, give endless interruptions. Figures of birth pervade the dialogue's representation of knowledge, explaining the extended concern with becoming.

> Their first principle, on which all that we said just now depends, is that the universe really is motion and nothing else. And there are two kinds of motion. Of each kind there are any number of instances, but they differ in that the one kind has the power of acting, the other of being acted upon. From the intercourse and friction of these with one another arise

> offspring, endless in number, but in pairs of twins. One of each pair is
> something perceived, the other a perception, whose birth always coincides
> with that of the thing perceived. . . . On the other side, the brood of things
> perceived always comes to birth at the same moment with one or another
> of these—with instances of seeing, colors of corresponding variety, with
> instances of hearing, sounds in the same way, and with all the other
> perceptions, the other things perceived that are akin to them. (Plato,
> *Theaetetus*, 156ac)[2]

These images of birth and generation are so powerful and recurrent, reminding us of places where Socrates speaks of *poiēsis,* that I wonder if what
is at stake in this dialogue is not knowledge and truth but bringing into
being from somewhere otherwise than being, as if the kind of account
Socrates is criticizing is one that remains within being, fixed by knowledge
as truth in being. The midwife does not give birth, but where Socrates and
Phaenarete participate, the birth is given from the good.

> in accordance with the account we accepted earlier, agent and patient give
> birth to sweetness and a sensation, both movements that pass simulta-
> neously. The sensation, on the patient's side, makes the tongue percipient,
> while, on the side of the wine, the sweetness, moving in the region of the
> wine, causes it both to be and to appear sweet to the healthy tongue.
> (Plato, *Theaetetus*, 159cd)[3]

We recall Socrates' suggestion in *Phaedrus* that writing and discourse
must be living to be true, where life is associated with *erōs* and *mania*,
intermediary figures. These accounts of coming into being in *Theaetetus*
are dead because they lack soul, lack intermediary movements, are births
that have forgotten the giving that gave them forth. Knowledge as perception lacks memory of the gods and the good. Socrates as midwife has to
resist such births in the name of gifts from heaven.

> Here at last, then, after our somewhat painful labor, is the child we have
> brought to birth, whatever sort of creature it may be. His birth should be
> followed by the ceremony of carrying him round the hearth; we must look
> at our offspring from every angle to make sure we are not taken in by a
> lifeless phantom not worth the rearing. Or do you think an infant of yours
> must be reared in any case and not exposed? Will you bear to see him put
> to the proof, and not be in a passion if your first-born should be taken
> away? (Plato, *Theaetetus*, 160e–161a)[4]

Throughout the dialogue are endless figures of giving birth, of gifts and
bringing into being from becoming, of *poiēsis* as a gift, as giving. The
dialogue ends with a return to birth before closing with the figure of the

midwife who gives a heavenly gift without giving anything, fostering the circulation. "Are we in labor, then, with any further child, my friend, or have we brought to birth all we have to say about knowledge?" (Plato, *Theaetetus*, 210b). The gift from the good gives from something without being and gives forth goods without issue. The giving is all, giving endlessly from the good, without determinate measure or being.

I am speaking of being's abundance, of heterogeneity, an abundance beyond any measure, impossible to fix in place, circulating endlessly, general economy. Our relation to heterogeneity, to the others composing the world, is given from the good as our being together, understanding being together as intermediary, endless movements and crossings, including truth and being. But endless crossings, intermediary movements, are resisted on every side, one side especially given by those who treat truth and being as possessions. Socrates the midwife, in memory of his mother, keeps the circulation moving, leading to his death. Disaster echoes throughout intermediary crossings, throughout our relations to others in memory of the good. The memory of the good is the burden of disaster, disturbing the gathering, reminding us of general economy.

With this thought we can consider the movement in *Theaetetus* as the endless bringing forth of knowledge, truth, and being from the good, resisting foreclosure, interrupting the gathering. Here, then, where Theaetetus names knowledge as perception, Socrates replies that such an account "is not, by any means, to be despised" (Plato, *Theaetetus*, 152a). It is a famous definition of knowledge, given by Protagoras. Socrates associates it with ontology, with Heraclitus and all other Greek philosophers save Parmenides: "All the things we are pleased to say 'are,' really are in process of becoming, as a result of movement and change and of blending one with another. We are wrong to speak of them as 'being,' for none of them ever is; they are always becoming" (152de). Now if being and becoming are binary opposites, then to criticize this claim that everything is becoming and not being is to support a being that does not become, leading to Parmenides. Yet nothing seems more clearly to close off the movement of bringing forth than Parmenides' view that being can never become. And Plato is traditionally interpreted as mediating between being and becoming, though I understand that mediation as intermediary, endless movement between and around binaries, heaven and earth, humans and gods, being and becoming, being-becoming and the good. This endless, intermediary circulation, the travels of angels and desire, gifts from the good, does not belong to being even in the form of becoming, exceeds being and becoming, knowledge and truth, defers all closure, including the paradoxical closure of endless time and becoming. General economy is not infinite restricted economy, not even that of becoming. The openness of becoming represents another closure.

That at least is how I read Socrates' critique of Protagoras, man the measure, far from Heraclitus's flux.

The alternative, to keep the movement of truth in being from closing, is to refuse to consider being and becoming in binary opposition, interrupting their gathering. Socrates begins his discussion with a repetition of the movement essential to body and soul, to all things.

> the healthy condition of the body is undermined by inactivity and indolence, and to a great extent preserved by exercise and motion, isn't it? . . .
>
> And so with the condition of the soul. The soul acquires knowledge and is kept going and improved by learning and practice, which are of the nature of movements. By inactivity, dullness, and neglect of exercise, it learns nothing and forgets what it has learned. . . .
>
> So, of the two, motion is a good thing for both soul and body, and immobility is bad. . . .
>
> Need I speak further of such things as stagnation in air or water, where stillness causes corruption and decay, when motion would keep things fresh, or, to complete the argument, press into its service that 'golden rope' in Homer, proving that he means by it nothing more nor less than the sun, and signifies that so long as the heavens and the sun continue to move round, all things in heaven and earth are kept going, whereas if they were bound down and brought to a stand, all things would be destroyed and the world, as they say, turned upside down? (Plato, *Theaetetus*, 153bd)

This is such a compelling picture of a mobile and changing universe, always flowing, that it is difficult to imagine that Plato is read by many to finally reject this picture in his critique of knowledge as perception. Indeed, that critique moves from the mobility of soul and body, truth and being, to the idea of measure. A measure that always moves does not measure. But measure does not belong to being alone; it comes from the good. Of being, Socrates says:

> The conclusion from all this is, as we said at the outset, that nothing *is* one thing just by itself, but is always in process of becoming for someone, and being is to be ruled out altogether, though, needless to say, we have been betrayed by habit and in observance into using the word more than once only just now. But that was wrong, these wise men tell us, and we must not admit the expressions 'something' or 'somebody's' or 'mine' or 'this' or 'that' or any other word that brings things to a standstill, but rather speak, in accordance with nature, of what is 'becoming,' 'being produced,' 'perishing,' 'changing.' For anyone who talks so as to bring things to a standstill is easily refuted. So we must express ourselves in

each individual case and in speaking of an assemblage of many—to which assemblage people give the name of 'man' or 'stone' or of any living creature or kind. (157ac)

We must not bring things to a standstill with any expression that halts the movement. That would leave us with no measure, no standard, of truth or knowledge, and what appears in dreams and madness is as true as what is perceived by sane interlocutors in the full light of day (Plato, *Theaetetus*, 158ab). The conclusion of this discussion is that "my perception is true for me, for its object at any moment is my reality, and I am, as Protagoras says, a judge of what is for me, that it is, and of what is not, that it is not" (Plato, *Theaetetus*, 160c). We halt the inexhaustible movement of truth and knowledge at the edges of my perception, filling being without voids.

> In general, I am delighted with his statement that what seems to anyone also is, but I am surprised that he did not begin his Truth with the words, The measure of all things is the pig, or the baboon, or some sentient creature still more uncouth. There would have been something magnificent in so disdainful an opening, telling us that all the time, while we were admiring him for a wisdom more than mortal, he was in fact no wiser than a tadpole, to say nothing of any other human being. What else can we say, Theodorus? If what every man believes as a result of perception is indeed to be true for him; if, just as no one is to be a better judge of what another experiences, so no one is better entitled to consider whether what another thinks is true or false, and, as we have said more than once, every man is to have his own beliefs for himself alone and they are all right and true—then, my friend, where is the wisdom of Protagoras, to justify his setting up to teach others and to be handsomely paid for it, and where is our comparative ignorance or the need for us to go and sit at his feet, when each of us is himself the measure of his own wisdom? (Plato, *Theaetetus*, 161c–162a)

A traditional reading of this critical summary remains within the rule of being, suggesting that Protagoras's claim to wisdom and truth cannot be sustained as a claim if every person's claim to truth has the same standing as any other's. Yet we may read it also as an account of epistemic authority. Here Protagoras's claim that knowledge is perception claims to possess an authority it has given away, an authority given from the good, placed in endless intermediary movement.

Socrates gives his own epistemic authority away wherever he can. And *Theaetetus* concludes with a barren birth, still claimed to be good. Is it possible to preserve the idea of avoiding coming to a standstill, keeping the flow of truth and knowledge alive, gifts from the gods that must be kept alive, in movement, intermediary figures, without halting at this claim?

Can the intermediary movement remain in movement without fixing authority? I read Socrates' critique of Protagoras as that he halts the movement of truth, followed by Socrates' urging Theaetetus not to give up the search for truth. Skepticism and relativism—if those are the names of what we have been discussing in Protagoras's name, for his enigmatic words can be given countless other interpretations—can halt the intermediary movement of truth. The doctrine—any doctrine, perhaps—that all is becoming, that truth is evanescent, becomes the doctrine that being, knowledge, and truth are impossible to gather, halting the circulation as thoroughly as the most dogmatic claims to possession of truth. As a doctrine, they fix truth in its place, in this case nowhere. The good resists that fixation, keeps truth and being on the move, not as becoming but as interruption. Stinging flies and torpedo fish interrupt the gathering of being, do so in memory of the good.

I will briefly consider the remaining moments in *Theaetetus* at which a definition of knowledge might bring us to fruition to see if they support the reading I have been developing. Immediately after the critique of Protagoras expressed above, that he should have said that pigs or baboons were the measure rather than men, disdaining any claim to wisdom, keeping truth always on the move, understanding our relation to the gods as endless intermediary movements, given as love, desire, and soul, Socrates recalls memory, another figure of endless movement, known to all who read Plato as recollection, *anamnēsis,* endless pursuit of what has been forgotten. Socrates' words in *Phaedrus* on *psuchē*'s self-movement are worth recalling, contrasted with Aristotle's unmoved mover, who gives movement only by not moving itself. Socrates' words are that

> All soul is immortal, for that which is ever in motion is immortal. But that which while imparting motion is itself moved by something else can cease to be in motion, and therefore can cease to live; it is only that which moves itself that never intermits its motion, inasmuch as it cannot abandon its own nature; moreover this self-mover is the source and first principle of motion for all other things that are moved. (Plato, *Phaedrus,* 245cd)

The nature of soul is to be immortal, an immortality of unending movement, moved by itself, impossible to bring to rest, endless life and commotion. The nature of immortal, heavenly being is motion, inexhaustible intermediary motion, giving movement to all other things. Soul, the good, the heavens express unending circulation, beyond any earthly identity.

And so with memory, with *anamnēsis,* though we must beware of memories of a memory so dead that it would come to halt, memories that would bring being and truth to rest, gathered in thought and being. Knowledge understood as perception halts the intermediary movement of truth in finite becoming, in your perception and mine, dead to divine recollection. Endless becoming is not endless intermediary movement because it has no memory of the gift of the good.

Knowledge as perception passes into knowledge as memory, under a certain view of remembering. "[C]an a man who has become acquainted with something and remembers it, not know it?" (Plato, *Theaetetus,* 163d). We remember that the dialogue begins with a risky and uncertain memory, bolstered by written notes, calling the very memory of which Socrates speaks here into question as truth.

> But what was this conversation? Could you repeat it? . . .
>   Certainly not, just from memory. But I made some notes at the time, as soon as I got home, and later on I wrote out what I could recall at my leisure. Then, every time I went to Athens, I questioned Socrates upon any point where my memory had failed and made corrections on my return. In this way I have pretty well the whole conversation written down. (143a)

From the beginning of the dialogue, expressing the possibility that there might be a dialogue that you and I might recall, we are brought face to face with memory and writing, reminding us of *Phaedrus,* where living memory is contrasted with writing. Here another contrast emerges, though not perhaps between writing and recollection. For there could be no *Theaetetus* without writing, both for us and for its interlocutors, a dialogue told in mimetic narrative, quite incompatible with Socrates' critique of *mimēsis* in *Republic* (Plato, *Republic,* 392–95).[5]

> This is the book, Terpsion. You see how I wrote the conversation—not in narrative form, as I heard it from Socrates, but as a dialogue between him and the other persons he told me had taken part. These were Theodorus the geometer and Theaetetus. I wanted to avoid in the written account the tiresome effect of bits of narrative interrupting the dialogue, such as 'and I said' or 'and I remarked' wherever Socrates was speaking of himself, and 'he asserted' or 'he did not agree,' where he reported the answer. So I left out everything of that sort, and wrote it as a direct conversation between the actual speakers. (Plato, *Theaetetus,* 143bc)

Memory frames the dialogue, as it frames perhaps all the dialogues, our memories, Plato's memory of Socrates, repeated throughout the dialogues as memories of past events, of time and loss, all together with *mimēsis.* Plato's dialogues represent time and loss so profoundly, I would say, that we must think of truth and knowledge in memory of loss, loss of the good I would say. A memory of loss, of forgetting, of which recollection is restitution, still mourning for loss. Truth is restitution for the loss of forgetting.

This is Heidegger's thought interrupted by an alteration. The loss is out of the good; the memory is endless interruption of the closure of being upon that wound. I add that desire, given from the good, for being, truth, and knowledge here, knows the joy of interrupting closure.

Could knowledge be memory, interrupted? Or, conversely, could we remember without knowing, without a gathering of truth and being, a memory of wounding? Socrates remembers, reminisces, recalls, and recollects, all to deny that he possesses knowledge. The transition he describes in *Theaetetus* is from perceiving something to remembering something, not nothing (Plato, *Theaetetus,* 163e). Everything that follows, on my reading, sustains this movement, this portrayal of knowledge as a memory of being, truth as truth of being, both something rather than nothing, contrasted with *anamnēsis,* memory of the lost divine. I pass over the details of the discussion that follows from this understanding of memory, that we must remember something that is not present, reintroducing nonbeing into being, absence into presence in the form of memory, still under the rule of being (Plato, *Theaetetus,* 164ac). Absence here belongs to being, nonbeing to being. I pass over the intermediary discussions in which knowing relates to not-knowing as being relates to nonbeing, non-oppositionally, undermining the binary opposition between truth and falsity, being and nonbeing. One can both know and not know the same thing at the same time, or, if that is too frightening or perplexing, at different times (Plato, *Theaetetus,* 166bc). That man is the measure acknowledges human diversity, differences between human beings and in nature. It does so, Socrates describes an alleged Protagoras saying, by regarding all experiences as true (167b). I pass over with but a passing glance the structure of the dialogue, made up of children except for Socrates and Theodorus, remarked upon by Socrates himself (168e). Age and youth replay intermediary and endless movements throughout the later dialogues, representing time. Youth represents contentiousness, binary oppositions, quickness of thought; age represents seriousness of purpose and tolerance for what cannot be thought oppositionally, slowness of thought (Plato, *Parmenides,* 128e).[6] Socrates' critique of Protagoras is that the opposition between truth and falsity, knowledge and ignorance, represents something inherent in our understanding of truth and knowledge (Plato, *Theaetetus,* 170b), though perhaps not central to being and nonbeing, being and becoming, to *anamnēsis.*

> Evils, Theodorus, can never be done away with, for the good must always have its contrary; nor have they any place in the divine world, but they must needs haunt this region of our mortal nature. . . . In the divine there is no shadow of unrighteousness, only the perfection of righteousness, and nothing is more like the divine than any one of us who becomes as righteous as possible. (Plato, *Theaetetus,* 176ac)

I read this nonbeing of unrighteousness within the opposition of good and evil as beyond binary opposition, comparable to Diotima's description of a nature beyond all measure. I read it as memory of the good. I take our relation to it to be unending intermediary movement. For again, Socrates denies that he has the knowledge in question.

I pass over all the further discussions of truth in being that prevent distinctions between true and false, knowledge and ignorance, including Socrates' references to coming to a halt (Plato, *Theaetetus*, 183ab). I pass over Socrates' suggestion that knowledge is not perception but judgment: "perhaps true judgment is knowledge" (187b); and the corresponding difficulty of understanding false judgments, of what is not, nonbeing (187d). We are still within the rule of being, struggling with the being of nonbeing and, correspondingly, with the truth of untruth, the not-knowing of knowledge. We find ourselves required to insist on the coexistence and being of binary oppositions and distinctions at the same time that we find that those oppositions make truth and being and the good unknowable, unintelligible, because these belong to the infinite, to the gods, beyond binaries and oppositions. If recollection, *anamnēsis*, repeats the play of knowing and not-knowing, being and nonbeing, for which it was offered in response, then it fails in the task assigned it, remains in being, struggling with nonbeing. We recollect the good beyond binary oppositions, while in our recollection we fall into such oppositions. Put another way, the gods know nothing of falsity, ignorance, and evil, do not participate in such oppositions. What we recollect, as sacred, given from the good, is this beyond, which is no thing and has no relation to time, sets no standard. Our relation to time is given in our intermediary movements around this memory of something beyond time, interrupting the hold of every opposition, every distinction, refusing closure, preventing our coming to halt, or thinking we come to rest, at a distinction or identity. The intermediary movement around the good is general economy, resisting the authority of every restricted economy. But we live in restricted economies, touching each other dyadically, in proximity, touched by intermediary and indefinite movements of desire and love. I read *Theaetetus* as inquiring into knowledge in intermediary movements between the good, beyond being, and our belonging to being in oppositional movements.

I pass over all these intermediary movements to return to memory. For after asking Theaetetus to search his memory (Plato, *Theaetetus*, 190b), Socrates discusses memory explicitly for the first time in the dialogue, reminding us of the Muses, whose mother is Memory (191d), reminding us of Socrates' mother, of the importance of mothers to time and being as well as the good, of the disruption we have seen of the closure of truth in being, all in that famous figure of wax that constitutes Descartes' understanding of identity.

> Let us call it the gift of the Muses' mother, Memory, and say that
> whenever we wish to remember something we see or hear or conceive in
> our own minds, we hold this wax under the perceptions or ideas and
> imprint them on it as we might stamp the impression of a seal ring.
> Whatever is so imprinted we remember and know so long as the image
> remains; whatever is rubbed out or has not succeeded in leaving an im-
> pression we have forgotten and do not know. (Plato, *Theaetetus,* 191de)

The wax is malleable to the point where to recall the trace of memory we
must acknowledge erasure. Memory is presence and absence, repetition and
erasure. Erasure, nonbeing, belongs to memory and being.

Socrates goes on to describe what appear to be cases in which error is
impossible, suggesting that we cannot err in memory without perception or
perception without memory, suggesting that error is midway between the
one and the other.[7] Where false judgment is possible, he says, is where we
perceive indistinctly and try to fit that perception into the wrong impression. The figure of wax imprints exercises a powerful hold on memory.

> When a man has in his mind a good thick slab of wax, smooth and
> kneaded to the right consistency, and the impressions that come through
> the senses are stamped on these tables of the 'heart'—Homer's word
> hints at the mind's likeness to wax—then the imprints are clear and
> deep enough to last a long time. Such people are quick to learn and also
> have good memories, and besides they do not interchange the imprints
> of their perceptions but think truly. These imprints being distinct and
> well spaced are quickly assigned to their several stamps—the 'real things'
> as they are called—and such men are said to be clever. Do you agree?
> (Plato, *Theaetetus,* 194cd)

> When a person has what the poet's wisdom commends as a 'shaggy heart,'
> or when the block is muddy or made of impure wax, or oversoft or hard,
> the people with soft wax are quick to learn, but forgetful, those with hard
> wax the reverse. Where it is shaggy or rough, a gritty kind of stuff con-
> taining a lot of earth or dirt, the impressions obtained are indistinct; so
> are they too when the stuff is hard, for they have no depth. Impressions
> in soft wax also are indistinct, because they melt together and soon be-
> come blurred. And if, besides this, they overlaps through being crowded
> together into some wretched little narrow mind, they are still more indis-
> tinct. All these types, then, are likely to judge falsely. When they see or
> hear or think of something, they cannot quickly assign things to their
> several imprints. Because they are so slow and sort things into the wrong
> places, they constantly see and hear and think amiss, and we say they are
> mistaken about things and stupid. (194e–195a)

I take this account, except for some details, to be as truthful an account as
possible of errors in memory as can be devised within the gathering of

being. Memory of things, of past perceptions, is like an imprint. Some can hold it firmly in mind; some cannot because their medium is too fluid and indeterminate. This is an account of remembered things, held in the mind as if in a block of wax, tempered perhaps by recalling that wax melts at a low temperature, lower perhaps than that of the brain. But the fundamental question for us, for Plato, is whether this figure gives us *anamnēsis*.

Theaetetus loves this figure of memory because it gives him a clear picture of true and false memory and judgment, a picture he can hold firmly in his mind—whether true or not. And indeed, perhaps every such story, true or not, can be held firmly in the mind, imprinted on the waxen surface of thought, as if it were true, as if it were owned, leaving us in error against the account given. Socrates returns to his refrain that he does not know what knowledge is, that "we are still destitute of knowledge" (Plato, *Theaetetus,* 196e) and remain so under the midwife's auspices. He shifts the discourse of imprinting, remembering and knowing something, given over entirely to being, to having, possessing knowledge (197b). Possession, I would say, not only belongs entirely to being, but in the name of property gathers things up, brings the flow of beings to a halt. What I possess ceases to move unless I permit it to do so. Private property, property of any kind, repeatedly halts the intermediary movement within the rule of being, the rule of my being, what belongs to me.

The figure of wax imprinted is not a figure of possession—or rather, does not become one until Descartes. The figure of possession here is taken up by that of an aviary.

> Now consider whether knowledge is a thing you can possess in that way without having it about you, like a man who has caught some wild birds— pigeons or what not—and keeps them in an aviary he has made for them at home. In a sense, of course, we might say he 'has' them all the time inasmuch as he possess them, mightn't we? (Plato, *Theaetetus,* 197cd)

This figure of bird knowledge, I insist, is a striking figure of memory. Socrates has no time for any knowledge here but that of memory, knowledge which we capture as it flies about to hold in our mental cage. This figure of memory explicitly expresses the understanding that to know, to remember something—always some thing—is to halt its circulation, to gather it into the aviary of our minds. Even so, to possess the memories as if they were birds is also not to possess them.

> But in another sense he "has" none of them, though he has got control of them, now that he has made them captive in an enclosure of his own; he can take and have hold of them whenever he likes by catching any bird he chooses, and let them go again, and it is open to him to do that as often as he pleases. (Plato, *Theaetetus,* 197cd)

We are to think of knowledge—now including teaching, learning, science: I would include all forms of *technē* (Plato, *Theaetetus*, 198ad)—as hunting for what we already possess, reaching into the aviary of the mind to grasp the ideas flying about.

Yet the image of possession fails to resolve the problem of error. We still may seize the wrong bird at times without knowing it or seize the bird we are looking for without recognizing it. All figures of possession, seizing, grabbing, holding, gathering are figures of halting the circulation. The striking and appealing figure of an aviary in which ideas fly about as they will, unrestricted, which we hope to bring to a halt when we need to know them, own them, gather them fails to resolve the problem of error. But more deeply, it represents an idea of memory incompatible with *anamnēsis*.

For remembrance arises as a need in a context in which we both know and do not know, where errors are common, and does not resolve, or overcome, the problem of error. The one problem that *anamnēsis* cannot overcome is that of error. Nor can it address the question to which Socrates leads Theaetetus subsequently, that of defining the account, the justification, that might turn true belief into knowledge. Theaetetus states this final, familiar definition of knowledge within another gesture of forgetting.

> I have heard someone make the distinction. I had forgotten, but now it comes back to me. He said that true belief with the addition of an account *(logos)* was knowledge, while belief without an account was outside its range. Where no account could be given of a thing, it was not 'knowable'—that was the word he used—where it could, it was knowable. (Plato, *Theaetetus*, 201cd)

He knew all the time but had forgotten. Memory belongs to forgetting. Knowledge and truth, as memory, also belong to forgetting. But forgetting is not always forgetting things, but sometimes is forgetting the gods, or being, or the good. *Anamnēsis* is a remembering within the wound of the forgetting that is *logos*, a forgetting that may not contain the name of anything forgotten. Recollection belongs to forgetting. And in the same vein, perhaps, we may return to Socrates' final words in which he again denies that he knows but suggests to Theaetetus that withholding claims to truth and knowledge recalls the good, that forgetting is at the heart of *anamnēsis, lēthe* of *alētheia*. These are not errors to escape but the soul of memory, knowledge, and truth, always moving. The forgotten good gives birth to being, a good which is nothing at all to remember or forget, nothing to hold in place. *Anamnēsis* joins *poiēsis* and *mimēsis* as figures of interruption, interrupting reason's truth. The truth of *mimēsis* and *poiēsis* interrupts the authority of reason's truth; the truth of *anamnēsis* interrupts the authority of remembered truth; untruth, *lēthe,* interrupts the reign of truth: all movements given from the good.

The question of truth for us here in not whether we can remember what we forgot, nor even whether we can think of remembering without forgetting, but of the movement of truth and memory in recollection of the good they serve, recollected as forgetting, intermediary figures. Memory and truth serve the good as gifts it gives to being, a giving that circulates, continues to circulate, against all attempts gather it up and to bring it to halt. Truth and memory, understood as possessions along with other human works and masteries, claim to bring the gift to rest. That is nature's endless struggle, endless movement, the injustice in memory of which we may hope to pursue restitution. Memory gathers up the movement, restricts the abundance; forgetting, together with interruption, is its movement toward abundance from within the restriction. It does not restore abundance; abundance does not need restoration, for it cannot be restricted. The restriction of nature's abundance restricts nothing. But it forgets its own limits. The rule of being over truth is the forgetting of the restriction of the gift of the good given over to being.

CHAPTER 3

Bat Ears

We began our journey in truth with Aristotle's implacable link of truth with being and saying, the journey I hope to undertake again but not to repeat. "To say of what is that it is not, or of what is not that it is, is false, while to say of what is that it is, and of what is not that it is not, is true" (Aristotle, *Metaphysics*, 1011). We have diverted ourselves with a passage through Plato to recall the possibility that the truth given by Aristotle to being and saying comes from the good, bears a relation unspeakable in being. Everything else I will have to say on truth bears a memory of this good that, wondrous in beauty, knows nothing of the opposition of good and bad, right and wrong, true and false, though all do their work in that memory.

The memory of the good is given to us in many ways, but one irresistible gift, endlessly giving, is that of desire. We have seen that Aristotle begins his *Metaphysics* not in being but in desire. "All men by nature desire to know" (Aristotle, *Metaphysics*, 980a), a desire bound to nature so tightly and excessively as to exceed every bond of truth to being. I read desire as excessive, reaching beyond any object, responding to gifts of abundance from the gods beyond the reach of being. Desire reaches beyond the gathering of being, beyond truth, toward the good. Truth and knowledge inhabit this reach, circulate as goods in the infinite yearning of desire—a hunger beyond the limits of any being including the infinite, any infinite. In this way, in Aristotle's words, desire for knowledge and truth betrays the rule of truth and being, as desire's excessive reach betrays every limit and object it would enfold. Nothing can encompass desire, neither truth nor being nor saying, nor the good. The good sets desire free beyond encompassment, beyond gathering, and in that movement, frees its objects from their limits, interrupting every limit.

In this way, in the desire for truth beyond any limits, we find desire beyond any limits, including the limits it sets for itself, powerfully described

by Deleuze and Guattari: " 'Why do men fight *for* their servitude as stub-
bornly as though it were their salvation?' " (Deleuze & Guattari, *A-O*, 29);
and in a more rigorous formulation:

> Hence the goal of schizoanalysis: to analyze the specific nature of the
> libidinal investments in the economic and political spheres, and thereby
> show how, in the subject who desires, desire can be made to desire its own
> repression—whence the role of the death instinct in the circuit connect-
> ing desire to the social sphere. (Deleuze & Guattari, *A-O*, 105)

Desire turns back on *(se rabattre sur)* itself in a movement beyond itself.
The movement beyond reaches back, falls back in an intermediary movement, interrupts its own gathering. In this reaching toward and back we
find the circulation of goods, gifts from the good, including truth and
saying and being, all demanding and exceeding their limits. That is how I
understand the force of the desire for truth that begins Aristotle's *Metaphysics*. I will call it the body of truth, truth's body expressed as desire.

We have seen that Aristotle does not always speak of desire when he
speaks of truth, and when he does not he follows the line of thought from
which I hope to depart, linking truth with being and saying, under the rule
of being. I read desire and gifts from the good as opening the possibility of
releasing the rule of being even as that opening turns back upon the possibility that desire might demand its own abjection, subordinating itself to
its own repression. This turning back is a subject to ponder at great length,
the body of truth given as desire, where desire can fall back upon itself in
the name of truth, repressing its relation to the good. And perhaps all
repression is forgetting the good, where the good is nothing, not a thing,
nor a no-thing, but the endless possibility of falling back and away, beyond,
in a turning back to the earth.

We remain, for the moment, within the rule of being. For Aristotle
speaks of truth away from desire and the good, within the *logos*, except for
repeated memories of the un-, the falling back and away, that haunt desire.
And perhaps we should not forget that metaphysics is, like physics, concerned with, rooted in, being, in a saying of being, where truth demands to
be founded. Carlo Sini reminds us of Aristotle's bat, embarking us upon a
journey in truth, including bats' and other truths (Sini, *IT*, 2–3).

> The investigation of the truth is in one way hard, in another easy. An
> indication of this is found in the fact that no one is able to attain the truth
> adequately, while, on the other hand, no one fails entirely, but every one
> says something true about the nature of things, and while individually
> they contribute little or nothing to the truth, by the union of all a con-
> siderable amount is amassed. Therefore, since the truth seems to be like

the proverbial door, which no one can fail to hit, in this way it is easy, but the fact that we can have a whole truth and not the particular part we aim at shows the difficulty of it.

Perhaps, as difficulties are of two kinds, the cause of the present difficulty is not in the facts but in us. For as the eyes of bats are to the blaze of day, so is the reason in our soul to the things which are by nature most evident of all. . . . (Aristotle, *Metaphysics*, 993b)

I halt this reading at the bat *(nukteris)*, who does not need eyes at all, who may never see the sun, or being, but hangs upside down in the dark during the day, in the light of being, devoid of interest in being's light, surrounded by his kind, millions of other bats, and who emerges in the dark to hunt by sound, to hear, and smell, to hear nothing but echoes of themselves, in truth. I temporarily give the name of Ari to this bat, Aristotle's left-handed bat, who knows nothing of the radiance of being, of the light of the sun, shuts his useless eyes to the sun in order to hear something else, otherwise than the order of light, on the left *(sinestra)* side of being.

Which is not to deny that we find something sinister in Aristotle, concerning bats.

In like manner we may infer that, after the birth of animals, plants exist for their sake, and that the other animals exist for the sake of man, the tame for use and food, the wild, if not all, at least the greater part of them, for food, and for the provision of clothing and various instruments. Now if nature makes nothing incomplete, and nothing in vain, the inference must be that she has made all animals for the sake of man. (Aristotle, *Politics*, 1256b)

Bats and other animals are for the sake of man as plants are for the sake of animals. The possibility that bats, and plants, and other animals, and more, exist for their own sake, not for others, and that this has something to do with truth, echoes to us from the good, interrupting the reign of use.

Aristotle, meanwhile, gestures beyond being to what?—more being. A gesture we have seen is given from the good, at least in Plato.

Now we do not know a truth without its cause; and a thing has a quality in a higher degree than other things if in virtue of it the similar quality belongs to the other things (e.g. fire is the hottest of things; for it is the cause of the heat of all other things); so that that which causes derivative truths to be true is most true. Therefore the principles of eternal things must be always most true; for they are not merely sometimes true, nor is there any cause of their being, but they themselves are the cause of the being of other things, so that as each thing is in respect of being, so is it in respect of truth. (Aristotle, *Metaphysics*, 993b)

The unmoved mover gives the cause of things to those things, gives them their truth and being, quite forgetful of the good. As each thing is in respect of being, so it is in respect of truth, gathered into its final cause. Being and saying each repeat truth endlessly, as does truth, repeating truth and being and saying. Yet if the cause of things is the idea of the good, then it is also the cause of truth. And if each thing is in respect of being as it is in respect of truth, then truth is a forgetting of the good. In being, and saying, and truth. All seen, and forgotten, I suggest, in the movement of desire. I postpone again the body of truth, falling away from the good.

For it will help us greatly in our quest for the truth and beauty of truth, gifts from the good, to fly with our bat, to join our journey with bats, for a while, interrupting the movement. I named the bat that does not see but hears himself and remembers the good, that flies from right to left, across being toward the good, I named him Ari: Aristotle's heir. I now name him Carlo, Ari Carlo Bat, in memory of a treatment of truth that deeply considers its mysteries in commemoration of the bat, yet does not remember its own desires and their repressions, does not recall the good, but recognizes truth's enchantment. For a little while I follow the human, Sini, who speaks of truth from Aristotle's bat to moonchild to the mystery, the enchantment of the world, all in the light of being, light and dark, while the bat flies by listening to himself reaching beyond light and dark to the good, desiring to fly.

Sini reads Aristotle in the light of being so that desire falls out of truth. He reads him backward to Parmenides and forward to Hegel, speaking of this journey and reading in memory of Heidegger, all in the light and shadows of being and saying, ignoring desire in Hegel where our bat recalls nothing else in Hegel, nothing beyond desire in Spirit's journey toward the gathering of being. With respect to Aristotle, and beyond, Sini says some remarkable things, caring and sensitive things on truth, without a glimmer of memory of the good. I follow his path with Ari Carlo the bat, who reads everything over again recalling the good, driven by mad desire for the good.

We return to Aristotle, who describes what is hard and easy about truth. Sini speaks of these in six "points," all lighted by being and saying, gathered in place.

> 1. *Anyone can say something about the truth (reality or the nature of things).* Man and his "speech" therefore, are always already placed in the truth. (Sini, *IT,* 3)

We are always already placed in the rule of being. For the bat, who does not see being, does not gather truth in the light, speaks a different language, that of the good, or desire, echoing in the dark. If we are always already in the good, torn by desire, we have no place there, find every place hard no matter how easy.

We human beings, perhaps all, perhaps some of us, are always already gathered in the lighting of being, still in the dark. The bat, however, the bats together, are in the ringing of being, happy to fly in the dark, listening and responding to the sound, the gift, of the good. Reason's response to what is most evident, not to see what lights the sky, is perhaps anything but like the useless eyes of the bat responding to the sun, not to see the sun but to hear many things, perhaps even to hear the sun—we do not know— always ringing back to the bat his own songs. Bats build a world together, teeming and abundant, large and small, a fetid, crowded, teeming world of bats, keeping the surrounding world sparkling clean.

How can a world of bats who build that world together not open upon the truth of being, the truth of being in the world of bats, bat-worlds among other worlds, other teeming and abundant worlds made so by bats? This ecological truth of being is, however, not a lighting but a ringing in the dark. The truth of being, ecologically speaking, is a plenitude of truths and beings, difficult, perhaps impossible to gather, where nature does not add up to a truth, hard or easy, part or whole, does not sum or add up. Any one, or any thing, including a bat or colony of bats, is always in the truth, but not by saying or speaking words, not in the light but in the dark, sonance rather than radiance. Or touch. The truth of being does not add up because other creatures and things, like bats, live in their and our worlds, make their worlds and thereby help to make ours, always in certain ways otherwise.

For us to mark this otherwise, to say, or to know otherwise without saying, as we may be overwhelmed in silence by swarms of millions of bats at dusk, darkening the air, making it harder for us to see, but filled with exact precision for them, who hear everything in every place; for us to have the slightest sense of this otherwise of truth and being is to know not merely that there are obscurities that we will never know, darknesses in light, but that our truth is the darkness of others, and conversely. And more. For this knowledge, this truth of the untruth of truth, marks not a darkness at the edges of light and saying, but the darkness of other truths and beings than saying and light, ungathered in the rays of the sun. For us to see and speak is not to know, to make impossible to know, what bats hear and sing, the world they know. And more. For to grant this truth of being is to grant something that eludes the truth, the gathering of being, as bats' calls elude our sight, and the sun eludes their hearing, perhaps; and also eludes being itself, as lighting, calling us to something otherwise. For we are called, are given as a gift, the possibility of reaching for what cannot show itself as truth in being, yet belongs to the being of bats, who themselves are called to live and act in being and truth by something that no collection of truths and beings can contain. The desire to be does not gather in being's light; for it may ring in being and truth. But lighting, ringing, and whatever more, all gather truth in being in response to the call of desire. Desire calls from the good, exposes us to others in their truth, and more, an exposure and debt to gather beyond gathering. For bats, this exposure to the good rings in being bringing swarms of bats together in community and desire. And this is so even as some of us may find bats repugnant. Repugnance and desire touch each other, hand and claw.

Anyone—human or animal or plant or thing—belongs in truth, gathered in being and otherwise than being. Human beings say and see; others sing and hear; still others touch, all openings onto and into being, interrupting its solidity. The solidity of being opens everywhere to truth in touch, and more. "Man and his 'speech'" (Sini's words) mark the smallest, thinnest, touch in being, opening being to the truth of saying, in the light, knowing little of the truth of touch, in the dark. Questions of man and being—"What does 'being' mean? What does 'man' mean? Can we explain either one of these terms without making reference to the other?" (Sini, *IT,* 3)—call for supplementation by remembering the bat, who displaces the hold of "man" (including woman?) on being, a call that being cannot offer except as given from the good. We recall Socrates' suggestion that not man but pigs and baboons, now bats, might be the measure of truth.

2. *Truth requires investigation, a theory.* (Sini, *IT,* 3)

> It is right also that philosophy should be called the science of truth. For the end of theoretical knowledge is truth . . . Now we do not know a truth without its cause . . . (Aristotle, *Metaphysics,* 993b)

With the bats whose blinding by the sun does not in the least impede their truth, their movement from building worlds to flight in the surrounding earth, day or night, we may read these words differently from Sini. Human truth requires a theory; human philosophy is the science of truth, demanding a cause. Forgetting the bat, cause and theory achieve the truth. Recalling the bat and bat's truth, cause and theory fall away from the good, achieving a truth that betrays the desire that gives rise to it, to know the truth. The truth of philosophy and science, of theory and cause (in being), is at the same time not the truth of being, is the untruth of the bat's truth and being, gathers truth in place against the call of infinite exposure. We must distinguish theory, science, and cause given over to being as saying, for human beings, and the cause of which Socrates speaks that gives forth the possibility of truth and being, for human beings and others, given in every place as endless exposure. In memory of the bat, given from the good, we read that human truth requires a theory enmired in being's causes, forgetting other truths and causes, forgetting that we are not all of being, that we do not own the good, that we are exposed to others beyond any gathering. We may hope to know that our unlimited desire for knowledge makes it impossible for us to know and admire other knowledges, knowledges we will never know, truths whose truth is beyond our reach. Our truth is within an untruth so far and wide as to interrupt the abundance of being.

> 3. *The cause of the difficulty in the investigation of truth is not in the things but in us.* Therefore, is there a "we" in man that is not in the truth or that does not know itself to be in it? Aristotle employs the image of the bat. But why, we should ask ourselves, is reason blind to the things most evident of all? Why does the most evident *(aletheia, alethestaton)* elude us? (Sini, *IT,* 3–4)

Being is free from the difficulty in truth; errors belong to us. "Perhaps . . . the cause of the present difficulty is not in the facts but in us" (Aristotle, *Metaphysics*, 993b). Perhaps. Aristotle does not claim as strongly as Sini that we are the cause of difficulties. Only perhaps. And with this thought that being is good enough in itself not to give forth error we embark upon a thought of truth in being that later passes into the goodness of God. All in the name of truth. From the beginning being is taken to be undivided in truth, by truth, undivided in error or goodness. Either being is good in the way of truth, free from untruth; or being is good, existence is good; or being is neither good nor bad, but arises in its goodness and truth in the light of saying. Perhaps. All these goods impede the circulation.

Aristotle employs the image of the bat, Sini says, without saying what that image tells us in relation to being's untruth. Why is reason blind to evident things, to any things, if they are not blind to themselves, in untruth as truth? The bat speaks and clicks and sings of truths to which reason must be blind to be reason, in the truth. The lighting of being shows itself as reason's truth deaf to the truths of bats, deaf to its own desires and bat desires. With the image of the bat, perhaps, we may think that the difficulty in truth belongs to truth, untruth to truth, not as truth rules over untruth, as it seeks to control and perhaps eliminate untruth, but a belonging together in which there cannot be the one without the other, in which the one interrupts the other, a belonging together that interrupts the gathering. And in this impossibility, being opens onto its nonbeing, not as if another being, circulating around being, within the rule of being, but as bat's truth is something to which reason is deaf, in its lighting and its darkness—for the darkness of reason still belongs to light, knows nothing of sound and silence—being's gift from the good belongs to being as an otherwise that knows nothing of either being or nonbeing. That is something

of what I understand Levinas to mean by speaking of "otherwise than being" instead of "being's *other*" (Levinas, *OB*, 3). The good touches being
otherwise as the bat's truth touches reason's truth across the lighting and
darkening of being, not another lighting or darkening. Ringing is otherwise. The music of the bat does not belong to the music of the spheres if
they belong to being, if music belongs to being, except as otherwise, as
interruption. Music, bats' and otherwise, interrupts the gathering of being
in the light of language.

> 4. *Aristotle clearly conceives the investigation of truth not just as
> fact but as a 'social' process.* . . . Everyone contributes to the search for
> truth . . . (Sini, *IT,* 4)

Every human but perhaps not every bat. Yet without the language of which
Aristotle and Sini speak so loudly and insistently, bats live a communal and
social world of greater density than human beings. Why should we not
grant that they are in the truth, a truth that is not just "theirs" any more
than "our" truth is "ours" alone, bat and human as if their worlds do not
touch, when we find bats around us and thrill at their exploits, if perhaps
with a touch of repugnance—not to mention jellyfish and molds? These
many and different truths and beings touch where different worlds touch,
filling the earth with abundance, interrupting the closure of every world.
This plenitude and displacement of things in nature, including human beings,
is what I mean by plenishment in the earth.[1] It is performed by human
beings together, socially, together as human, together with other things. It
is performed by bats and jellyfish together and apart. Plenishment is the
gift of the good given to those who gather in and upon the earth, gathering
and interruption, exposure to abundance. Truth belongs to plenishment as
given in its work, always and everywhere, but not the only thing, not
plenishment itself. For truth knows too little of the good—so Aristotle's bat
says to the human Sini and to most of the others.

> 5. *Philosophy is the science of truth.* (Sini, *IT,* 4)

But perhaps not truth itself, not even in human terms. For Sini tells
us, every one of us (men), what we desire in truth. "[E]very man desires
that the loving words of the woman he loves are the expression of her
sincere feelings without lies, design, or reserve. And every woman wishes
the same from the man she loves" (Sini, *IT,* 4). Every woman and every man
desires sincerity and truth above all, without qualification. Yet every woman
and man lies, perhaps marking something in desire that interrupts this rule
of truth as sincerity. And many animals lie, deceive, and mask. What if the

desire for truth, the inexhaustible desire to know, were at the very same time and indistinguishably an inexhaustible and unlimited desire to lie, to interrupt the rule of truth, to wear masks, to be in untruth? A Nietzschean thought. I speak for the moment of desire and emotion, suggesting that as they offer themselves in sincerity, they wear masks: desire desiring its own interruption. I suggest that truth offers another trap to desire, which reaches beyond sincere feelings to another sincerity, given from the good, described by Levinas as referring to "the glory of infinity": "the anarchic identity of the subject flushed out without being able to slip away" (Levinas, *OB*, 144). If this glory is touched with a subjectivity that forgets the ears of the bat, still it brings desire into a relation to the infinite other beyond the reach of any human truth. Desire wants what it wants, as Deleuze and Guattari say (Deleuze & Guattari, *A-O*, 116), and that is revolutionary, against the gathering of all the work of social forces, which seek to trap desire, to restrict abundance. Truth, even as the lighting of being, in its mystery and enchantment, traps and resists desire. I speak here not of the eyes nor even the ears of the bat, but of bat-desires other than human-desires, wanting what he wants, when he wants, giving birth to truth.

6. *Everything has as much being as it has truth.* (Sini, *IT*, 5)

It would be wonderful to take this statement in the spirit of the bat, telling us first of the absolute identity between being and truth, so that all truth, even the truth of being and nonbeing, and the untruth of truth, remains trapped within the closure and rule of being and the lighting and darkening of being as truth and untruth, endlessly repeating the gathering of being, knowing nothing of the good, given in endless memory of a yearning for a truth that has forgotten all recollection of the desire that calls it and the giving that gives it forth. The truth of the good does not belong to truth, or untruth, or being, or nonbeing. Perhaps there is no truth of the good. Perhaps there is no place or being of the good. But desire reaches away from being to otherwise in abundance. Being and truth trap desire within a closure endlessly and infinitely betraying the good, in that double sense of betrayal.

And telling us second, still in the spirit of the bat, that the truth of the bat, who hears where we see, and sings where we reason, who knows more of music and song than human beings, almost as much as Plato's cicadas (Plato, *Phaedrus*, 230b, 258e),[2] gathers in truth and being interrupting the gathering of any truth of the good. If there is no truth of the good, still the good in its giving of truth interrupts the identity of truth and being not by denying its identity but by insisting on its abundance against any gathering. If truth and being are identical in truth, then that truth and that being count for nothing, or if not nothing then for too little to say. They fail to account for the good, that is, fail in the name of the good to account for the unaccountable in profusion. The bat, whose truth interrupts our truth, points to another truth in and of being, points to the untruth of that and every truth, and to what is otherwise than being and truth, a pointing that belongs to desire, bats' and others', given from the good. The good belongs in truth neither to being nor to us and bats, but interrupts every gathering, including ours and bats'. Truth leads us beyond itself, displacing the identity and calculability of truth together with being, the endless movement of desire.

Sini's journey continues from Aristotle through Parmenides to Hegel, avoiding Plato and Descartes. Aristotle's bat, our bat, named Ari after Aristotle, named Carlo remembering his left-clawed insistence that he not be left out, began with Plato, where we found something otherwise in the gathering of truth and being, though we had not known at the time that our journey was led by a bat. Let us with our bat continue reading Aristotle for a moment, on to Descartes, before retracing Sini's journey.

We begin again with Aristotle's further words in *Metaphysics* concerning truth, summarized by Sini (but not the bat) as follows: "being is above all by itself, in itself, and for itself the true from the moment that it 'is'" (Sini, *IT,* 9). Aristotle's own words are:

> since that which *is* in the sense of being true, or *is not* in the sense of being false, depends on combination and separation, . . . it is another question, how it happens that we think things together or apart; . . . for falsity and truth are not in things—it is not as if the good were true, and the bad were in itself false—but in thought; while with regard to simple things and essences falsity and truth do not exist even in thought: . . . since the combination and the separation are in thought and not in the things, and that which is in this sense is a different sort of being from the things that are in the full sense (for the thought attaches or removes either the 'what' or quality or quantity or one of the other categories), that which *is* accidentally and that which *is* in the sense of being true must be dismissed. . . . Therefore let these be dismissed, and let us consider the causes and the principles of being itself, *qua* being. (Aristotle, *Metaphysics,* 1027b–1028a)

Being in and by itself is true. "But in the *logos* which speaks being, in the affirmation and negation of judgment, we encounter another type of truth (and its opposite which is falsehood) . . ." (Sini, *IT,* 9). The bat, who hears and sings but does not speak the words of human language, may perhaps be said also and in that same way not to judge, not to be in judgment's truth, affirmation and negation, but is nevertheless in being's truth, together with all creatures and things. To which our bat, Aristotle's bat, responds that he chooses, marks, a different fork in the road upon which Aristotle considers being itself *qua* being. Aristotle desires that we consider being *qua* being, in itself and in general. The bat desires to build his world, with others, scouring the landscape, listening for clues.

It seems that Aristotle demands being twice at the point at which we recall the good. For truth and falsity divide into good and bad, with qualifications, and being *qua* being, which is no genus, emerges where no genus can be the true because falsity and truth are nothing, nothing in being and things. Being calls, gives rise to the desire for knowledge, opens to the reach of desire, toward the good, given as the true, as truth, and being, and more, because it is given beyond the lighting of truth as ringing and hearing and song. Among other gifts.

The qualifications repeat this fork in the road at the mundane level, where good and bad do not repeat true and false but join them at their junction. This junction is judgment, spoken of by Aristotle without the name, in relation to good and bad.

> the belief about the good that it is good and that about the not good that it is not good are alike; and so, too, are the belief about the good that it is not good and that about the not good that it is good. What belief then is contrary to the true belief about the not good that it is not good? Certainly not the one which says that it is bad, for this might sometimes be true at the same time, while a true belief is never contrary to a true one. (There is something not good which is bad, so that it is possible for both to be true at the same time.) Nor again is it the belief that it is not bad, for these also might hold at the same time. There remains, then, as contrary to the belief about the not good that it is not good, the belief about the not good that it is good. Hence, too, the belief about the good that it is not good is contrary to that about the good that it is good. (Aristotle, *De Interpretione*, 23b–24a)

True and false meet good and bad without identity in the logic of judgment, subsuming the good, in part, to the rule of truth. The good is either good or not good. And this proposition is either true or false. The possibility, expressed in Plato, that the good knows nothing of good and not good, true and false, binary oppositions, includes all things in their abundance, is overcome in Aristotle's theory of judgment, where being gathers together with saying in truth. True and false belong to judgment, that is, to combination and separation, to distinction and to *technē*, all gathered together. But that very belonging, Sini notes, evokes being's truth, being gathered in the true, as distinguished, separated, from judgment.

> Since being is revealed to the intuition of the senses and of thinking it is *alethes*: manifest, not latent, *i.e.*, true. But in the *logos* which speaks

> being, in the affirmation and negation of judgment, we encounter another
> kind of truth (and its opposite which is falsehood); it is thus that truth and
> falsehood take place in the soul's reason, since judgment says *how* the
> being which is is, says being in all its manifold meanings. (Sini, *IT,* 9)

Ari Carlo the bat reminds us that being cannot be said or seen or gathered
in all its meanings, that being cannot show all its meanings, that we are
called from somewhere other than judgment to know the limits of judgment and truth.

Aristotle himself says something similar, still evoking the name of
being in the envelope of identity.

> Thought is itself thinkable in exactly the same way as its objects are.
> For in the case of objects which involve no matter, what thinks and what
> is thought are identical; for speculative knowledge and its object are iden-
> tical. (Why thought is not always thinking we must consider later.) In the
> case of those which contain matter each of the objects of thought is only
> potentially present. It follows that while they will not have thought in
> them (for thought is a potentiality of them only in so far as they are
> capable of being disengaged from matter) thought may yet be thinkable.
> (Aristotle, *De Anima,* 430a)

This identity of thought thinking itself, *nous* nousing *nous,* is so supreme
and overarching an identity within the rule of being as to eliminate the very
possibility of judgment, which requires separation and combination, which
calls for saying. Aristotle speaks of thought thinking itself as object under the
form of identity, and of actual knowledge within the identity of being as
immortal and eternal, and more, in words largely incomprehensible from the
standpoint of separation and combination, that is, of words and judgment.

> And in fact thought, as we have described it, is what it is by virtue
> of becoming all things, while there is another which is what it is by virtue
> of making all things: this is a sort of positive state like light; for in a sense
> light makes potential colours into actual colours.
> Thought in this sense of it is separable, impassible, unmixed, since it
> is in its essential nature activity (for always the active is superior to the
> passive factor, the originating force to the matter). (430a)

Thought becomes all things under the rule of being, giving truth; to the creative emerging from which all things are given, which I take, with Plato, to be
given from the good, Aristotle continues the rule of being, though it is not
being over thought but the gathering of thought that makes being, thought in
its pure activity, not its passivity, pure beyond the reach of the *logos.*

The question given to us by our bat, on his journey from Aristotle to Sini, on the left hand so to speak, is whether the being of separation and combination is perhaps passive being, associated with truth as judgment. The being that makes and gives being is impassible and unmixed, reminding us of Diotima's nature or being of wondrous beauty, a nature I associate with the abundance of the good, reminding us of the soul's intermediary journeys, the journeys of the bat. This abundance of thought is in its essential nature activity, abundance, in being, nature, not under the rule of being, but circulating in displaced and intermediary movements of desire. To introduce desire into active thinking, creative emergence, is to bring being in its purity into the intermediary movements I understand to be given from the good. Aristotle describes active *nous* exactly as Socrates describes the gift of the good to being. Soul belongs to heaven in memory of the good. I add that Spinoza, who speaks of this activity of being as deeply as any philosopher, relates it to body as well as soul, always in memory of the good. He calls it ethical.

Sini's journey leads from Aristotle back to Parmenides, still within the rule of being, before soaring over the founding of modern science and its idea of truth to Hegel, oblivious to Descartes among others, including Spinoza and Hume, for example. Aristotle's bat does not fly so fast, and touches down here and there on the right as he retraces Sini's flight on the left. Before leaving Aristotle, however, we may recall what rule means to human beings, echoing its meaning to bats and other creatures. I echo these famous (or infamous) words, at undue length.

> Thus it is clear that household management attends more to men than to the acquisition of inanimate things, and to human excellence more than to the excellence of property which we call wealth, and to the excellence of freemen more than to the excellence of slaves. A question may indeed be raised, whether there is any excellence at all in a slave beyond those of an instrument and of a servant—whether he can have the excellences of temperance, courage, justice, and the like; or whether slaves possess only bodily services. And, whichever way we answer the question, a difficulty arises; for, if they have excellence, in what will they differ from freemen? On the other hand, since they are men and share in rational principle, it seems absurd to say that they have no excellence. A similar question may be raised about women and children, whether they too have excellences; ought a woman to be temperate and brave and just, and is a child to be called temperate, and intemperate, or not? ... For the slave has no deliberative faculty at all; the woman has, but it is without authority; and the child has, but it is immature. ... Clearly, then, excellence of character belongs to all of them; but the temperance of a man and of a woman, or the courage and justice of a man and of a woman, are not, as

Socrates maintained, the same; the courage of a man is shown in com-
manding, of a woman in obeying. . . . as the poet says of women,

Silence is a woman's glory,

but this is not equally the glory of man. (Aristotle, *Politics*, 1259b–1260b)

Aristotle speaks of household management *(oikos)* here, but we know that
he speaks of being, being by nature, where nature denies freedom and
authority to human beings, to slaves and women, whose "excellence" denies
them all the goodness of humanity. And so with animals and the rest of
nature.

To which I add a heinous thought linking slavery and truth. For slavery in Greece was linked with truth. Slaves, and only slaves, were tortured
in Greece to ascertain their master's truth. The word *basanos*, touchstone
of truth, changed its meaning from a mark of gold, rubbed on stone, to a
mark of truth, marked on the body of the slave, by whose smell, we are told,
we know the stranger. We know the strange body by smell. In Latin, we
know family and familiarity in the name of the *famulus*, the slave. The
oikos is a place of pain in truth.

Foucault describes this seventeenth-century memorial of truth on the
body, reinscribed by Kafka in the penal colony, visiting the truth on the
body of the condemned, reminding us of "the political question":

> The tortured body is first inscribed in the legal ceremonial that must
> produce, open for all to see, the truth of the crime. (Foucault, *DP*, 35)
>
> every penalty of a certain seriousness had to involve an element of torture,
> of *supplice*. (33)
>
> If torture was so strongly embedded in legal practice, it was because it
> revealed truth and showed the operation of power. (55)

Such torture was an ancient practice, with the difference, in Greece, that
free citizens were never tortured, but their household slaves were tortured
if the citizens were accused. I offer a single quotation, from Demosthenes.

> Now, you consider *basanos* the most reliable of all tests both in private
> and in public affairs. Wherever slaves and freemen are present and facts
> have to be found, you do not use the statements of the free witnesses, but
> you seek to discover the truth by applying *basanos* to the slaves. Quite
> properly, men of the jury, since witnesses have sometimes been found not
> to have given true evidence, whereas no statements made as a result of
> *basanos* have ever been proved to be untrue. (Demosthenes 30.37; quoted
> in duBois, *TT*, 49–50)

Slaves in Greece were prisoners of war, or abandoned children, or those unprotected by Greek law. Most slaves were strangers, non-Greek, or were made strangers by exile. The right of strangers was to be enslaved in the home and subjected to torture.

Aristotle rejects Demosthenes' argument that the torture of slaves guarantees truth (Aristotle, *Rhetoric*, 1376b–1377a). But he defends slavery, in passages at the heart of the *oikos*. Household management was the management of slaves. And he defends a technique of truth, if not a technique of torture. Scientific *technē* is the management of truth, calling for the most effective techniques if truth demands it, including torture if sufficiently reliable. Yet even where we understand truth as a possession, belonging to *technē*, owned by men of wisdom, *sophoi*, the possibility of truth, in Plato and Aristotle, is framed by gifts of the gods beyond the reach of *technē*. In Plato, *poiēsis* interrupts the rule of *technē*, *mimēsis* interrupts *diēgesis*, propositional reason, truth circulates from the good interrupted by disturbing movements of *erōs*, *mania*, and Pharmakeia, love and madness, intermediary figures, interrupting every technique of truth. Pharmakeia interrupts the rule of law. In Aristotle, the unmoved mover and active *nous* far surpass the rule of *technē*, and *mimēsis* interrupts *technē*'s rule over truth and household management.[3]

This is to recall to our attention, never I hope to escape it, that the thought of truth and being is an ethical thought, of freedom and authority, still in memory of this active soul beyond combination and separation, beyond the distinctions by nature of which Aristotle speaks in truth. Active *nous* touches something that interrupts the authority of combination and separation, touches a nature untouched by distinction, a nature that moves from and toward itself with no trace of the distinctions and oppositions by nature, an intermediary movement given in memory of the good, a good that interrupts the authority of every limit. For that which gives the limit must give the possibility of its interruption. The presence of women and slaves, like bats and jellyfish, give the possibility of interrupting the identities of women and slaves, bats and jellyfish, and men and others, all the identities of being and truth.

I close this discussion with a return to Sini, who as I have said evokes Parmenides' *Way of Truth*, perhaps the critical moment in Greek thought at which being gained ascendance over the good. For Parmenides speaks in the voice of being of that which Aristotle speaks in the same voice, of being, while Socrates speaks of the good.

> One way remains to be spoken of: the way how it is. Along this road here are very many indications that what is is unbegotten and imperishable; for it is whole and immovable and complete. Nor was it at any time,

nor will it be, since it is now, all at once, one and continuous. (Simplicius, *Phys.* 145, 1 [DK 28 B 6]; Robinson, *EGP*, 113)

Remaining the same, and in the same place, it lies in itself, and so abides firmly where it is. For strong necessity holds it in the bonds of the limit which shuts it in on every side, because it is not right for what is to be incomplete. For it is not in need of anything, but not-being would stand in need of everything. (Simplicius, *Phys*, 145, 27 [DK 28 B 8]; Robinson, *EGP*, 115)

It is not right for being as such to be incomplete, a rightness born from something other than being or saying, and with respect to a need that knows more than being. The way of truth looks beyond being to what is right and good, in the movement of desire. For desire is the first of the gods, the intermediary movement which is the only relation possible to the limit: "And love she framed the first of all the gods" as Phaedrus says (Plato, *Symposium*, 178b).

We cannot speak of being or truth except in relation to something that reaches beyond the distinctions and judgments of truth, beyond being and becoming, to what Parmenides still names as being: being beyond its oppositions. But our naming and reach remain linked to these oppositions at the same time that they interrupt them, to extricate us from the bonds of identity. Eros, or desire, reaches from truth and being to what? To being, as Parmenides suggests, or to the good? Or perhaps the name does not matter so long as we remember Diotima's description of the wondrous beauty that can be inhabited only in memory of the good, as beautiful, and right, without need. The greatest risk of Parmenides' thought is that being, what is, in its truth, will be understood to lack nothing because it has everything. As the good it lacks nothing and has nothing because it is not a possession and does not possess, knows nothing of property and propriety.

This refusal of lack is where Sini finds "the Parmenidean knot which ties together being, thinking, and truth and which lies at the origin of our entire culture. The question of truth is at the center of this knot" (Sini, *IT*, 10). Oblivious to the possibility that this link and every one of its members, the very possibility of this knot, evokes memory of the good. "The force of this statement lies precisely in the absolute character of its truth, namely, that the non-being of being cannot even be thought" (Sini, *IT*, 10). In memory of the forgetting of nonbeing in the thought of being, to which Heidegger devoted so many of his writings, still within the rule of being, I resist Sini's tying of the knot. The nonbeing of being cannot be thought and must be thought, where the impossibility and necessity are ethical, responses demanded from the good.

The place where we may say all this thinking goes astray is with the reading of Plato.

> With Plato we have the birth of what we could call onto-logy: the science of discourse, of truth and falsity, since it is founded on beings or, better, on the being of beings, that is, on the relations among beings that constitute their being, their way of being, and, finally, the reason that makes them be what they are. (Sini, *IT,* 11)

The Plato whose Socrates said as clearly as could be said that being comes from the good, led by desire and love, is assigned the role of closing being on itself in what Heidegger calls "ontotheology," reminding us of God where Plato speaks incessantly of divine gifts. I have resisted this reading of Plato. I am now suggesting that the idea of the rule of being that Sini names as lying "at the origin of our entire culture" is present in that culture everywhere and nowhere. Being permeates every Western philosophic thought, perhaps gives us the idea of philosophy itself as the truth of being, the science of the truth of being, and the truth of that science, and more, all knotted in being, but always driven by a desire that crosses each knot with something otherwise, in memory of a good whose gifts make the knotting of that knot impossible, interrupt every knot with loose ends, every truth with untruth. The knot has at its center, tied up within its entanglements, what makes it impossible to knot the knot with the demand to do so.

The bat, Aristotle's bat, moves throughout the world in memory of this impossibility, moves in being in memory of what being cannot assemble. The bat reminds us of our obligation, given from the good, to question ontology and ontotheology, as Sini describes them: "The foundation of onto-logy and thus of science, both ancient and modern, is the Parmenidean knot of being, thinking and truth" (Sini, *IT,* 13). To question, however, is not to refute, not to abrogate, but to interrupt. Perhaps science is tied in this knot as tightly as possible, within the gift from the good that makes it impossible to accept this knot as tied. For Sini recognizes that the statement that ties the knot inverts it, if it does not untie it. "[W]hat is the truth of the Parmenidean knot? The truth of its truth is exactly the opposite of what it says" (p. 14). The opposite, I would say, is not the deepest question we may uncover. For Sini reevokes the priority of saying. "[T]he original place of truth is not the being that is and which then is revealed in judgment. The original place is precisely the *logos,* judgment" (p. 14). The knot of being, saying, and truth remains unbroken, pulling first on one strand and then another.

Yet Sini hopes to untie this knot, even as he ties it up too tightly. He turns to Hegel to pursue the possibility that truth does not belong to judgment or to being, but echoes in the abyss first named as such by Kant. "The first step toward the abyss is taken by Hegel, as he is the first to declare and to show that judgment *is not* the place of truth" (Sini, *IT,* 15). We will follow Aristotle's bat retracing Sini's journey after we have considered the one crucial thought I find that Sini never thinks, that the knot of being, truth, and saying has been tied in oblivion, forgetting the good, but an oblivion that reemerges in every gathering of being and truth. Ari Carlo, the bat, touches down on other places in the European tradition, for a moment, on Descartes, Spinoza, and Hume for example, before resuming its flight with Sini, the man of truth.

I close this discussion with a return to Aristotle who, speaking of the good as if belonging to being, reminds us that it has nothing to do with truth.

> Now to know anything that is noble is itself noble; but regarding excellence, at least, not to know what it is, but to know out of what it arises is most precious. For we do not wish to know what bravery is but to be brave, nor what justice is but to be just, just as we wish to be in health rather than to know what being in health is, and to have our body in good condition rather than to know what good condition is. (Aristotle, *Eudemian Ethics,* 1216b)

We wish not the truth of virtue, of health and justice—though that truth is excellent—but to be just and good. If truth belongs to being then the desire of which Aristotle speaks, if it is a desire to be, does not come from being, does not belong to being, if it points toward it, comes from the gods, if with a hesitation, a maybe:

> Now if there is any gift of the gods to men, it is reasonable that happiness should be god-given, and most surely god-given of all human things inasmuch as it is the best. But this question would perhaps be more appropriate to another inquiry; happiness seems, however, even if it is not god-sent but comes as a result of excellence and some process of learning or training, to be among the most godlike things; for that which is the prize and end of excellence seems to be the best thing and something godlike and blessed. (Aristotle, *Nicomachean Ethics,* 1099b)

The gift of virtue calls forth desire from us for being that is not satisfied by any truth, not even the truth of our being virtuous and good. The good, the nature of wondrous beauty, evokes desire in us as finite, temporal creatures to be in other, productive ways. The desire, I say, recognizes a memory of something otherwise than being, otherwise but pointed at being, linking being with something other. That is the work of desire. Against the idea that the intermediary link named desire belongs to judgment and its truth I ask us to think that the intermediary is desire, linking beyond any closure being with the good.

CHAPTER 4

Brute Truth

Aristotle's bat, named Ari when he joined us, also labeled Carlo, to be renamed at another time, flies from one end of the Western tradition to the other in the name of the good seeking truth, seeking left-handed, *Chiroptera* truth, and more, always more truth than any present given from the good. He flies from Aristotle to Descartes, from the Greeks to modernity, surveying scientific truth, flying over God's truth in the Middle Ages, though his truth is named by Aquinas in a deeply contaminated way,[1] remembering Aristotle, to come to rest for a while in Descartes, who also names him, has bats and other animals in mind, from the beginning, in the name of truth. For in the very moment in which Descartes disclaims his own perfection of reason, he claims the absolute superiority of human beings over animals, bats included. Supremely democratic sentiments, that all human beings are equal in truth and reason, join the absolute rule of humanity over nature.

> as regards reason or sense, since it is the only thing that makes us men and distinguishes us from the beasts, I am inclined to believe that it exists whole and complete in each of us. Here I follow the common opinion of the philosophers, who say there are differences of degree only between the accidents, and not between the forms (or natures) of individuals of the same species. (Descartes, *DM*, 111)

Human beings, except for accidents, minor differences, are equal in mind. But all, except for accidents, minor differences, are in kind superior to animals, bats included, in the way of reason and truth. A democratic principle that all human beings share reason in common, differing only in their accidents, embodies a supreme principle of preeminence of kin and kind, human beings over beasts. At this moment, opening his *Discourse on the Method,* thinking of "the method of rightly conducting one's reason and seeking the truth in the sciences" (Descartes, *DM*, 111), Descartes interposes a figure of sovereignty and rule, of authority in truth and reason, expressing the good that gives the gift of truth. The democracy of reason belongs to it profoundly, a democracy that guarantees the despotic authority of humanity over animals and the rest of nature. I will return to nature in general. Here I am concerned with the ethical rule of reason instituting truth and with the political governance of animals by human reason, denied to animals in their nature, without reason's deepest interrogation. I add that it requires stretching to the extreme to institute the rule of reason so as to exclude many kinds of human beings, women or people of other tribes and cultures, whose rationality is not high or pure enough. Reason's institution evokes authority throughout the most glorious moments of Descartes's account of rational method, encompassing "the search for truth" (Descartes, *DM,* 126). This search strives for the good, institutes authority, is driven by unlimited desire.

I would hate to moderate Descartes's immoderation, which is beyond question splendid in its way. Immoderate equality has much to praise even where we would withhold unqualified assent. Immoderate desire for truth is likewise admirable. "I thought that, provided we refrain from accepting anything as true which is not, and always keep to the order required for deducing one thing from another, there can be nothing too remote to be reached in the end or too well hidden to be discovered" (Descartes, *DM,* 120). Nothing is beyond, too far, too big or small, or too well hidden, to be beyond human truth. The Greeks called such expectations *hubris.* Yet Descartes knows as well as we the importance of restraint to forestall the destructions of untempered enthusiasm. He insists on moderation two pages later. "Where many opinions were equally well accepted, I chose only the most moderate" (p. 122). Elsewhere he tells us explicitly that he knows that his immoderate method of doubting everything risks no danger. "I know that no danger or error will result from my plan, and that I cannot possibly go too far in my distrustful attitude" (Descartes, *M,* 1, 15). Yet he warns that some people cannot follow such a method, for they are either too precipitate or too modest to do so, a political description of sovereign rule. And he claims absolute rational authority. "I will add that these proofs are of such a kind that I reckon they leave no room for the possibility that the human mind will ever discover better ones" (Descartes, *M,* Ded. Let., 4). Immoderate enthusiasm for democracy and reason is justified where democracy and reason encourage moderation. Where democracy overwhelms all relations of difference it engenders tyrannies.

Democracy in reason means the governance of animals by human beings and of plants by animals, using them in any way whatever. Descartes's democratic, rational spirit undermines the togetherness of nature, the shared world of natural kinds. Human beings differ in the least ways because they belong to the same species, but differ in the greatest ways from every other kind of creature. God's world is divided into species and kinds, divided from the beginning into kinds by authority and rule.

Descartes speaks repeatedly of "animal spirits," describing the body machine:

> The parts of the blood which penetrate as far as the brain serve not only to nourish and sustain its substance, but also and primarily to produce in it a certain very fine wind, or rather a very lively and pure flame, which is called the animal spirits . . .
>
> Indeed, one may compare the nerves of the machine I am describing with the pipes in the works of these fountains, its muscles and tendons with the various devices and springs which serve to set them in motion, its animal spirits with the water which drives them, the heart with the source of the water, and the cavities of the brain with the storage tanks. (Descartes, *TM*, 100)

The human body is a machine run by animal spirits which give it its vitality and movement, in the manner of a machine without reason. And animals, bats included, know nothing of truth, of the world, because they possess "no intelligence at all" (Descartes, *DM*, 140), are nothing but machines moved by their animal spirits, which human beings would be if they did not possess reason. All of us, all human beings. Descartes treats all things that lack reason as automata, occasionally wonders if human shapes have souls or are simulacra.[2] This idea of automata, of machines that move without volition or desire, is perhaps the thought of being most oblivious to the good in the Western tradition. Aristotle understands self-movement very differently, bearing marks of yearning and desire, if remaining predominantly within the gathering of being. I interrupt my discussion of Descartes for just a moment to recall the gathering of being in Aristotle, joined with something otherwise.

For in Aristotle things move by "chance" *(tuchē)* and "spontaneity" *(automaton)*, against those who insist on necessity everywhere in nature. But *tuchē* and *automaton* (self-movement, self-origination) must be understood as actions for the sake of something.

> But chance and spontaneity are also reckoned among causes: many things are said both to be and to come to be as a result of chance and spontaneity. (Aristotle, *Physics*, 195b)
>
> Hence it is clear that events which belong to the general class of things that may come to pass for the sake of something, when they come to pass not for the sake of what actually results, and have an external cause, may be described by the phrase "from spontaneity." (197b)
>
> A difficulty presents itself: why should not nature work, not for the sake of something, nor because it is better so, but just as the sky rains, not in order to make the corn grow, but of necessity? . . .

> . . . Yet it is impossible that this should be the true view. . . . There-
> fore action for an end is present in things which come to be and are by
> nature. . . .
>
> And since nature is twofold, the matter and the form, of which the
> latter is the end, and since all the rest is for the sake of the end, the form
> must be the cause in the sense of that for the sake of which. (198b–199a)

All things, including *tuchē* and *automaton*, are for the sake of something,
typically the final cause or end, and if they do not contain this "for the sake
of" within themselves, they cannot be causes, cannot belong to nature, even
though we say, and say truly, that some things are from *tuchē* and *automaton*, if only as accidental causes.

Aristotle typically speaks of movement for the sake of the end. Yet that
which moves from itself comes to pass for the sake of something even when
it comes to pass not for the sake of what actually results, the actual end.
For just a moment Aristotle distinguishes coming to pass for the sake of a
result, an end, gathered in being, traditionally understood as "teleological,"
from coming to pass for something otherwise, what does not gather, does
not include the end. I understand the good as that for which things emerge
and act, to which they are indebted and toward which they incline, where
the good is no being, does not gather, composes no end. Among the multiple senses of "for the sake of," at least one does not entail gathering beings
together as means and ends. Gifts from the good give different sakes for
which things may come and go. One, perhaps the most important to Aristotle,
is the end, though we may also speak of other causes. The causes include
the different origins of movement, for the sake of which things move, the
ends they bring to pass and from which they come forth. Traditionally, this
movement toward an end in being is known as natural teleology, the gathering and assembling of being as means and ends. But Aristotle acknowledges, however obliquely, that natural things may move for the sake of
something that does not come to pass, something perhaps non-teleological,
but still for the sake of something, responding to a call, quite different from
a natural necessity that moves without a debt. *Tuchē* and *automaton* move
for the sake of something, indebted to something other, though they do not
appear to, though they do not bring particular ends to pass. They force us
to distinguish the sake of the end from the sake of something from which
things emerge, their matter but also that which gives their movement
forth, which does not gather in being. The good remains in Aristotle, retaining the sense of end toward which things incline as that being which
they strive to bring about, and another sense of desire toward that which
has nothing to do with being brought about, nothing to do with gathering
in being, with means and ends, but calls and beckons to things for which
they move and to which they are indebted as they touch and respond to

other things. *Automata* respond to touch, sensitively and responsively, for the sake of something.

Automata, machines, in Descartes work very differently, severed entirely from will and desire, soul and reason, in the extreme devoid of all yearning for the good.

> I suppose the body to be nothing but a statue or machine made of earth, which God forms with the explicit intention of making it as much as possible like us. (Descartes, *TM,* 99)

> I should like you to consider, after this, all the functions I have ascribed to this machine . . . I should like you to consider that these functions follow from the mere arrangement of the machine's organs every bit as naturally as the movements of a clock or other automaton follow from the arrangement of its counter-weights and wheels. In order to explain these functions, then, it is not necessary to conceive of this machine as having any vegetative or sensitive soul or other principle of movement and life, apart from its blood and its spirits, which are agitated by the heat of the fire burning continuously in its heart—a fire which has the same nature as all the fires that occur in inanimate bodies. (p. 108)

> I might consider the body of a man as a kind of machine equipped with and made up of bones, nerves, muscles, veins, blood and skin in such a way that, even if there were no mind in it, it would still perform all the same movements as it now does in those cases where movement is not under the control of the will or, consequently, of the mind. (Descartes, *M,* 6, 58)

Descartes understands *automata* as machines that move without the least sense of debt or call, any sense of desire or the good. He ascribes reason, or mind and soul, to that which moves by will and desire. And soul belongs to human beings only, absolutely excluding all other natural things including animals and plants. We might recall Plato's understanding that all things are in the care of soul, or Aristotle's understanding that all things act for the sake of something, even where that something is no end. Descartes proposes a mechanical assembling of being gathered without soul or end, beings gathered together in time without the slightest memory of injustice, given from the good. In Anaximander's name, I hope to recall the good in nature, not a being which moves beings, gathered together, but the giving the debt all things owe to each other, and more, where they touch together.

This barren idea of mechanical being proposed by Descartes, oblivious to the good, was, I believe, a European calamity, tempered, I hope to argue, by recurrent marks of the good, of will and desire, elsewhere in Descartes and his successors. Descartes's resistance to natural teleology, immensely plausible from the standpoint of natural causation gathered under the view of modern science he was so instrumental in inaugurating, remains gathered in being. Efficient and final causation remain gathered in being, alternative accounts of beings in temporal relation. Within this important and beneficial resistance, Descartes's understanding of mechanical self-movement contains a far more ruinous exclusion, having nothing to do with being gathered, with scientific truth. For he excludes at this moment every vestige of the good, though he must include the good in every thing given from the perfection of God, under God's authority. This division, between mechanical causation on the one hand and the rule of God on the other, represents the oblivion to the good we may associate with the gathering of being into modern science and technology—with the qualification that it betrays the giving of the good in the excesses of the gathering, in the will to the truth that founds it. Descartes's will to truth expresses something far exceeding the gathering of being as science's or any other truth. For the will, human or otherwise, reflects the infinite and exceptional nature of God. I postpone discussion of God and free will to the next chapter. The good appears otherwise in Descartes, in relation to the domination and subordination he links with reason.

For we may note at the edges of Descartes's picture of human reason, warding off the claims of bats and other creatures, that we might suppose within the same gestures of exclusion of natural kinds, allowing human beings to use animals in any way whatever, that women or humans of other races do not possess quite the same reason as European men.[3] Everything depends on what we take to be the "same species," defined perhaps in biological, perhaps in political terms, perhaps by reason, perhaps in relation to truth, or race, or gender. Reason's distinctions impose political tyrannies, gathered up into the movement of being.

From the first, then, in Descartes the framing of the question of reason and reason's truth is ethical|political, concerned, as in Aristotle and Aquinas, with the rule of human beings over others, using them to human purposes, provided that we can tell with reason's certainty that they are unlike us. We have an argument that at any moment can expand to divide human beings from strangers who, unlike us, are not in reason's truth, not deeply or truly enough. Bodies are machines, are not in the truth, entirely lack reason. First and foremost, animal bodies. An infinite gulf, an abyss of essence, divides animal bodies moved by animal spirits from human bodies moved by reason as well as by animal spirits. Reason is here a supplement, something beyond and higher than animal spirits, not considered as perhaps costly, diminishing our sensory awareness, our mobility, or our emotional sensitivity. Descartes never imagines that reason might be our shortcoming.

Aristotle's bat reminds us that he does not see but hears, and hears very well, that bats live in social colonies and tend their children, male and female bats. What if reason deprived us of a belonging together that bats and wolves and lions know? And what if that were an infinite loss? What price do we pay to be in the true? What sacrifice in the good is required for truth? And what if bats were in the truth, their truth, as well as human beings, if not in what Descartes calls rational truth?

Plants and animals, bats included, Descartes says, are absolutely without rationality. He offers two familiar arguments so contemptuous of life and nature apart from humanity as to be laughable when we stop crying for bats and other maligned living creatures. For it is not enough that animals be regarded as *automata*, but they are machines that feign to be other, have no life or dignity of their own. Descartes's eye is not, like God's, upon the sparrow except to deprive it of its worth.

> I made special efforts to show that if any such machines had the organs and outward shape of a monkey or of some other animal that lacks reason, we should have no means of knowing that they did not possess entirely the same nature as these animals; whereas if any such machines bore a resemblance to our bodies and imitated our actions as closely as possible for all practical purposes, we should still have two very certain means of recognizing that they were not real men. The first is that they could never use words, or put together other signs, as we do in order to declare our thoughts to others. . . . Secondly, even though such machines might do some things as well as we do them, or perhaps even better, they would inevitably fail in others, which would reveal that they were acting not through understanding but only from the disposition of their organs. (Descartes, *DM*, 139)

Descartes made special efforts to show that we can always tell animal machines from human beings, to the detriment of living animals. Aristotle's bat urges us to recognize and resist Descartes's special efforts to organize his discourse on truth around the disjunction of animals and human beings. The discourse on truth has a special requirement, to separate and divide human beings from animals, with certainty, so that human beings may be sure of their superiority, so that they may rule. I say that this special demand for human authority does not belong to truth, but comes from the good, not good itself—I regard it as heinous—but bearing responsibility and driven by a desire for superiority. I say this is the first of many special efforts in modernity to ensure the superior authority of human beings in the light of divine authority, despite the memory that God's eye is on the sparrow and bat, not just on human beings.

Descartes makes so extreme an effort to institute human authority that we may imagine, even claim to know, all sorts of ways in which it falls short of truth. For example, writers and artists have imagined that a machine might simulate a human being or animal, as if it were delightful, or incredible, or wonderful that we might be persuaded by a simulacrum, even within the rule of truth. Descartes insists that we must know where we frequently are charmed not to know; yet typically we are not fooled at all. Machines do not pass themselves off as humans or animals—or rather, we do not pass them off. What if we could not always tell? Would that shake the fabric of the world? Artificial intelligence workers hope to fool us with a machine that appears to think and speak, perhaps one that actually thinks and speaks. Against Turing tests and criteria, perhaps we may imagine being fooled without the world crumbling into dust. Or perhaps it is not being deceived, but granting the possibility that reason might belong to machines or animals. For Descartes imagines that we (or he) will always be able to tell the deficiencies of machines. And what of the deficiencies of human beings? Must we be superior to be good? In all these ways, rational truth is a criterion of human superiority, driven by a desire to rule beyond any possible achievement of reason or truth.

This insistence on the superiority of human beings becomes absolute in Descartes, even extremely absolute, far exceeding any sense that can be made of rational authority.

> Now in just these two ways we can also know the difference between man and beast. For it is quite remarkable that there are no men so dull-witted or stupid—and this includes even madmen—that they are incapable of arranging various words together and forming an utterance from them in order to make their thoughts understood; whereas there is no other animal, however perfect and well-endowed it may be, that can do the like. . . . This shows not merely that the beasts have less reason than men, but that they have no reason at all. (Descartes, *DM,* 140)

Yet we can find in the continuation of this passage some of the unease Descartes appears to feel at this discussion, not so much at the inadequacy of the arguments he gives for the superiority of humans, but at the question of superiority itself.

> It is also a very remarkable fact that although many animals show more skill than we do in some of their actions, yet the same animals show none at all in many others; so what they do better does not prove that they have any intelligence, for if it did then they would have more intelligence than any of us and would excel us in everything. It proves rather that they have no intelligence at all, and that it is nature which acts in them according to the disposition of their organs. (p. 140)

Animals do some things better than human beings, and if that proved intelligence they would be superior to us, able to excel us in everything.

The issue is one of superiority and authority. The purpose of reason is to rule. Descartes speaks similarly in the dedicatory letter of his *Meditations* of the need for reason to compel obedience from the disobedient.

> For us who are believers, it is enough to accept on faith that the human soul does not die with the body, and that God exists; but in the case of unbelievers, it seems that there is no religion, and practically no moral virtue, that they can be persuaded to adopt until these two truths are proved to them by natural reason. (Descartes, *M,* Ded. Let., 3)

And he alludes a few pages later to "atheists" who deny the existence of God: "provided only that we remember that our minds must be regarded as finite, while God is infinite and beyond our comprehension, such objections will not cause us any difficulty" (p. 7). We may be sure that the question of the existence of God to believers and unbelievers is not one of truth but of life and being. The issue is of the authority that should guide our life, including the pursuit of truth. Certainty becomes the touchstone of the good life.

> For since our will tends to pursue or avoid only what our intellect represents as good or bad, we need only to judge well in order to act well, and to judge as well as we can in order to do our best—that is to say, in order to acquire all the virtues and in general all the other goods we can acquire. And when we are certain of this, we cannot fail to be happy. (Descartes, *DM,* 124)[4]

This is to acknowledge that within truth we find the mark of the good in the work of exclusion, domination, and authority. Descartes's reason is not presented in its pristine purity, which could not grant it authority, but is sought to rule, to govern, to dominate and exclude, to make sure that human beings exercise God's authority over nature, and that European men exercise reason's authority over unbelievers. The theme of reason's truth which marks an absolute difference between human beings and animals continues throughout Descartes's writing, inherent in the absolute distinction between mind and body, instituting an absolute rule of mind over body, human beings over animals. Within his apparently inoffensive rejection of the possibility that human beings are rational animals—"I should have to inquire what an animal is, what rationality is, and in this way one question would lead me down the slope to other harder ones, and I do not now have the time to waste on subtleties of this kind" (Descartes, *M,* 2, 17)—we may see an absolute and total rejection of the essence of humanity as animal and of the essence of truth as embodied.

This leads to the second disclosure of the truth of truth in Descartes, where we are led by Aristotle's bat, who passionately strives for truth against the will to authority that has successfully deprived bats of reason, but perhaps not so successfully deprived bats of truth. For the reason Descartes describes as evoking the possibility of certain truth is one undisturbed by emotion. "So today I have expressly rid my mind of all worries and arranged for myself a clear stretch of free time. I am here quite alone, and at last I will devote myself sincerely and without reservation to the general demolition of my opinions" (Descartes, *M*, 1, 12). Emotion, passion, will, and desire all interfere with the movement of truth, are associated by Descartes with madness, a madness he cannot allow to enter into his consideration of reason.

> how could it be denied that these hands or this whole body are mine? Unless perhaps I were to liken myself to madmen, whose brains are so damaged by the persistent vapours of melancholia that they firmly maintain they are kings when they are paupers, or say they are dressed in purple when they are naked, or that their heads are made of earthenware, or that they are pumpkins, or made of glass. But such people are insane, and I would be thought equally mad if I took anything from them as a model for myself. (Descartes, *M*, 1, 12)[5]

Descartes could not be mad. Yet no one has suffered more from that "other form of madness" described by Foucault than Descartes, if not "madness itself": "We have yet to write the history of that other form of madness, by which men, in an act of sovereign reason, confine their neighbors, and communicate and recognize each other through the merciless language of non-madness" (Foucault, *MC*, ix). I speak less of the madness of confinement than that of sovereign reason, a madness that cannot tolerate the possibility of its own madness. This is its extremity, why it must be called "other," claiming to know and control the truth of madness, including its own. Ari Carlo, Aristotle's bat, mad for truth as perhaps are you and I, knows that madness belongs to every truth it finds, driven by its will to truth, causing its bat's body to tremble.

Descartes owns a will to truth greater than almost any other we may imagine, a will that demands certitude at any price. For he moves from what we may suppose is a modest sanity concerning truth to a madness beyond all madnesses. From Rule Two of *Rules for the Direction of the Mind*—"We should attend only to those objects of which our minds seem capable of having certain and indubitable cognition" (Descartes, *RDM*, 10)—he passes through a desire for certitude—Dewey calls it the "quest for certainty" (Dewey, *QC*)—to something beyond a quest, to what shows itself as madness.

> I tried to expose the falsity or uncertainty of the propositions I was examining by clear and certain arguments, not by weak conjectures; and I

> never encountered any proposition so doubtful that I could not draw from
> it some quite certain conclusion, if only the conclusion that it contained
> nothing certain. (Descartes, *DM*, 125)

The madness is to want, to desire, a certainty so great that even the uncertain bends itself to certainty, first providing us with the certainty that
nothing is certain, then transforming what we thought was uncertain into
certainty, undergoing a transformation greater perhaps than that of the
world into God. "The eventual result of this doubt is to make it impossible
for us to have any further doubts about what we subsequently discover to
be true" (Descartes, *M*, Syn. 9). In the extreme, he will take as false what
is perhaps uncertain. "Anything which admits of the slightest doubt I will
set aside just as if I had found it to be wholly false; and I will proceed in
this way until I recognize something certain, or, if nothing else, until I at
least recognize for certain that there is no certainty" (Descartes, *M*, 2, 16),[6]
knowing full well that such a practice is mad. In another extreme, he
claims to be clear in what he knows cannot be clear, as if inclarity might
be understood clearly in its obscurity. For the moment I ignore the criterion of clear and distinct ideas with his own qualifications, linking dreams
with madness. I will discuss this conjunction later.

> can it be objected that I have in the past regarded as true and certain
> many things which I afterwards recognized to be false? But none of these
> were things which I clearly and distinctly perceived: I was ignorant of this
> rule for establishing the truth, and believed these things for other reasons
> which I later discovered to be less reliable. (Descartes, *M*, 5, 48)

I ignore the possibility that dreaming might overthrow all of Descartes's
certainty as profoundly as madness. I would point out instead that if he did
not recognize clear and distinct ideas as clear and distinct before, or took
erroneous ideas as clear and distinct, nothing could overcome the possibility of similar errors in the future. As he concedes in closing his *Meditations.*

For he acknowledges his own madness twice, a mad desire for certainty and a mad fascination with human frailty. "[I]t must be admitted that
in this human life we are often liable to make mistakes about particular
things, and we must acknowledge the weakness of our nature" (Descartes,
M, 6, 61). In his hands, in relation to practice, to ethics and the good,
probability becomes certainty in an act of legerdemain or madness. "Even
when no opinions appear more probable than any others, we must still
adopt some; and having done so we must then regard them not as doubtful,
from a practical point of view, but as most true and certain, on the grounds
that the reason which made us adopt them is itself true and certain"
(Descartes, *DM*, 123). Whatever he says of God recalls the madness of his
malicious demon, both excessive beyond the limits of sense.

We may consider two such extreme claims, tantamount to derangement. One is that despite the infinite nature of God and God's incomprehensibility, the idea of God is clear. "I though it was quite proper for me to inquire . . . how God may be more easily and more certainly known than the things of this world" (Descartes, *M*, Ded. Let., 3); "I have taken careful note of the fact that there is very little about corporeal things that is truly perceived, whereas much more is known about the human mind, and still more about God" (*M*, 4, 37); "For what is more self-evident than the fact that the supreme being exists, or that God, to whose essence alone existence belongs, exists?" (*M*, 5, 47). If this is not madness it must be blasphemy. The idea of a clear idea of God is incompatible with everything Descartes passionately believes and with the idea of an infinite God.

The second extreme claim comes from this clear and distinct idea of God's nature, and while far more compatible with Descartes's excessive desire for truth, it touches another extreme close to madness. Here our idea of ourselves and our limits leads us to God, the totality of all perfections. "This idea of a supremely perfect and infinite being is, I say, true in the highest degree. . . . The idea is, moreover, utterly clear and distinct; for whatever I clearly and distinctly perceive as being real and true, and implying any perfection, is wholly contained in it" (Descartes, *M*, 3, 31). The claim I regard as excessive here is that every perfection is wholly contained in the idea of God. The extreme is "wholly," for it implies that truth and being close in God around every perfection and imperfection. This is indeed Foucault's "other madness," that which does not know that the good makes such closure impossible, interrupts the gathering of being, places every perfection and imperfection, good and bad, in endless circulation, never to be wholly contained, in nature or God. The inclusion is not containment but endless movement, endless excess. Descartes's madness is the endless anarchy of things, resisting the gathering and containment of truth and being and saying together.

We come to Descartes's confrontation with his madness, which he hopes to put away, but cannot do successfully. He summarizes the lunacy, knowing full well that it is dangerously insane, but denies its danger like any madman.

> I think it will be a good plan to turn my will in completely the opposite direction and deceive myself, by pretending for a time that these former opinions are utterly false and imaginary. I shall do this until the weight of preconceived opinion is counter-balanced and the distorting influence of habit no longer prevents my judgement from perceiving things correctly. In the meantime, I know that no danger or error will result from my plan, and that I cannot possibly go too far in my distrustful attitude.

> This is because the task now in hand does not involve action but merely the acquisition of knowledge. (Descartes, *M*, 1, 15)

He claims that he will not completely tear down the house in which we live in order to rebuild it (Descartes, *DM*, 122), yet that is exactly what he proposes in relation to doubt. Only someone crazy would think that he could tear down his house while living within it. Only someone mad would think that by believing everything uncertain is false he "should at least be sure not to fall" (Descartes, *DM*, 116). We may pass over the certainty with which Descartes guards against disaster. Disaster, I would say, threatens no matter what. Anyone who claims to be sure to avoid disaster is either naive or mad. I emphasize instead that concern for disaster is ethical. Truth and certainty come as gifts from the good and do their work in its memory.

Descartes's project is mad as a project, interweaving moments of lucidity and insanity. I have spoken of the madness of certainty, which insists that if a belief is not certain it must be false. If I cannot prove you are human with complete certainty I must think you are a machine. Only God can save us from such madness. But I am interested for the moment in the figure of the project, described as building an edifice to heaven, in a repeated figure of foundations and God, gathering truth in being. In reply to Bourdin (Descartes, *OR*, Obj. 7, 366), Descartes likens himself to an architect, building upon solid rather than sandy foundations.

> Throughout my writings I have made it clear that my method imitates that of the architect. When an architect wants to build a house which is stable on ground where there is a sandy topsoil over underlying rock, or clay, or some other firm base, he begins by digging out a set of trenches from which he removes the sand, and anything resting on or mixed in with the sand, so that he can lay his foundations on firm soil. In the same way, I began by taking everything that was doubtful and throwing it out, like sand; and then, when I noticed that it is impossible to doubt that a doubting or thinking substance exists, I took this as the bedrock on which I could lay the foundations of my philosophy. (Descartes, *OR*, Obj. 7, 366)

This tempered account of his method bears exalted expectations.

> Above all I delighted in mathematics, because of the certainty and self-evidence of its reasonings. But I did not yet notice its real use; and since I thought it was of service only in the mechanical arts, I was surprised that nothing more exalted had been built upon such firm and solid foundations. On the other hand, I compared the moral writings of the ancient pagans to very proud and magnificent palaces built only on sand and mud. (Descartes, *DM*, 114)

The desire for solid foundations so that a serviceable and commodious habitation might be built passes into images of palaces and towers, public buildings instituting the authority of great civilizations, gathering all their subjects under their rule. The figure framing this desire for greatness comes from enforced solitude, another figure of madness.

> I stayed all day shut up alone in a stove-heated room, where I was completely free to converse with myself about my own thoughts. Among the first that occurred to me was the thought that there is not usually so much perfection in works composed of several parts and produced by various different craftsmen as in the works of one man. Thus we see that buildings undertaken and completed by a single architect are usually more attractive and better planned than those which several have tried to patch up by adapting old walls built for different purposes. (Descartes, *DM*, 116)[7]

The agenda of Descartes's project to search for truth and follow reason bears upon unbelievers and faith in God, the superior authority of great civilizations built upon firm foundations and laid out according to plan, reaching from the ground to God, gathering together their territorial possessions. All these gestures instituting divine authority in the rule of reason over truth commemorate the good. At the moment, my concern is with whether the good bears the weight of the edifice Descartes hopes to build. I add that the figure of an architect cannot be taken lightly, for Descartes does not forbear granting it political weight. When he speaks of tearing everything down that was once thought true, but that allowed for doubt, his image of building becomes explicitly political.

> Admittedly, we never see people pulling down all the houses of a city for the sole purpose of rebuilding them in a different style to make the streets more attractive; but we do see many individuals having their houses pulled down in order to rebuild them, some even being forced to do so when the houses are in danger of falling down and their foundations are insecure. This example convinced me that it would be unreasonable for an individual to plan to reform a state by changing it from the foundations up and overturning it in order to set it up again; or again for him to plan to reform the body of the sciences or the established order of teaching them in the schools. (Descartes, *DM*, 117)

Such a measure, tearing down the walls of church and state to build anew, is not only impossible—something Descartes does not quite acknowledge— but blasphemous and traitorous. Perhaps even those who would condone violence and revolution against tyranny might acknowledge that new beginnings are impossible and exceedingly dangerous. Yet while Descartes agrees that this is so, he also begins again, and represents a pure beginning, instituting the truth of reason's certainty where certainty was not possible before. Descartes builds his edifice of reason in an ethical world filled with political demands. We may recall that Ari the left-winged bat builds no tower but inhabits existing caves with millions of his friends and family, inhabits nature without dividing bats into us and them. Descartes's method is not for all.

> The simple resolution to abandon all the opinions one has hitherto accepted is not an example that everyone ought to follow. The world is largely composed of two types of minds for whom it is quite unsuitable. First, there are those who, believing themselves cleverer than they are, cannot avoid precipitate judgements and never have the patience to direct all their thoughts in an orderly manner. . . . Secondly, there are those who have enough reason or modesty to recognize that they are less capable of distinguishing the true from the false than certain others by whom they can be taught; such people should be content to follow the opinions of these others rather than seek better opinions themselves. (Descartes, *DM*, 118)

The purpose of a method of arriving at truth here is to let those who should rule do so and to encourage those who should not to obey. Obedience and authority permeate reason. The democratic rational principle that divided human beings from other species returns to divide human beings from each other, perhaps Europeans from non-Europeans and men from women, humans from bats.

Let us return to the bat who flies through history looking for truth but who finds it where he and other bats live, in surrounding places in nature, always in circulation. Such creatures cannot imagine for a moment that reason or truth might call for the destruction of everything they hold dear. Nor can Descartes, when he is sane. But he is mad for reason and truth most of the time in his writings. Even so, when he is sane he remembers the gift of the good. But when he is mad he claims to be sane.

> I formed for myself a provisional moral code consisting of just three or four maxims, which I should like to tell you about.
>
> The first was to obey the laws and customs of my country. . . . Where many opinions were equally well accepted, I chose only the most moderate, both because these are always the easiest to act upon and probably the best (excess being usually bad), and also so that if I made a mistake, I should depart less from the right path than I would if I chose one extreme when I ought to have pursued the other. (Descartes, *DM*, 122)

He claims to be moderate and to obey the laws and customs of his country. Yet where custom and law demand appeal to perception and memory,

Descartes departs, in a departure that cannot be thought moderate, where to think it moderate is to be mad. For Descartes may deny that he will tear down the edifice of custom to build another based on reason. Yet that is what he does, and does gladly.

> So, for the purpose of rejecting all my opinions, it will be enough if I find in each of them at least some reason for doubt. And to do this I will not need to run through them all individually, which would be an endless task. Once the foundations of a building are undermined, anything built on them collapses of its own accord; so I will go straight for the basic principles on which all my former beliefs rested. (p. 12)

We may recall that his architectural work, said to be in the service of building an edifice, serves the good and right, "the right path" above, and elsewhere. Truth is no end in itself in Descartes, nor is building a tower. They serve the good—or rather, because I regard the good as giving rather than ruling, they are called to the good by its giving as gifts. Truth interrupts this calling, I would say madly. Those who think that truth serves the good without remainder are mad. If anyone thinks that. Can the right path be given by truth and knowledge? Descartes says it can. "[W]e need only to judge well in order to act well" (Descartes, *DM*, 124). At the point at which he will become his own deceiver, taking on the role of a malicious demon (Descartes, *M*, 1, 15), he knows it will not matter because his activity involves knowledge only, not action, though he clearly believes that truth and knowledge are on the right path, on the way to the good. Whatever he thinks about the likelihood of danger, he knows that he must think about the danger in the light of the good. Not to think so is mad; and to think that there is no danger at all is also mad.

Descartes is contemptuous of Bourdin for many of the observations I am making here.[8] Bourdin frames his objections in an architectural voice, asking if the leaking building can be repaired (Descartes, *OR*, Obj. 7, 365). Only God knows the madness of his project. Or Kant. Another architectural figure of gathering.

> We have found, indeed, that although we had purposed to build for ourselves a tower which should reach to Heaven, the supply of materials sufficed merely for a habitation, which was spacious enough for all terrestrial purposes, and high enough to enable us to survey the level plain of experience, but that the bold undertaking designed necessarily failed for want of materials—not to mention the confusion of tongues, which gave rise to endless disputes among the laborers on the plan of the edifice, and at last scattered them over all the world, each to erect a separate building for himself, according to his own plans and his own inclinations. (Kant, *CPR*, 397)

Except that Kant accepts the project Descartes defines, to build a glorious tower reaching toward the heavens established on absolute foundations, if without quite enough materials at hand. For the Tower of Babel must stand even if it does not reach far enough, stand against the possibility of scattered laborers with habitations throughout the world. Civilization demands a tower against the threat of mad confusion, driven by another, Archimedean madness.

For Bourdin reminds Descartes repeatedly of his Archimedean point whereby he may move the world although he has no body to press the lever, no body and no mind.

> This is excellent, my distinguished friend! You have found your "Archimedean point," and without doubt you can now move the world if you so wish. Look: the whole earth is already shaking. But since, I gather, you are cutting everything back to the bone, so that your method may include only what fits and is coherent and necessary, may I ask why you refer to the mind (I mean in the phrase "whenever it is conceived in my mind")? Did you not banish both mind and body? (Descartes, *OR*, Obj. 7, 322)

Bourdin may be more concerned with Descartes's madness than his materiality, having cast away everything that goes with sanity. How can there be a point on which we stand if we stand nowhere? We may remain within the excesses of madness by reminding ourselves of Descartes's own words on Archimedes.

> It feels as if I have fallen unexpectedly into a deep whirlpool which tumbles me around so that I can neither stand on the bottom nor swim up to the top. Nevertheless I will make an effort and once more attempt the same path which I started on yesterday. Anything which admits of the slightest doubt I will set aside just as if I had found it to be wholly false; and I will proceed in this way until I recognize something certain, or, if nothing else, until I at least recognize for certain that there is no certainty. Archimedes used to demand just one firm and immovable point in order to shift the entire earth; so I too can hope for great things if I manage to find just one thing, however slight, that is certain and unshakable. (Descartes, *M*, 2, 16)[9]

In the midst of overwhelming confusion, Descartes will find a single point on which to move the world, overlooking in his enthusiasm that Archimedes had to stand somewhere and to place his lever somewhere, not to mention where the other end touches the world—three material points in all. What arrogance to claim to be Archimedes—an arrogance history regards as just! What arrogance to forget the body Archimedes so carefully weighed! What madness to forget the tumbling whirlpool of madness.

CHAPTER 5

Mad Will

We have barely touched Descartes's extreme madness, senselessly denying the body. What else but derangement can it be to "abandon all the opinions one has hitherto accepted" knowing that that cannot be right, even possible, for most people? What but a lunacy we would not tolerate in others? How sane can it be to treat "anything which admits of the slightest doubt . . . just as if I had found it to be wholly false" (Descartes, *M*, 2, 16)? What moderation? What resistance to overwhelming passion and excessive will? For precisely emotion and will are excluded when Descartes excludes his body, when he considers himself "as not having hands or eyes, or flesh, or blood or senses, but as falsely believing that I have all these things" (Descartes, *M*, 1, 15). In the name of truth he excludes the excesses of passion and will that would interfere with reason's authority—in the name of an excessive passion and will for reason's truth.

This madness for truth beyond the bounds of truth is acknowledged by Descartes himself, if obliquely, remembering his desire to free himself from worries and cares, seeking a reason and truth uncontaminated by emotion, by bodily matters. For no one knows better than Descartes, if in a different place, that the will cares nothing for what reason demands. This will, infinitely free, represents God in humanity. "It is only the will, or freedom of choice, which I experience within me to be so great that the idea of any greater faculty is beyond my grasp; so much so that it is above all in virtue of the will that I understand myself to bear in some way the image and likeness of God" (Descartes, *M*, 4, 39). Even here, facing this limitless will beyond containment, Descartes imposes his own excessive desire for truth and certainty. "For if I always saw clearly what was true and good, I should never have to deliberate about the right judgement or choice; in that case, although I should be wholly free, it would be impossible for me ever to be in a state of indifference" (Descartes, *M*, 4, 39). We may pause upon this idea of indifference.

For Descartes has shown that action calls upon us to pursue both moderation and conviction, that we cannot in relation to action seek to make ourselves indifferent. But we can do so in relation to reason and truth when action is not required. Indifference has then a double nature. On the one hand, it represents the lowest grade of freedom. "[T]he indifference I feel when there is no reason pushing me in one direction rather than another is the lowest grade of freedom; it is evidence not of any perfection of freedom, but rather of a defect in knowledge or a kind of negation" (Descartes, *M,* 4, p. 39). His passion for truth shows that he seeks a higher freedom. On the other hand, this indifference is anything but neutral in relation to error.

> So what then is the source of my mistakes? It must be simply this: the scope of the will is wider than that of the intellect; but instead of restricting it within the same limits, I extend its use to matters which I do not understand. Since the will is indifferent in such cases, it easily turns aside from what is true and good, and this is the source of my error and sin. (Descartes, *M,* 4, 40)

Descartes claims reason's indifference when he must be anything but indifferent to reason and its truths, and moreover, regards indifference as the lowest grade of freedom. We must be indifferent when we do not know with certainty.

> I happen to be in doubt as to whether the thinking nature which is in me, or rather which I am, is distinct from this corporeal nature or identical with it. I am making the further supposition that my intellect has not yet come upon any persuasive reason in favour of one alternative rather than the other. This obviously implies that I am indifferent as to whether I should assert or deny either alternative, or indeed refrain from making any judgement on the matter. (Descartes, *M,* 4, 41)

I wonder if he may claim indifference only in the context of a total absence of indifference, in the throes of a passion, a will, for reason's authority so overwhelming that no other passion or will can compete. The infiniteness of the will is required by the quest for truth. Both will and truth demand unlimited commitment. Yet Descartes claims reason's indifference when reason is not sure, passionately insists on indifference. What indifference is possible in God's world, within nature? That question comes from the good to fall within the gathering of being. Even so, indifference is not the absence of passion but the infiniteness of emotion and desire for truth. We may be indifferent, I would say, concerning what is superior and inferior, resisting domination and exclusion. In the name of the good, we cannot be indifferent to the endless call of things to us to respond, in our desire for truth.

The will, an image of God, cannot be limited, is unlimit, power itself.[1] In this way, it overrides truth in the name of God. At this point we seem to have no choice but to grant that error is the excess of desire over being, truth, and saying, exceeding the gathering of truth in the name of the good, the excess of God over humanity, of the good over truth. Except that we desire truth beyond anything else. This desire for something beyond, which exceeds any limits including the limits of truth and being, comes from the good as a gift. Descartes reminds us that truth is given as a gift within excessive desire. We desire beyond any truth, except that we desire truth more than that. "From these considerations I perceive that the power of willing which I received from God is not, when considered in itself, the cause of my mistakes; for it is both extremely ample and also perfect of its kind" (Descartes, *M,* 4, 40); "it is clear by the natural light that the perception of the intellect should always precede the determination of the will" (p. 41).

This natural light, if it insists that the intellect reign over the will where the will is the infinite image of the divine, presents a boundless and excessive authority, overriding the power of God in the name of God's authority. Surely this cannot be taken for granted except as another account of limitless and excessive will—the will for truth—and another sign of madness. This madness for truth, resting in the natural light of being, recalls our memory of the good in the name of God. If it is true that we should subordinate our wills and passions to our intellect, it is in virtue of the gift of truth from the good.

> even if I have no power to avoid error in the first way just mentioned, which requires a clear perception of everything I have to deliberate on, I can avoid error in the second way, which depends merely on my remembering to withhold judgement on any occasion when the truth of the matter is not clear. Admittedly, I am aware of a certain weakness in me, in that I am unable to keep my attention fixed on one and the same item of knowledge at all times; but by attentive and repeated meditation I am nevertheless able to make myself remember it as often as the need arises, and thus get into the habit of avoiding error. (Descartes, *M,* 4, 43)

I would speak instead not of a weakness in me but of an infinite yearning, a desire for truth, that overrides every other object of desire. The gift, God's gift, is the will. The will to truth, beyond limit, is the only resistance to the excessive authority of reason produced by the limitless will to truth.

Descartes insists that the gift is reason's truth against all the evidence of his own argument of the excessive force of the will. He argues for the existence of God in the name of truth, that God is no deceiver and that knowledge is a perfection. Error and falsity are imperfections. "I saw clearly that it is a greater perfection to know than to doubt" (Descartes, *DM,* 127); "it is manifest by the natural light that all fraud and deception depend on some defect" (Descartes, *M,* 3, 35); "I know by experience that there is in me a faculty of judgement which, like everything else which is in me, I certainly received from God. And since God does not wish to deceive me, he surely did not give me the kind of faculty which would ever enable me to go wrong while using it correctly" (Descartes, *M,* 4, 37).

The argument from perfection in Descartes is an ethical argument, given from the good. Truth is better than deceit. I might wish to argue in return that great deceptions have something sublime in them, that a great lie far exceeds in worth a tepid truth. I would argue that truth and error— truth and lie in Nietzsche's sense—are so inextricably entwined that we cannot choose one over the other in general or in principle, but only here and there in local and particular circumstances. In either case, however, the claim of the truth upon falsity belongs to the good. Descartes spells this out in detail in his account of error and the will. The reason why we are not to chafe at the unlimitedness of a will that leads us into error, why we are not thereby to regard the will as imperfect, is that God wills what is best. The argument is based on superiority. "There is, moreover, no doubt that God could have given me a nature such that I was never mistaken; again, there is no doubt that he always wills what is best. Is it then better that I should make mistakes than that I should not do so?" (Descartes, *M,* 4, 38). From the standpoint of the universe as a whole, it may be better that I err than that I do not. "It also occurs to me that whenever we are inquiring whether the works of God are perfect, we ought to look at the whole uni- verse, not just at one created thing on its own. For what would perhaps rightly appear very imperfect if it existed on its own is quite perfect when its function as a part of the universe is considered" (p. 39). This famous— or infamous—argument concerning the goodness of the world has little to recommend it, in my opinion, for I grant neither the superiority of truth without qualification nor that of the aggregate. I resist thinking of the good as a claim to superiority. Even so, truth's privilege demands that we grant the good as giving gifts that allow for the institution of privilege. Truth's superiority is an ethical claim. In this light, Descartes's privileging of truth is either blasphemy or madness.

I add two further points of privilege in Descartes, still mad we might say, touching this site of the authority of truth. One is his search for the nature of things, appearing twice. One appearance concerns the nature of The Human, who "I" am by nature. In Meditation 2 a human being is a thinking thing; in Meditation 6, a human being is "a combination of mind and body" (Descartes, *M*, 6, 61). The second portrayal of nature is of nature itself, not things by nature but nature in general, gathered into totality. "[I]f nature is considered in its general aspect, then I understand by the term nothing other than God himself, or the ordered system of created things established by God. And by my own nature in particular I understand nothing other than the totality of things bestowed on me by God" (Descartes, *M*, 6, 55). This nature in general reminds us of the *phusis* that moves from itself toward itself and of *phusin kalon*, Diotima's nature of wondrous beauty. Yet we are not to speak of nature in general without another sense of nature limited, of things by nature, identities and boundaries, what things are.

> I must more accurately define exactly what I mean when I say that I am taught something by nature. In this context I am taking nature to be something more limited than the totality of things bestowed on me by God. For this includes many things that belong to the mind alone—for example my perception that what is done cannot be undone, and all other things that are known by the natural light; but at this stage I am not speaking of these matters. It also includes much that relates to the body alone, like the tendency to move in a downward direction, and so on; but I am not speaking of these matters either. My sole concern here is with what God has bestowed on me as a combination of mind and body. (Descartes, *M*, 6, 56)

In relation to this sense of things in nature bounded by their identities, all relations are in terms of good and bad, to seek or avoid.

> a further problem now comes to mind regarding those very things which nature presents to me as objects which I should seek out or avoid... (Descartes, *M*, 6, 58)

> Admittedly, when I consider the purpose of the clock, I may say that it is departing from its nature when it does not tell the right time; and similarly when I consider the mechanism of the human body, I may think that, in relation to the movements which normally occur in it, it too is deviating from its nature if the throat is dry at a time when drinking is not beneficial to its continued health. But I am well aware that "nature" as I have just used it has a very different significance from "nature" in the other sense. As I have just used it, "nature" is simply a label which depends on my thought; it is quite extraneous to the things to which it is applied, and depends simply on my comparison between the idea of a sick man and a badly-made clock, and the idea of a healthy man and a well-made clock. But by "nature" in the other sense I understand something which is really to be found in the things themselves; in this sense, therefore, the term contains something of the truth. (p. 58)

Descartes assimilates to truth this distinction between nature in general, to which binary oppositions are irrelevant, and things by nature, whose identities are bounded by oppositions and limits. Yet on his account both allude to the good, bear ethical weight. For nature both institutes and alludes to oppositions where we must choose between the better and worse, are drawn to the good away from the bad, and includes what is good and true because it belongs to God, the totality of things given from God. Nature bears a double meaning, one related to privilege and superiority, bounded by identities and limits, the other the totality beyond any superiority, exceeding privilege and authority. To privilege truth over the good is impossible on this second reading, given Descartes's own sense of the gift of things from God. The privilege of truth exceeds truth as the will exceeds truth, leading to madness.

It follows that Descartes is indeed mad, as are all who seek truth so passionately with him, mad for truth, as Socrates is, where that very madness is a sign of something other than the truth to which it is responsible and from which it is given, and where that something may be nothing, no thing or being. Descartes names it God, and that name has force. Yet even here it is the question of the existence of God, thereby granting divine authority. The good has nothing to do with existence and imposes no authority, but, rather, gives from itself authority to the questions of being that underlie the authority of truth. If the good failed to exist, that would in no way halt the gifts that circulate in its name. The good does not need to exist to give its gifts, does not insist on gathering into being, does not need to exercise being's authority. It is blasphemy, I believe, to insist that what calls us to truth and justice is a being, the blasphemy of being's authority as if without excess, as if authority were not beyond limit. Existence and being are nothing without the authority given them from the good. Truth is nothing without desire, will, and emotion. Or without imagination. All remind us of the body that Descartes has killed, the excessive body beyond the limits of time and skin.

They also remind us of his parents, humanly embodied. For even they pass into the madness of a mind that does not know its kinship with its body.

> Lastly, as regards my parents, even if everything I have ever believed about them is true, it is certainly not they who preserve me; and in so far as I am a thinking thing, they did not even make me; they merely placed certain dispositions in the matter which I have always regarded as containing me, or rather my mind, for that is all I now take myself to be. So there can be no difficulty regarding my parents in this context. (Descartes, *M*, 3, 35)

When Christ said "Follow me!" he did not dismiss the formative and emotional relation of children to their parents. He willed something greater.

It is as if we were living in a dream, we might say. And dreams are everywhere in Descartes's writing, linked with madness, perception, and imagination, interrupting the gathering of truth. He seems to worry that he might be living in a dream, or that he could not tell that he was dreaming, and proposes worlds of thoughts and images, malevolent demons, that we cannot encounter save in dreams or madness. To make his case that the intellect can reach truth independent of the deceptive imagination, Descartes must dream, or imagine, or imagine that he is dreaming, proposing as dreamlike a state as we may find in any writing.

"Suppose then that I am dreaming, and that these particulars—that my eyes are open, that I am moving my head and stretching out my hands— are not true. Perhaps, indeed, I do not even have such hands or such a body at all" (Descartes, *M*, 1, 13). Yet must I not be dreaming, or mad, to think that I have no hands or body? At least I must have an overheated imagination. "What else am I? I will use my imagination. I am not that structure of limbs which is called a human body. I am not even some thin vapour which permeates the limbs—a wind, fire, air, breath, or whatever I depict in my imagination; for these are things which I have supposed to be nothing" (*M*, 2, 18); "I will suppose then, that everything I see is spurious. I will believe that my memory tells me lies, and that none of the things that it reports ever happened. I have no senses. Body, shape, extension, movement and place are chimeras" (p. 16).

> I will suppose therefore that not God, who is supremely good and the source of truth, but rather some malicious demon of the utmost power and cunning has employed all his energies in order to deceive me. I shall think that the sky, the air, the earth, colours, shapes, sounds and all external things are merely the delusions of dreams which he has devised to ensnare my judgement. I shall consider myself as not having hands or eyes, or flesh, or blood or senses, but as falsely believing that I have all these things. (Descartes, *M*, 1, 15)

Descartes is obsessed, haunted, by dreams and madness. Here I might briefly question the dispute between Derrida and Foucault on whether Descartes accounts for or excludes madness (Foucault, *FD;* Derrida, *CHM*).[2] I would say that he gives himself wholly, madly, obsessively, over to madness and imagination, as if insanely dreaming, at the same time that he asks us to imagine that imagination is never able to establish truth, insists that madness is irreconcilable with truth. He asks us to imagine the destruction of imagination, to dream the overwhelming presence of dreams,

at the same time that he institutes the authority of reason under God and
the destruction of the body, only to gather the body under God.

Imagination, together with memory, dreaming, and perception, is one
of the points at which truth touches the good embodied. For if Descartes
must imagine or dream of unreality in order to establish first the unreality
and then the reality of the corporeal world, the reality and veracity of
imagining and dreaming, we must ask how and with what he dreams and
imagines when he imagines himself without body. He says that imagination
is corporeal, along with memory, even that what we are able to dream and
think requires corporeality. "Just as the imagination employs figures in
order to conceive of bodies, so, in order to frame ideas of spiritual things,
the intellect makes use of certain bodies which are perceived through the
senses, such as wind and light. By this means we may philosophize in a
more exalted way, and develop the knowledge to raise our minds to lofty
heights" (Descartes, *EW*, 4); "The things which are perceivable by the senses
are helpful in enabling us to conceive of Olympian matters" (p. 5).

We cannot know without imagination and sense-perception, though
all such knowledge depends on the intellect, described in extreme images
of gathering, surveying and enumerating, reminding us of humanity's
architectural|political project.

> Once he has surveyed everything that follows immediately upon knowl-
> edge of the pure intellect, among what remains he will enumerate what-
> ever instruments of knowledge we possess in addition to the intellect; and
> there are only two of these, namely imagination and sense-perception. He
> will therefore devote all his energies to distinguishing and examining
> these three modes of knowing. (Descartes, *RDM*, 29)[3]

Rule Twelve presents the dependence of reason and knowledge on imagination and memory, on the senses, so completely that it is difficult to understand why Descartes privileges reason and the intellect.

> Finally we must make use of all the aids which intellect, imagination,
> sense-perception, and memory afford in order, firstly, to intuit simple
> propositions distinctly; secondly, to combine correctly the matters under
> investigation with what we already know, so that they too may be known;
> and thirdly, to find out what things should be compared with each other
> so that we make the most thorough use of all our human powers.
> (Descartes, *RDM*, 39)

We think with and through the imagination, together with sense-perception
and memory. The intellect is among the faculties we employ, perhaps con-
tiguous and inseparable from the others. Yet though we are to make use in
every case of all our human powers together—and who would doubt it?—

Descartes emphasizes the distinctness of the different powers. Moreover, we are to devote all our energies, not to the most thorough use of all our human powers, wherever they may lead, but to distinguishing and examining the different powers. No wonder that Gassendi objects, "But, my good Mind, can you establish that there are several internal faculties and not one simple and universal one, which enables us to know whatever we know?" (Descartes, *OR*, Obj. 5, 186).

This issue of autonomous faculties, to which Descartes never quite replies, suggests two things; one that although for some analytic purposes it may be useful to think of the human mind as divided into distinct faculties, in every case we use all our powers. Descartes himself suggests as much. The separation and distinctness of faculties is neither clear and distinct nor functionally defensible, but a proximate and tentative distinction. The second is that although for some analytic purposes we may distinguish mind from body, in every case we work with mind and body together. Descartes himself suggests as much.

> in so far as our external senses are all parts of the body, sense-perception, strictly speaking, is merely passive, even though our application of the senses to objects involves action, viz. local motion; sense-perception occurs in the same way in which wax takes on an impression from a seal. It should not be thought that I have a mere analogy in mind here: we must think of the external shape of the sentient body as being really changed by the object in exactly the same way as the shape of the surface of the wax is altered by the seal. (Descartes, *RDM*, 40)

This extreme view, if we understand that to think is to think through memory and imagination, goes far beyond any empiricism to the body. We think as our bodies are pressed by other bodies. This leads directly to Spinoza, and is not absent in Descartes despite his contrary claims.

> Fourthly, the motive power (i.e. the nerves themselves) has its origin in the brain, where the corporeal imagination is located; and the latter moves the nerves in different ways, just as the "common" sense is moved by the external senses or the whole pen is moved by its lower end. This example also shows how the corporeal imagination can be the cause of many different movements in the nerves, even though it does not have images of these movements imprinted on it, but has certain other images which enable these movements to follow on. (Descartes, *RDM*, 42)

Here a "purely corporeal imagination" is one without intellect. Descartes says nothing about a purely mental intellect that entirely lacks corporeal imagination. To the contrary.

the power through which we know things in the strict sense is purely
spiritual, and is no less distinct from the whole body than blood is distinct
from bone, or the hand from the eye. It is one single power, whether it
receives figures from the "common" sense at the same time as does the
corporeal imagination, or applies itself to those which are preserved in the
memory, or forms new ones which so preoccupy the imagination that it is
often in no position to receive ideas from the "common" sense at the same
time, or to transmit them to the power responsible for motion in accordance with a purely corporeal mode of operation. (Descartes, *RDM*, 42)

There is one power, sometimes called intellect, imagination, memory, or
sense-perception, intimately related to corporeal imagination, that is, to
the body. Descartes comes very close to the shocking truth that we understand by means of imagination, whose omission is said in our time to be
shocking.

> Without imagination, nothing in the world could be meaningful. With-
> out imagination, we could never make sense of our experience. Without
> imagination, we could never reason toward knowledge of reality. . . .
>   It is a shocking fact that none of the theories of meaning and ratio-
> nality dominant today offer any serious treatment of imagination. (Johnson,
> *BM*, ix)

I add sense-perception and memory, including dreams.
    Descartes dreams that he is dreaming, imagines that his imaginings
are unreal, and can dream and imagine and remember only because he has
a body. How then does the intellect become an autonomous faculty, separate from the body? It is no more separate from imagination, I believe, than
it is from the will, not separate at all, capable of truth in virtue of the
infinite demands of the will and the cacophony of bodily sensations.

> All the modes of thinking that we experience within ourselves can be
> brought under two general headings: perception, or the operation of the
> intellect, and volition, or the operation of the will. Sensory perception,
> imagination and pure understanding are simply various modes of percep-
> tion; desire, aversion, assertion, denial and doubt are various modes of
> willing. (Descartes, *PP*, 204)

I could go on at length to show that Descartes knows as well as anyone
that we are fully embodied and that knowledge and truth work through a
corporeal imagination, even that this corporeal imagination, together with
memory and sense-perception, exceeds the sense we have, including
Descartes's, of the limitations of bodies. In this way I suggest that we
approach Spinoza, where Ari Carlo our bat will find himself, returning to

bodies and their materiality. Delaying that flight for just a moment, I conclude this discussion with Descartes's recognition of the unity that composes mind and body, intellect and imagination: "the mind is proved to be really distinct from the body, but is shown, notwithstanding, to be so closely joined to it that the mind and the body make up a kind of unit . . . " (Descartes, *M,* Syn., 11). Descartes recognizes this unity, knows the impossibility of thinking without a body, perhaps of embodying without thought, held up by an overweening passion for something beyond knowledge.[4]

Descartes ends his *Meditations* in memory of dreams, supplemented by the weakness of reason.

> I now notice that there is a vast difference between the two, in that dreams are never linked by memory with all the other actions of life as waking experiences are. If, while I am awake, anyone were suddenly to appear to me and then disappear immediately, as happens in sleep, so that I could not see where he had come from or where he had gone to, it would not be unreasonable for me to judge that he was a ghost, or a vision created in my brain, rather than a real man. But when I distinctly see where things come from and where and when they come to me, and when I can connect my perceptions of them with the whole of the rest of my life without a break, then I am quite certain that when I encounter these things I am not asleep but awake. . . . But since the pressure of things to be done does not always allow us to stop and make such a meticulous check, it must be admitted that in this human life we are often liable to make mistakes about particular things, and we must acknowledge the weakness of our nature. (Descartes, *M,* 4, 61)

We know the difference between dreams and sense-perception because we remember, and we remember through our bodies, memories imprinted on our bodies. Dreams disrupt the gathering of truth in sense-experience, taking us in memory to our bodies. Without physical marks our memories would be empty. In Descartes, the thought that mind is disembodied, and that correspondingly, *automata,* machines, are devoid of soul, is a disaster of cosmic proportions, the like of which we have only dreamed of, extreme oblivion to the good. It is a disaster I hope to remember.

CHAPTER 6

Full Body

Ari, the left-winged bat, flies for truth, touching down on a moment in Spinoza where bats and other creatures find marks of their truth. We do not know what bodies can do: "For indeed, no one has yet determined what the Body can do, i.e., experience has not yet taught anyone what the Body can do from the laws of nature alone. . . . This shows well enough that the Body itself, simply from the laws of its own nature, can do many things which its Mind wonders at" (Spinoza, *E,* 3, P2, Sch). Including bats, Ari laughs and screams, bats and bat bodies. And other bodies. But touching down in Spinoza offers bats little rest (*acquiescentis*: Spinoza, *E,* 5, P26). For Spinoza speaks of animals for human use, recalling Aristotle and Aquinas.

> Apart from men we know no singular thing in nature whose Mind we can enjoy, and which we can join to ourselves in friendship, or some kind of association. And so whatever there is in nature apart from men, the principle of seeking our own advantage does not demand that we preserve it. Instead, it teaches us to preserve or destroy it according to its use, or to adapt it to our use in any way whatever. (Spinoza, *E,* 4, App 26)

I will discuss bodies in Spinoza in another place.[1] Here I touch down with Ari the bat upon Spinoza's ethical understanding of embodied truth. Yet before I begin to explore the scene upon which Spinoza's account of truth is displayed in relation to the good, I must reflect on several ways in which Spinoza understands nature, joins truth with being we might say, as if gathered under one substance, God. One is that everything follows from God, taking nature as a whole as *natura naturans* and *natura naturata* together, nature naturing, infinite, necessary, composed of nature natured, infinite numbers of infinite kinds:

> In nature there is nothing contingent, but all things have been deter-
> mined from the necessity of the divine nature to exist and produce an
> effect in a certain way. (Spinoza, *E*, 1, P29)

> it is already established that by *Natura naturans* we must understand
> what is in itself and is conceived through itself, or such attributes of
> substance as express an eternal and infinite essence, i.e. (by P14C1 and
> P17C2), God, insofar as he is considered as a free cause.
>   But by *Natura naturata* I understand whatever follows from the ne-
> cessity of God's nature, or from any of God's attributes, i.e., all the modes
> of God's attributes insofar as they are considered as things which are in
> God, and can neither be nor be conceived without God. (P29, Sch)

All things, finite and infinite, follow from Nature's unlimited power
(potentia). But finite things, or modifications *(affectiones),* also follow from
other finite things in infinite succession.

> Every singular thing, or any thing which is finite and has a determinate
> existence, can neither exist nor be determined to produce an effect unless
> it is determined to exist and produce an effect by another cause, which is
> also finite and has a determinate existence; and again, this cause also can
> neither exist nor be determined to produce an effect unless it is deter-
> mined to exist and produce an effect by another, which is also finite and
> has a determinate existence, and so on, to infinity. (Spinoza, *E*, 1, P28)

Throughout his *Ethics*, in every Part, Spinoza moves between and
across these two registers, two related kinds or varieties of causality, in
relation to knowledge and truth, good and evil, justice and injustice, perfection and imperfection. Moreover, crossing these registers at an unfamiliar angle, by no means their repetition, is his understanding of the relation
between mind and body, expressed at one extreme in the proposition that
"The order and connection of ideas is the same as the order and connection
of things" (Spinoza, *E*, 2, P7). This (near) identity of ideas and things,
thought and extension, joins his understanding that we do not know what
bodies can do, that infinite powers reside in bodies that we do not, cannot,
know, but that belong to nature and to any of its truths. The infinite nature
of God cannot be gathered in truth. Its truth divides into infinite numbers
of infinite attributes. "By attribute I understand what the intellect perceives
of a substance, as constituting its essence" (Spinoza, *E*, 1, D4), perhaps
even the divine intellect. God is not to be understood in infinite totality, but
as divided into infinite attributes. That is the plenitude of things, general
economy, an unlimited abundance of unlimited kinds. "By God I understand a being absolutely infinite, i.e., a substance consisting of an infinity
of attributes, of which each one expresses an eternal and infinite essence"

(Spinoza, *E*, 1, D6); "I say absolutely infinite, not infinite in its own kind" (D6, Exp). The plenitude does not gather even in relation to God. It pertains to bodies and ideas, and countless other kinds. The totality of God and nature, *natura naturans* and *natura naturata*, provides whatever truth may be known, but does not gather into truth. Nature's plenitude divides into infinite numbers of infinite kinds, beyond any saying or knowing, including God's. All embodied.

At the other extreme, related to this understanding of the plenitude of bodies, is what is sometimes regarded as Spinoza's most paradoxical thought, that disposing the body in many different ways disposes the mind to adequate ideas, to God's truth. I list three examples among many others.

> in proportion as a Body is more capable than others of doing many things at once, or being acted on in many ways at once, so its Mind is more capable than others of perceiving many things at once. And in proportion as the actions of a body depend more on itself alone, and as other bodies concur with it less in acting, so its mind is more capable of understanding distinctly. (Spinoza, *E*, 2, P13, Sch)

> Whatever so disposes the human Body that it can be affected in a great many ways, or renders it capable of affecting external Bodies in a great many ways, is useful to man; the more it renders the Body capable of being affected in a great many ways, or of affecting other bodies, the more useful it is; on the other hand, what renders the Body less capable of these things is harmful. (4, P38)

> He who has a Body capable of a great many things has a Mind whose greatest part is eternal. (5, P39)

We might call this thought "paradoxical," after many of Spinoza's commentators. Yet I regard it now as fundamental in Spinoza's thought where truth and the good circulate around each other. These are the movements around which I hope to turn Spinoza's understanding of truth, hoping to understand it in his terms as ethical, in my terms as given from the good. From the beginning we may imagine that these different registers and movements compose Spinoza's ethics. With Ari I seek the embodied good in this incarnate ethics, that is, in nature.

I return for just a moment to the beginning of Spinoza's *Ethics* to recall two thoughts in Latin (and French) that do not appear in English translation, do not allow themselves to be thought openly in English, as much of Spinoza's thought seems to me to remain unthought in English, buried in the Latin. A human without Latin will not understand Spinoza very deeply, I believe. A bat may understand things in a different way. For Spinoza's *Ethics* opens with the definition of self-causation *(causam sui)* as "that whose essence involves *[involvit]* existence" (Spinoza, *E*, 1, D1), where *involvit* means, as "involve" no longer means in English, "to enfold, envelope." The French translation is *enveloppe*. What is self-caused, shown to be nature or God, enfolds its existence in a material and embodied way that we do not know how to think, that perhaps we may never quite know how to think or say.

Similarly, Definition 6, on the attributes, which I have noted with a different regard, defines God as a substance with infinite numbers of infinite attributes (see also Spinoza, *E*, 1, P9–10, Dem and Sch), "of which each one expresses *[exprimit]* an eternal and infinite essence" (D6). Again, *exprimit* exposes not only the sense of expressing as showing, saying, revealing— propositional truth—but also as squeezing out, pressing forth, extruding. Substance, God, enfolds itself in material ways, squeezing its essence out into infinite numbers of infinite attributes, including thought and extension. Truth, the truth of nature and being, is material, not a truth of matter but a truth enmattered, a matter of truth, a matter touched in truth and flesh.

I take this further expression of the materiality of nature in Spinoza to bear upon and express in tangibly material ways the ethical side of truth, the relation of truth to the good. With Aristotle's bat, I hope to think of truth in Spinoza as it has, I believe, never been thought before or elsewhere, as what I might call here the bat-tering of truth. This means more than the materiality of truth, though that is included, enfolded, expressed. I mean more than the beating of truth by force, though that is expressed, included, but also the enfolding of truth in the lives and desires of bats and others: truth touched by the materiality of bats and other creatures and things.

Spinoza's idea of truth is expressed immediately following a number of lemmas on the composition of bodies, concluding with all of nature regarded as an individual with infinite abundance, portraying abundance in a striking way. "And if we proceed in this way to infinity, we shall easily conceive that the whole of nature is one Individual, whose parts, i.e., all bodies, vary in infinite ways, without any change of the whole Individual" (Spinoza, *E*, 2, P13, L7, Sch). Abundance is nature's infinite variety of individuals, parts, and kinds.

These lemmas follow the connection of the human mind and its ideas to the human body. "The object of the idea constituting the human Mind is the Body, or a certain mode of Extension which actually exists, and nothing else" (Spinoza, *E*, 2, P13). As a consequence, all human ideas are inadequate and confused, following from external causes. Spinoza develops this thought at length.

> The human Mind does not know the human Body itself, nor does it know that it exists, except through ideas of affections by which the Body is affected. (Spinoza, *E,* 2, P19)
>
> The human Mind does not involve adequate knowledge of the parts composing the human Body.
>
> The idea of any affection of the human Body does not involve adequate knowledge of an external body. (P25)
>
> The ideas of the affections of the human Body, insofar as they are related only to the human Mind, are not clear and distinct, but confused. (P28)
>
> We can have only an entirely inadequate knowledge of the duration of the singular things which are outside us. (P31)

I understand this account of knowledge to belong to a single register, that of *natura naturata,* infinite numbers of finite things in infinite succession, about which our knowledge is and must be inadequate and confused, battered and bruised. I take it that this knowledge and truth, of finite things in infinite succession, is not confused because we human beings, we knowers, are confused but because the knowledge itself is, because the things are, because infinite numbers of things in infinite succession, related by external causes, do not have an adequate truth *as finite,* as modifications, *affectiones.* Finite things as finite modes, affected by other things, do not admit of adequate truth in this succession of affects. Finite things resist gathering.

This extended expression of the fragmentary and confused nature of the truth of external things and causes is immediately followed by a radical reversal. "All ideas, insofar as they are related to God, are true" (Spinoza, *E,* 2, P32), recalling a similar thought expressed somewhat earlier. "There is also in God an idea, or knowledge, of the human Mind, which follows in God in the same way and is related to God in the same way as the idea, or knowledge, of the human Body" (P20), followed by "The human Mind has an adequate knowledge of God's eternal and infinite essence" (P47), reaching culmination of a sort in Part 5: "There is no affection of the Body of which we cannot form a clear and distinct concept" (5, P4), that is, an adequate and true idea.

This last proposition shows us that Spinoza's understanding of the two registers, *natura naturans* and *natura naturata,* infinite and finite perhaps, temporal and eternal, *potentia* and *potestas,* creative power and power of acting, requires bridging, linking, movements similar to the one I described above as "paradoxical." I will note others in due course, all intermediary movements resistant to the gathering of truth into thinking and saying.

For the moment I am concerned with the play of inadequate and adequate ideas, two registers of truth expressing the two registers of *natura naturans* and *natura naturata*. The lemmas of bodies together with the propositions following them expressing the inadequacy and confusion of all ideas of finite things in relation to the modifications of the body enfold two thoughts of a quite different order, on two different registers. One is where Proposition 20 joins Proposition 32, suggesting that for every inadequate idea there is a corresponding true and adequate idea in God, and that both follow by necessity (Proposition 36); the other that we may think of nature as a single composite individual of infinite variety, endless abundance. I take these thoughts to be closely linked, and add that where we may find two registers of truth corresponding to substance and its modifications, we may find two registers of being corresponding to the unity of God and endless infinites and infinite varieties of individuals and kinds. The thought of God appears to gather all things under God's being and truth, expressed in infinite ways. It is a gathering of infinite variety which is expressed in infinite numbers of infinite kinds. It is a gathering that fails to gather, a one composed of infinite variety and heterogeneity, an assembling whose abundance disassembles (and dissembles) its assembly. This is the thought I take to bring together two thoughts in Spinoza: the thought of truth with the thought of the good. It is a thought of truth's abundance, beyond any gathering, an embodied general economy.

But first, let me note that where in Part 2 knowledge and truth are presented in the two registers of causation, a harsh and uncompromising view of the inadequacy of truth for finite things followed by the adequacy of truth in God, in Parts 3 and 4 Spinoza passes into a harsh and extreme view of the subjection of finite human beings to passions and to external causes followed by the ways in which human beings can touch the eternal part of themselves and understand themselves in relation to eternity. Here we find the thought that crosses from the human ethical world to the ethics embodied in nature and God.

In Part 3, from the *conatus*, the striving that belongs to every thing, finite or infinite, Spinoza takes us through the vicissitudes and hatreds of desire escalating to the greatest and most intransigent hatred of all in historical human memory, animosity toward strangers. I follow the development briefly.

> Each thing, as far as it can by its own power *(potentia)*, strives to persevere in its being. (Spinoza, *E*, 3, P6)

> When this striving is related only to the Mind, it is called Will; but when it is related to the Mind and Body together, it is called Appetite. This Appetite, therefore, is nothing but the very essence of man, from whose

nature there necessarily follow those things that promote his preservation. And so man is determined to do those things. (P9, Sch)

He who imagines that what he hates is destroyed will rejoice. (P20)

If we imagine someone to affect with Joy a thing we love, we shall be
affected with Love toward him. If, on the other hand, we imagine him to
affect the same thing with Sadness, we shall also be affected with Hate
toward him. (P22)

He who Hates someone will strive to do evil to him, unless he fears that
a greater evil to himself will arise from this; and on the other hand, he
who loves someone will strive to benefit him by the same law. (P39)

If someone has been affected with Joy or Sadness by someone of a class,
or nation, different from his own, and this Joy or Sadness is accompanied
by the idea of that person as its cause, under the universal name of the
class or nation, he will love or hate, not only that person, but everyone of
the same class or nation. (P46)

Where in Part 2 all human knowledge is knowledge of what affects the human body, and all knowledge of what affects the human body is inadequate,
fragmented, and confused, in Part 3 the *conatus* leads through desire to
hatred and love toward other people, arriving at the greatest cause of war,
hatred toward those who differ from us by nation, class, or tribe, loving only
our kind, hating every other kind. Spinoza expresses an apocalyptic view of
religion and the state, expresses the ferocity of belonging to a kind.

Yet this is not the whole story in either part, because there are adequate ideas through God of all things, including finite things that affect
our finite bodies. In Part 2, inadequate ideas give way to adequate ideas in
God. In Part 3, love replaces hatred and breeds a greater love. "Hate is
increased by being returned, but can be destroyed by Love" (Spinoza, *E*, 3,
P43); "Hate completely conquered by Love passes into Love, and the Love
is therefore greater than if Hate had not preceded it" (P44). And it is followed by an affirmation of variety and difference among human beings and
other things that recalls us to Spinoza's sense of nature's abundance.

There are as many species of Joy, Sadness, and Desire, and consequently
of each affect composed of these (like vacillation of mind) or derived from
them (like Love, Hate, Hope, Fear, etc.), as there are species of objects by
which we are affected. (Spinoza, *E*, 3, P56)

Each affect of each individual differs from the affect of another as much
as the essence of the one from the essence of the other. (P57)

I am speaking of where he concludes his lemmas concerning body with an
image of the unity of God and nature embodied in a single composite

individual "whose parts, i.e., all bodies, vary in infinite ways." The two registers meet here in a coupling with immense practical and ethical implications. We are led by desire to hate all strangers. We are led through God and nature's abundance to love infinite variety, to cherish abundance and general economy.

Part 4 reveals a similar structure. It begins strongly framed by the limits of external causes, repeating the account of inadequate and confused truth in Part 2 in the language of emotion. I understand Spinoza's entire *Ethics*, including both registers, to be linked by the Latin idea of emotion, *affectiones*, translated as "modification," combined with *affectibus* in Part 3, where its root, *adfectio*, is "to be affected" and "to strive." To be finite is to be subject to external causes, infinitely, that is, to be affected by and to affect, that is, to be emotional, active or passive, to endeavor, to desire.

> It is impossible that a man should not be a part of Nature, and that he should be able to undergo no changes except those which can be understood through his own nature alone, and of which he is the adequate cause. (Spinoza, *E*, 4, P4)

> An affect cannot be restrained or taken away except by an affect opposite to, and stronger than, the affect to be restrained. (P7)

> A Desire which arises from a true knowledge of good and evil, insofar as this knowledge concerns the future, can be quite easily restrained or extinguished by a Desire for the pleasures of the moment. (P16)

> A Desire which arises from a true knowledge of good and evil, insofar as this concerns contingent things, can be restrained much more easily still by a Desire for things which are present. (P17)

It would seem that external causes overpower the most adequate knowledge of contingent things, including everything that affects individual human bodies and other bodies. It would seem that we must therefore be extremely cautious in engaging on that level or plane of life which is concerned with practical things and events, including politics and ethics. As contingent beings, we cannot avoid such ethical and political judgments, but nothing, not even true knowledge of good and evil, and not even the desire, the love, that arises from that knowledge, can restrain the pressures of contingent things present before us and pleasures that attract us face to face. Gathering up finite things is a treacherous endeavor.

With this understanding, perhaps, we can read Spinoza's account of a contingent ethics and politics, reminiscent of Hobbes indeed, but bearing something else. For it takes Hobbes hundreds of pages to explain the force and authority of sovereignty. Spinoza takes but a page or two, in the con-

text of the force of present desire, directed again at strangers but aug-
mented by an even greater violence toward animals and other natural things
who are not "like us."

> Any singular thing whose nature is entirely different from ours can nei-
> ther aid nor restrain our power of acting *(potestas),* and absolutely, no
> thing can be either good or evil for us, unless it has something in com-
> mon with us. (Spinoza, *E,* 4, P29)

> it is clear that the law against killing animals is based more on empty
> superstition and unmanly compassion than sound reason. The rational
> principle of seeking our own advantage teaches us the necessity of joining
> with men, but not with the lower animals, or with things whose nature
> is different from human nature. We have the same right against them that
> they have against us. Indeed, because the right of each one is defined by
> his virtue, or power, men have a far greater right against the lower ani-
> mals than they have against men. Not that I deny that the lower animals
> have sensations. But I do deny that we are therefore not permitted to
> consider our own advantage, use them at our pleasure, and treat them as
> is most convenient for us. For they do not agree in nature with us, and
> their affects are different in nature from human affects. (P37, Sch 1)

The principle of infinite variety in nature becomes in law a justification for
using animals and every other natural thing in any way whatever (Spinoza,
E, 4, App 26). Even so, the normative ideas on which such extreme judgments are based are "extrinsic," not "intrinsic." Spinoza says this almost
immediately after condemning animals to our use in any way whatever
because they are different, followed by a remarkable phrase: "From this it
is clear that just and unjust, sin and merit, are extrinsic notions, not attributes that explain the nature of the Mind. But enough of this" (Spinoza,
E, 4, P37, Sch 2). *Sed de his satis.* Enough of what, we may ask, perhaps.

The same phrase appears at the close of another heinous and repugnant passage concerning the contingencies of human social life, closing the
Political Treatise. There Spinoza speaks of women ruled by men in his
"perfectly absolute dominion, which we call democracy" (Spinoza, *PT,* 385)
from which he excludes "women and slaves, who are under the authority
of men and masters, and also children and wards, as long as they are under
the authority of parents and guardians" (Spinoza, *PT,* 386).

> But, perhaps, someone will ask, whether women are under men's author-
> ity by nature or institution? . . . For there has never been a case of men
> and women reigning together, but wherever on the earth men are found,
> there we see that men rule, and women are ruled, and that on this plan,
> both sexes live in harmony. . . . And since this is nowhere the case, one

> may assert with perfect propriety, that women have not by nature equal
> right with men: but that they necessarily give way to men, and that thus
> it cannot happen, that both sexes should rule alike, much less that men
> should be ruled by women. (Spinoza, *PT,* 386–87)

This passage seems as plain as possible, that Spinoza claims that men
should rule over women for men's and women's benefit, in the nature of
things, reminiscent of Aristotle and Aquinas. Yet he continues, followed by
the phrase in question:

> But if we further reflect upon human passions, how men, in fact, generally
> love women merely from the passion of lust, and esteem their cleverness
> and wisdom in proportion to the excellence of their beauty, and also how
> very ill-disposed men are to suffer the women they love to show any sort
> of favour to others, and other facts of this kind, we shall easily see that
> men and women cannot rule alike without great hurt to peace. But of this
> enough. (Spinoza, *PT,* 387)

Men must rule women, to the benefit of men and women, because of human passion and the lusts of men, who are ill-disposed toward the judgments of women, jealous and controlling. But enough of this, because it is
not a subject responsive to nature and God, perhaps. Perhaps all these
contingent things must be said because they reflect the best that contingency can provide, and we must not expect more of them. Perhaps we say
enough of this because we must say more, in a different register, for these
claims belong to inadequate and confused ideas, to human bondage, *de
servitute humana.*

Even here, Spinoza does not leave these conclusions to rest in their
most oppressive and heinous form. He says no more in *A Political Treatise,*
perhaps because it ends unfinished. He follows his remarks on animals and
strangers in his *Ethics* with the claim that all such remarks, all contingent
judgments of good and bad, are extrinsic, asking us to think of what is
intrinsic. The proposition immediately following is one of the central bridging thoughts whereby the two registers, *natura naturans* and *natura
naturata,* join in a single voice, however "paradoxical."

> Whatever so disposes the human Body that it can be affected in a great
> many ways, or renders it capable of affecting external Bodies in a great
> many ways, is useful to man; the more it renders the Body capable of
> being affected in a great many ways, or of affecting other bodies, the more
> useful it is; on the other hand, what renders the Body less capable of these
> things is harmful. (Spinoza, *E,* 4, P38)

Moreover, such a disposition into variety brings humanity closer to eternity.
Contingency reaches toward necessity through the register of infinite variety.

But there is more. For Spinoza follows this account, still we might imagine with one side grounded in contingency, with a thought of freedom, leading to an entirely different understanding of the relation of individual human beings to their social world. "If men were born free, they would form no concept of good and evil so long as they remained free" (Spinoza, *E,* 4, P68); "A man who is guided by reason is more free in a state, where he lives according to a common decision, than in solitude, where he obeys only himself" (P73). External causes require that we submit ourselves to a state with authority over us, threaten us to accept the common good. Freedom knows nothing of good and evil, even within a state. "He who is guided by Fear, and does good to avoid evil, is not guided by reason" (Spinoza, *E,* 4, P63). Some of the confusion many today experience in reading Spinoza, I believe, comes from the way words have come down to us. "Love and Desire can be excessive *(excessum)*" (Spinoza, *E,* 4, P44), where *excessum* suggests being away from, outside oneself, another reference to what is extrinsic. What is intrinsic is beyond good and evil. On my reading, what is beyond good and evil is the good. Freedom is beyond finite gathering.

With this thought we come to Part 5, which I understand to retain a similar structure. It begins with formulas for contingent life, leading to love of God.

> An affect which is a passion ceases to be a passion as soon as we form a clear and distinct idea of it. (Spinoza, *E,* 5, P3)

> Insofar as the Mind understands all things as necessary, it has a greater power over the affects, or is less acted on by them. (P6)

> He who understands himself and his affects clearly and distinctly loves God, and does so the more, the more he understands himself and his affects. (P15)

This section concludes with two striking passages, one an explanation of how it is possible, despite the contingencies of truth, external causes, and passions, that the passions may be remedied.

> And with this, I have covered all the remedies for the affects, or all that the Mind, considered only in itself, can do against the affects. From this it is clear that the power of the Mind over the affects *[Mentis in affectus potentiam]* consists:
>
> I. In the knowledge itself of the affects (see P4S);
>
> II. In the fact that it separates the affects from the thought of an external cause, which we imagine confusedly (see P2 and P4S);
>
> III. In the time by which the affections related to things we understand surpass those related to things we conceive confusedly, or in a mutilated way (see P7);

IV. In the multiplicity of causes by which affections related to common properties or to God are encouraged (see P9 and P11);

V. Finally, in the order by which the Mind can order its affects and connect them to one another (see P10, and in addition, P12, P13, and P14). (Spinoza, *E,* 5, P20, Sch)

I add that while Spinoza occasionally speaks of reason or mind restraining or combating the affects or emotions, the Latin phrase which he repeats again and again is *mentis in affectus potentiam,* the power of the mind or reason *in* emotion (see Spinoza, *E,* 5, P42, Sch). I do not believe that Spinoza shares Descartes's view of the battle between emotion and reason. Rather, he has another and more complicated view of their relation, enjoyed by Ari the bat as well as human beings.

He concludes the Scholium of Proposition 20 with a doubly astonishing claim:

> With this I have completed everything which concerns this present life. Anyone who attends to what we have said in this Scholium, and at the same time, to the definitions of the Mind and its affects, and finally to IIIP1 and P3, will easily be able to see what I said at the beginning of this Scholium, viz. that in these few words I have covered all the remedies for the affects. So it is time now to pass to those things which pertain to the Mind's duration without relation to the body. (Spinoza, *E,* 5, P20, Sch)

One is that he has finished with this life, the life of contingency and external causes. Yet we know that he cannot be finished, that the wise and free human being still belongs to that order and register. Even so, perhaps we have finished with Spinoza's theory of contingent practice, in a single register. The second astonishing claim is that the mind may endure without relation to the body, despite the principle that the order and connection of ideas is the same as the order and connection of things, and that all human ideas are ideas of the body. Later he restates this as "the things I have decided to show concerning the Mind, insofar as it is considered without relation to the Body's existence" (Spinoza, *E,* 5, Sch). This does not help resolve the difficulty of the idea of a mind without relation to the body unless we understand it in another register containing attributes, including corporeal extension, but not a human body.

The difficulty I take to be insurmountable is not the suggestion of another register, that of eternity, but that Spinoza does not consider the eternity of the body, of corporeal extension, as deeply as he considers the eternity of the mind. "The human Mind cannot be absolutely destroyed with the Body, but something of it remains which is eternal" (Spinoza, *E,* 5, P23). And the Body, I would say, which cannot be absolutely destroyed, but passes into the infinite abundance and variety of bodies. For we do not know what bodies can do, and what they can do, must do in Spinoza's theory, is to belong to both registers, as individual corporeal things and as corporeal substance, embodied nature, full of infinite variety, eternal and abundant. I cross the intellectual love of God with an endless flow of materiality, endless crossings and circulations, given from nature and the good. I postpone this subject to another time.

Nevertheless, this thought, with or without the corresponding thought of bodies, bridges temporality and eternity, crosses the two registers however impossibly or aporetically. With the thought that something in human mind or body is eternal, bridging and crossing two registers, finite and infinite, that cannot be crossed, but that Spinoza's entire theory crosses, we may add two additional crossings. "The more we understand singular things, the more we understand God" (Spinoza, *E,* 5, P24); "He who has a Body capable of a great many things has a Mind whose greatest part is eternal." (P39). I take these crossings, impossible as they may be, to express the aporia at the heart of nature's abundance, its infinite variety. I take the crossing, not either register alone, to express the gift of the good. Another intermediary movement that abets the circulation.

With this gift we may return with Ari to Spinoza's view of truth, doubly given in the two registers. Nothing of this registration gives us either a correspondence or coherence theory of truth, or any other theory of truth. I believe that Spinoza has no theory of truth. But he knows truth when he encounters it, as he takes us to do, in another impossible thought within the register of *natura naturata.*

I have noted the succession of Propositions 16–31 describing inadequate knowledge of things related to the human body, reaching culmination in the claim that "We can have only an entirely inadequate knowledge of the duration of the singular things which are outside us" (Spinoza, *E,* 2, P31). This succession of propositions concerning truth establishes that knowledge pertaining to the body as a finite mode, of things affecting the human body, is always inadequate. This is the story of knowledge on the register of *natura naturata.* Yet all such inadequate knowledge of finite things is produced by the infinite and eternal power of nature, the register of *natura naturans,* is given its existence and essence from that register, given its truth. Moreover, this account is not the last word on truth or on the register of *natura naturata.* For Spinoza's account of inadequate knowledge is preceded by two extraordinary thoughts I have noted bridging the two registers. One is that of nature as a single individual whose parts "vary in infinite ways" (Spinoza, *E,* 2, P13, L7, Sch). The other is that "The human Mind is capable of perceiving a great many things, and is the more capable, the more its body can be disposed in a great many ways" (Spinoza, *E,* 2, P14). On this reading, all our knowledge of things external to and affecting our bodies is inadequate, except that nature is a single, unchanging individual throughout all the infinite changes of its parts and the inadequacies of knowledge of those parts, and bodies can be disposed in ways that make its knowledge more adequate. The truth of nature associated with nature as a composite individual bears upon eternity. The truth of nature's parts in their infinite variety bears upon temporal succession. The truth of nature's abundance relates to the impossibility of gathering all things up in time, in place, circulating from the good.

The succession of Propositions 16–31, largely concerned with truth as *natura naturata,* is followed by a famous succession of propositions that suggest a complete inversion of the preceding account, culminating in an absolute account of the truth of truth.

> All ideas, insofar as they are related to God, are true. (Spinoza, *E*, 2, P32)
>
> There is nothing positive in ideas on account of which they are called false. (P33)
>
> Every idea that in us is absolute, or adequate and perfect, is true. (P34)
>
> He who has a true idea at the same time knows that he has a true idea, and cannot doubt the truth of the thing. (P43)

The immediate question for us and most other readers is how it can be true at one and the same time that all knowledge of external finite things is inadequate and that ideas in us can be absolute, perfect, and true. My answer here is in terms of the two registers. Knowledge in relation to *natura naturata* is always inadequate; knowledge in relation to *natura naturans,* to God, is absolute, perfect, and true, leaving no room for doubt. These two registers compose nature and God, including every part of nature and every modification of God.

The question becomes how we are to understand truth in this double register, whether truth might be something different in relation to *natura naturata* from *natura naturans,* and how we are to understand the movements that bridge the registers in relation to truth. We may find two different kinds of accounts in Spinoza, one what he says directly about knowledge, the other related to the double register and bridging movements I have been exploring. The first appears in the context of common notions and intuition, famous expressions of traditional rationalism.

> Those things which are common to all, and which are equally in the part and in the whole, can only be conceived adequately. (Spinoza, *E*, 2, P38)
>
> From what has been said above, it is clear that we perceive many things and form universal notions:

I. from singular things which have been represented to us through the senses in a way that is mutilated, confused, and without order for the intellect (see P29C); for that reason I have been accustomed to call such perceptions knowledge from random experience;

II. from signs, e.g., from the fact that, having heard or read certain words, we recollect things, and form certain ideas of them, which are like them, and through which we imagine the things (P18S). These two ways of regarding things I shall henceforth call knowledge of the first kind, opinion or imagination.

III. Finally, from the fact that we have common notions and adequate ideas of the properties of things (see P38C, P39, P39C, and P40). This I shall call reason and the second kind of knowledge.

In addition to these two kinds of knowledge, there is (as I shall show in what follows) another, third kind, which we shall call intuitive knowledge. And this kind of knowing proceeds from an adequate idea of the formal essence of certain attributes of God to the adequate knowledge of the essence of things.

I shall explain all these with one example. Suppose there are three numbers, and the problem is to find a fourth which is to the third as the second is to the first. Merchants do not hesitate to multiply the second by the third, and divide the product by the first, because they have not yet forgotten what they heard from their teacher without any demonstration, or because they have often found this in the simplest numbers, or from the force of the Demonstration of P7 in Bk. VII of Euclid, viz. from the common property of proportionals. But in the simplest numbers none of this is necessary. Given the numbers 1, 2, and 3, no one fails to see that the fourth proportional number is 6 and we see this much more clearly because we infer the fourth number from the ratio which, in one glance, we see the first number to have [to] the second. (Spinoza, *E,* 2, P40, Sch 2)

I quote at length to show again that Spinoza speaks on both registers at once although he appears to distinguish and separate them. We arrive at knowledge from singular things, always in a mutilated and confused way. We arrive at knowledge from signs, words, memory, and imagination, all representations, also inadequate. But we have common notions and adequate ideas, in relation to God, of what is universal, infinite, and eternal. These ideas are what we call reason, and we reason upon them, through them, with them, deducing other ideas from them (Spinoza, *E,* 2, P40). But beyond, or other to reason, is intuitive knowledge, known "in one glance" and without the slightest possibility of doubt. The example Spinoza gives, of a ratio or proportion of numbers, bridges all these different kinds of knowledge. It follows, or at least is suggested, that knowledge of such a proportion crosses all the different kinds of knowledge. Spinoza's example offers another bridging thought.

How is it possible to think of truth pertaining to God and eternity and also to finite things? How is it possible to think of finite, inadequate, and mutilated truth as also, or potentially, infinite and adequate? One answer is that all ideas are true insofar as they are related to God but false insofar as they are related to finite things, false as privation. The relevant proposition, "Falsity consists in the privation of knowledge which inadequate, or mutilated and confused, ideas involve" (Spinoza, *E*, 2, P35), does not define a distinct relation of privation from which falsity is derived, a binary relation of possession and lack, but defines falsity as inadequacy, that is as finiteness and its modifications, resistant to binary relations. Truth is positive, without lack or privation, knows nothing of binarity and opposition, is inclusive rather than exclusive. *Natura naturans* is the creative movement of the universe, including everything in infinite variety. Everything that pertains to it is true. *Natura naturata* is the result of this movement, God's and nature's work. Everything that pertains to it is true, but as infinite and eternal, as embodying *natura naturans*. Truth is to be found where the two registers meet, in a joining that gives rise to falsity as the privation of that meeting, the gap or difference between the registers, the space between inclusion and exclusion, where these define no binary opposition. In this way, wherever finiteness is present, everywhere in *natura naturata*, truth is untruth, dispersing the totality. And everywhere in *natura naturans*, taken apart from *natura naturata*, truth is never the truth of *natura naturata*, so it is another, quite different untruth. On this double register reading, the truth we encounter as absolute is absolute because it has nothing to do with us, nothing to do with our bodies, and consequently, nothing to do with our minds.

I say this baldly, but the truth in Spinoza is that the two registers are as intimately related, belong together, as closely as do ideas and things. *Natura naturata* follows from *natura naturans* and "Inadequate and confused ideas follow with the same necessity as adequate, or clear and distinct ideas" (Spinoza, *E*, 2, P36). Truth inhabits the double register in which nature is one large and composite individual whose parts compose an infinite variety, beyond any assembling. Truth is absolute and infinitely varied, is one only containing an endless abundance and heterogeneity. Eternity and its truths have nothing to do with time, with succession or striving or modifications, but modifications have everything to do with time and emotions and eternity and its truths. Here I would venture to consider the possibility that God's truth is less the truth whose absoluteness we can know, than can be known at all, than the absoluteness of an unchanging individual that changes in its parts in infinite variety. The truth of nature itself is abundance and heterogeneity, resisting every closure, including the enclosure of truth. Closure, limit, pertains to inadequate ideas and inadequate truths, truths that lack the truth of abundance. Nature's general economy does its work in restricted economies, interrupting their limits.

This understanding follows the thought of the good I have suggested in which the use and advantage to which Spinoza subjects animals and everything nonhuman belongs to a register in a voice that constantly calls from another register, demands another voice, that in which we strive to adapt ourselves as widely as we can, including all those things and creatures we otherwise subject to our purposes, to give ourselves to eternity, where we have always been, in body and soul, part of something larger, so infinite that it cannot change, infinite with everything in it changing constantly. Including every individual truth. The double register of truth is given in memory of the good, given reflecting the double register of the good. Everything involving truth is to be told in another voice, the voice of the good, that which allows Spinoza's *Ethics* to be an ethics. It is an ethics because it speaks of what is good for humanity, advantageous and useful according to the model of humanity we set before us (Spinoza, *E,* 4, Pref). But all such knowledge of humanity, its models, and what is advantageous, is inadequate and confused. This truth, joined with the truth that truth and humanity and the good belong to the double registers of *natura naturans* and *natura naturata*, is the gift of the good, is profoundly ethical. Put another way, truth reflects the ethical truth that ethics, good and evil, belong to a double register, where the good of one register has nothing to do with good and evil, good and bad, justice and injustice. Nothing to do but altogether inseparable from it, bridged by understanding that we must dispose our bodies in innumerable ways to approach eternity, must live as well as we can in as many ways as we can in participating in the double register. This participation is given from the good, given as truth among other things.

Ari arrives at truth from the good with the understanding that his arrival is an endless departure. Truth is at once endlessly limited, determined by the limits of things, inadequate and confused, pervaded by something with its truth beyond limits, a truth of infinite creativity, an adequate truth of endless inadequacy and creativity. All this truth expresses the double register where the truth of nature and God speak of the creativity beyond the limits of finite values and finite truths. God's truth is the good. Emotion, *affectus*, crosses, bridges, truth with untruth and truth and untruth together with the abundance of nature, abundance given from the good beyond any binary opposition. Spinoza's truth knows nothing and everything of binary oppositions, knows nothing and everything of the limits of truth, truth's privation. All this returns us to know that we do not know what bodies can do, that truth expresses—in the doubly multiple senses of expression—this truth of what we know and what we do not know, all expressions—again in this doubly multiple sense of truth and bodies and multiply double registers—of the good. Truth belongs to the heterogeneous body of the good.

CHAPTER 7

True Experience

We began our discussion with Aristotle's words on truth: "To say of what is that it is not, or of what is not that it is, is false, while to say of what is that it is, and of what is not that it is not, is true" (Aristotle, *Metaphysics*, 1011). Whether or not these words designate a correspondence theory of truth, they establish a gathering of being and saying in truth that has haunted the Western tradition, setting off bats and other creatures on endless flights shrieking for their truth. Even so, it waited for Hobbes and Locke to unfold another wrinkle in the matter of saying that has come to haunt the truth of truth. Truth belongs to words and not things. This far from indisputable revision of the truth of saying in the saying of truth is a radical alteration of the truth of being given as the being of truth. The space between these two inverted movements, which I understood as given from the good, is filled by words in Hobbes, Locke, Hume, and their followers, not all empiricists by any means. I retrace this well-known movement here to return it to the good, away from which it has fallen. The fall into language, understood in metaphysical terms as a fall away from being, is a falling away from the good, still given from the good, falling away from bodies and places into disembodied concepts and words, as if we might speak and write without bodies in their places.

Let us first recall the truth of truth as words, the words of truth:

> Now these words true, truth, and true proposition, are equivalent to one another; for truth consists in speech, and not in the things spoken of; and though true be sometimes opposed to apparent or feigned, yet it is always to be referred to the truth of proposition . . . (Hobbes, *EOP,* 35)

> Seeing then that truth consisteth in the right ordering of names in our affirmations, a man that seeketh precise truth had need to remember what every name he uses stands for, and to place it accordingly; or else he will find himself entangled in words, as a bird in lime twigs, the more he struggles the more belimed. (Hobbes, *L,* Pt. 1, 105)

111

I interpose a brief digression in the name of birds who do not find themselves entangled in words, as Ari does not find himself blinded by the sun,
against their truth. For in the grand academy of Lagado, Swift tells us, we
may find

> a scheme for entirely abolishing all words whatsoever; . . . since words are
> only names for *things*, it would be more convenient for all men to carry
> about them such *things* as were necessary to express the particular busi-
> ness they are to discourse on. . . .
>   Another great advantage proposed by this invention was that it would
> serve as an universal language to be understood in all civilised
> nations . . . (Swift, *GT*, 150)

Truth cannot belong to things as such, things we can carry around with us,
because something escapes us when we present things as if their being
were the same as their truth. Truth cannot belong to things without words,
or without something else excessive, does not equate with being, does not
gather without surplus. Truth cannot belong to words without things, or
something else, does not equate with language. "What do you mean by that
thing?" "What is the truth you wish to show in showing that thing?" Truth
and being are not univocal, are not just what they are in their truth. They
are interrupted by and interrupt the circulation of goods, gifts of the good.
They circulate in endless interruptions.
     In the extreme, attached so tightly to names, Hobbes must say some-
thing so implausible that we may wonder how it is possible for anyone to
believe it. I begin with his "correspondence" theory of truth, though I
might have passed over it, given its irrelevance to our project here.

> When two names are joined together into a consequence, or affirma-
> tion, as thus, a man is a living creature; or thus, if he be a man, he is a
> living creature, if the latter name living creature, signify all that the former
> name man signifieth, then the affirmation, or consequence is true; other-
> wise false. For true and false are attributes of speech, not of things. And
> where speech is not, there is neither truth nor falsehood. Error there may
> be, as when we expect that which shall not be, or suspect what has not
> been: but in neither case can a man be charged with untruth. (Hobbes, *L*,
> Pt. 1, 104)

If when we speak we say what is, we speak the truth; otherwise we say what
is false. And truth and falsehood belong to speech, to words and language,
to propositions. But there can be error, we can err without language, in
thought or practice, but we cannot be charged with untruth. How, we may
wonder, can error belong to a different plane of reality or judgment than

truth and falsehood? How can we think of falsehood without error, or error without falsehood, and truth?

In anticipation of the rest of this chapter, to be postponed for just a moment, we may ask what is at stake in restricting truth to words. What if truth belonged to things, to nature and being, even to sparrows and God? What loss is incurred when we forget that truth is given from the good, perhaps to words, to the said in Levinas's language, but always from something unsaid, beyond words, perhaps beyond saying? What of the interruption by words of the gathering of being?

Locke carries Hobbes's love of words into a somewhat different place, distinguishing propositions from words. In this moment, truth's belonging to language and words passes into a different place, without words, without speech, much closer to being, though denied.

> 1. Though truth and falsehood belong, in propriety of speech, only to propositions; yet ideas are oftentimes termed true or false (as what words are there, that are not used with great latitude, and with some deviation from their strict and proper significations?) Though, I think, that when ideas themselves are termed true or false, there is still some secret or tacit proposition, which is the foundation of that denomination ... (Locke, *E*, 514)

It is not quite true to say that truth belongs to words, because it belongs to propositions and these may be mental or verbal (Locke, *E*, 514n). Even so, propositions are not things, but made up of ideas or words, though of no particular words exactly. I interpose another interruption, this time from Wittgenstein, who leads this understanding of truth back to where it belongs.

> 1.   The world is all that is the case *[der Fall]*.
> 1.1   The world is the totality of facts *[Tatsachen]*, not of things
> 2.04   The totality of existing states of affairs is the world.
> 3.01   The totality of true thoughts is a picture of the world. (Wittgenstein, *TLP,* 7, 13, 19)

If we do not return to things, still we cannot dissociate truth and things, truth and the world. If truth belongs to propositions, being is made up of propositions, or if not quite propositions, then of proposition-like facts, propositions and facts. What else could be true of a correspondence, picturing, theory of truth? If that is Wittgenstein's view of truth.

Truth and falsehood belong to words, to pictures and models, to propositions. But even so, they belong to things, if in a degenerate, metaphysical sense.

> 2. Indeed both ideas and words may be said to be true in a metaphysi-
> cal sense of the word truth, as all other things, that any way exist, are said
> to be true, i.e. really to be such as they exist. (Locke, *E,* 514)

I use the word "degenerate," suggesting that something of that sort must guide Locke's understanding of truth, given that there is a sense of truth in which everything that is is really what it is, is true.

> 3. But it is not in that metaphysical sense of truth which we enquire
> here, when we examine whether our ideas are capable of being true or
> false; but in the more ordinary acceptation of those words . . . For truth or
> falsehood lying always in some affirmation, or negation, mental or verbal,
> our ideas are not capable, any of them, of being false, till the mind passes
> some judgment on them; that is, affirms or denies some thing of them.
> (Locke, *E,* 515)

Locke's equation of truth with judgment follows our reading of Aristotle, a reading that we have seen excludes Spinoza, who identifies truth with God, thought and extension together, through the order and connection of ideas and things. This order and connection of ideas and things expresses (in Spinoza's double sense of expelling and showing) something of the good, cannot be thought or envisaged except as given from the good. In Spinoza. Where is the good in Locke, that which gives the gift of truth? Locke and Hume give somewhat different answers, both reminiscent of Descartes. It may be worth considering each, given in prefatory explication of the project.

> 4. If, by this enquiry into the nature of the understanding, I can
> discover the powers thereof; how far they reach; . . . If we can find out
> how far the understanding can extend its view, how far it has faculties
> to attain certainty, and in what cases it can only judge and guess; we
> may learn to content ourselves with what is attainable by us in this
> state. (Locke, *E,* 28)

This is the language of authority. Locke's project is related to the establishment of truth's authority. We may make those who understand us less credulous, less accepting of the authority of reason, less demanding of its authority, contented with what is attainable, possessing just so much authority and certainty as is possible. The undertaking to inquire into reason, truth, and understanding is related to truth's authority.

Hume says something similar in a different voice. He begins his *Enquiry* by distinguishing two different kinds of philosophy, for just a moment suggesting that we might be content with either.

> Moral philosophy, or the science of human nature, may be treated after two different manners; each of which has its peculiar merit, and may contribute to the entertainment, instruction, and reformation of mankind. The one considers man chiefly as born for action; and as influenced in his measures by taste and sentiment; pursuing one object, and avoiding another, according to the value which these objects seem to possess, and according to the light in which they present themselves. . . .
> The other species of philosophers consider man in the light of a reasonable rather than an active being, and endeavour to form his understanding more than cultivate his manners. (Hume, *EHU*, 9–10)

If there are two such different ways of treating human nature, perhaps both offer a species of truth, and perhaps both may be joined in human experience. Hume comes close to such a suggestion, opening the possibility of an entirely different relation to truth and reason, born in *praxis*. Indeed, he expresses the possibility of a Nietzschean critique of metaphysical reason in eloquent terms.

> It seems, then, that nature has pointed out a mixed kind of life as most suitable to the human race, and secretly admonished them to allow none of these biasses to draw too much, so as to incapacitate them for other occupations and entertainments. . . . Be a philosopher; but, amidst all your philosophy, be still a man. (Hume, *EHU*, 12)

Yet he contemptuously dismisses one pole of the mixed life as "easy and obvious philosophy" (p. 10), and joins forces against this life and its allures (p. 9), replying in violently adversarial terms. What is at stake is superstition.

> But is this a sufficient reason, why philosophers should desist from such researches, and leave superstition still in possession of her retreat? Is it not proper to draw an opposite conclusion, and perceive the necessity of carrying the war into the most secret recesses of the enemy? In vain do we hope, that men, from frequent disappointment, will at last abandon such airy sciences, and discover the proper province of human reason. (p. 15)

Philosophy, hard philosophy, is at war; reason is at war against superstition and dogma on the one hand, against skepticism on the other. Reason's task is to undermine and defeat obscurity and dogmatism, to cure the disease of life and thought that claims authority without the right to do so. "Accurate and just reasoning is the only catholic remedy, fitted for all persons and all dispositions; and is alone able to subvert that abstruse philosophy and metaphysical jargon, which, being mixed up with popular superstition, renders it in a manner impenetrable to careless reasoners, and gives it the air of science and wisdom" (Hume, *EHU*, 15).

Socrates speaks repeatedly of entering battle on the side of reason, presenting reason as engaged in war. And we may read Book I of Plato's *Republic* as expressing this intrinsically embattled condition of reason and truth.[1] For Thrasymachus violently bursts out against Socrates' rationality, demanding that Socrates overcome him by force and denying that Socrates has the power to do so. He accuses Socrates of treating him unfairly in the use of argument, suggesting that reason contains an unfair force in its nature.[2] Moreover, the line between reason's coercion and physical force remains blurred, as Thrasymachus complains: "And how am I to persuade you? he said. If you are not convinced by what I just now was saying, what more can I do for you? Shall I take the argument and ram it into your head?" (Plato, *Republic*, 345bc). This exchange ends with peace, but it is not a peace based on reason's intrinsic authority but permeated with the communal and consensual force that lies behind it. "Revel in your discourse, he said, without fear, for I shall not oppose you, so as not to offend your partisans here" (Plato, *Republic*, 352b).

In this picture, reason is embattled, adversarial, engaged in war. And with it, we may assume, comes an adversarial sense of truth, always at war with error and falsehood, with superstition and unreason. We recall that Socrates died for his truths against the Athenian multitude and that Hume writes in memory of the Inquisition. Reason was at war when Descartes, Hobbes, and Spinoza wrote; Galileo was condemned; Hume remembered. In this view, the embattled language of reason and truth reflects the historical condition that reason was at war for its life and authority. We have to ask ourselves, recalling Hume's suggestion of a mixed life, whether the time has come, if the time will ever come, to end reason's war. Like the modern state, modern reason is forever at war. That at least is what Hobbes says. And Hume. The enemy must be expelled.

> Reason is the discovery of truth or falsehood. Truth or falsehood consists in an agreement or disagreement either to the real relations of ideas, or to real existence and matter of fact. Whatever therefore is not susceptible of this agreement or disagreement, is incapable of being true or false, and can never be an object of our reason. (Hume, *T*, 458)

Mill offers a different thought, though within the image of an embattled reason and a conflicting truth, it may be passed over lightly.

> We have hitherto considered only two possibilities: that the received opinion may be false, and some other opinion, consequently, true; or that, the received opinion being true, a conflict with the opposite error is essen-

tial to a clear apprehension and deep feeling of its truth. But there is a commoner case than either of these; when the conflicting doctrines, instead of being one true and the other false, share the truth between them; and the nonconforming opinion is needed to supply the remainder of the truth, of which the received doctrine embodies only a part. (Mill, *L*, 43)

Understood in adversarial and conflicting terms, Mill's concern for shared truth is a resolution of conflict in an intrinsically controversial space. Truth wars with falsehood; reason wars with superstition; science wars with religion. Binaries are bred in conflict and open onto war. This idea of truth embodies in its warlike nature indirect acknowledgment that truth is at war to establish its authority, and must do so by force. Reason fought the Church by transforming faith and Church authority into superstition. In place of this image of war in which one party must win, Mill suggests a space shared by truth with others, requiring the others for its truth.

It is time to take stock of this movement of empiricism, reflecting three vital principles among many others.

1. Reason is at war against its enemies, superstition and unreason, exemplified by its double relation to skepticism. It is skeptical of all unwarranted claims to epistemic authority, skeptical against all superstitions; it is skeptical of all extreme skepticisms, establishing reason's authority. Truth belongs to reason in this doubly adversarial movement.
2. All knowledge comes from experience, reflecting that same double movement. For experience sets the limits of truth, undermining superstitious authority; and experience unleashes truth, instituting experience's authority.
3. Truth inhabits a warlike, adversarial realm, always at war with untruth, reason at war with unreason. In both cases, the conflict makes peace impossible, makes impossible the belonging together of truth and untruth, reason and unreason. Truth gathers into being and saying in a violent act of exclusion.

These principles obliquely define what may be called the epistemological project, to undermine all forms of epistemic authority that do not begin with a deep and skeptical view of the problem of knowledge and, in the same gesture, instituting trustworthy grounds for epistemic authority that annihilate the remaining residue of skepticism toward authority. Reason here destroys dogmatism in the same gesture that it institutes its own authority—I would say dogmatically. Truth here demands complete disengagement, under the threat of a warlike and destructive conflict, from untruth and unreason. The overriding appeal of a correspondence theory of truth is that it succeeds in structurally instituting this disengagement as no other thought of truth can, instituting truth's authority. Heidegger's thought that truth and untruth belong together, and Nietzsche's thought that truth is perspectival, to be won by feints and misdirection, both relinquish truth's authority. As perhaps does Mill, in a different voice, insisting on continuing the circulation of truth with untruth.

But all this talk of authority, the institution of epistemic authority at the heart of the Western European modern project, cannot belong to truth as such, cannot come from reason or being. Epistemology and ontology carry no authority over life and experience—empiricism's deepest insight—without being granted that authority from elsewhere, perhaps from life and experience, perhaps beyond them, gifts from the good. Locke's critique of innate ideas may be read as instituting another site of epistemic authority than reason alone, but also as repudiating any privileged site of epistemic authority. Authority comes from experience in its richness and immediacy, in its mobility and circulation, undermining any fixing of authority. Against the authority of the Church, experience destroys any institutionalized authority. Yet to resist the destruction of all authority, experience must be confined within limits that institute its own supreme authority.

All knowledge of matters of fact comes from experience. All truth of world and things is given from experience. Experience releases the hold of dogmatic authority. Yet within the frame of the epistemological project, experience institutes another authority, that of scientific rationality. The authority of experience is given by repetition, at least in Hume, a repetition so repeatedly instituted as to exceed any possible experiential authority. The great principle of Hume's epistemology, instituting science's authority against the skepticism that pervades his mind and thought, is repetition. Experience's truth is repetition; as a consequence, only what is or can be repeated can be known, can be claimed as true. Hume's theory of experience is framed entirely and almost without exception in terms of copies and repetitions.

> All the perceptions of the human mind resolve themselves into two distinct kinds, which I shall call impressions and ideas. The difference betwixt these consists in the degrees of force and liveliness, with which they strike upon the mind, and make their way into our thought or consciousness. (Hume, *T,* 1)

Impressions and ideas resemble each other exactly except for force and vivacity, which do not disturb that resemblance.

> Thus we find, that all simple ideas and impressions resemble each other; and, as the complex are formed from them, we may affirm in general, that these two species of perception are exactly correspondent. (Hume, *T,* 4)

all our simple ideas in their first appearance, are derived from simple impressions, which are correspondent to them, and which they exactly represent. (p. 8)

since all ideas are derived from impressions, and are nothing but copies and representations of them, whatever is true of the one must be acknowledged concerning the other. Impressions and ideas differ only in their strength and vivacity. (p. 19)

to express myself in philosophical language, all our ideas or more feeble perceptions are copies of our impressions or more lively ones. (Hume, *EHU*, 22)

This copy machinery, framing Hume's epistemology, between ideas and impressions, is repeated everywhere, on every level, instituting repetitions of repetition virtually without interruption. Yet an exception is mentioned by Hume, discounted as having no force, though with Whitehead and Kant, we may regard it as destroying the theory of repetition.

Suppose, therefore, a person to have enjoyed his sight for thirty years, and to have become perfectly well acquainted with colours of all kinds, excepting one particular shade of blue, for instance, which it never has been his fortune to meet with. . . . Now I ask, whether it is possible for him, from his own imagination, to supply this deficiency, and raise up to himself the idea of that particular shade, though it had never been conveyed to him by his senses? I believe there are few but will be of opinion that he can . . . (Hume, *T*, 5)

This exception proves the possibility of a creative imagination, we might say, if that were what concerned us. I would rather say that it establishes a principle of iterability, that knowledge, truth, and meaning all presuppose repetition, but every repetition is different. Every repetition gathers; every repetition interrupts the gathering.

This principle reflects deeply upon Hume's understanding of memory and experience. First memory.

We find, by experience, that when any impression has been present with the mind, it again makes its appearance there as an idea; and this it may do after two different ways: either when, in its new appearance, it retains a considerable degree of its first vivacity, and is somewhat intermediate betwixt an impression and an idea; or when it entirely loses that vivacity, and is a perfect idea. The faculty by which we repeat our impressions in the first manner, is called the memory, and the other the imagination. (Hume, *T*, 8)

It is evident, that the memory preserves the original form in which its objects were presented, and that wherever we depart from it in recollecting any thing, it proceeds from some defect or imperfection in that faculty. (p. 9)

Memory's task here is to copy, repeat, and preserve, and departure is a defect. To speak of imperfection may remind us of Descartes's claim that falsity is an imperfection, impossible for God, where we humans revel in misdirection to the point where we may imagine that truth without falsity and error could be no perfection. In relation to memory, however, Hume grants nothing of a memory that in remembering remembers loss, knows that to remember is not to have, is of what cannot be present, a memory that carries the thought of the impossibility of preservation *as memory*. Disaster and destruction lie at the heart of this memory, which succeeds in its task, we may say, when it fails to present the past as if it were present, but presents it in its departures.

We may say much the same of experience, which almost certainly does not bear responsibility for repeating itself endlessly, or does so in endless departure, iterability again, except that this account too closely repeats the premises of the epistemological project. First Hume's account of this epistemic frame, within the association of ideas, then applied to experience.

> As all simple ideas may be separated by the imagination, and may be united again in what form it pleases, nothing would be more unaccountable than the operations of that faculty, were it not guided by some universal principles, which render it, in some measure, uniform with itself in all times and places. . . . The qualities, from which this association arises, and by which the mind is, after this manner, conveyed from one idea to another, are three, viz. resemblance, contiguity in time or place, and cause and effect. (Hume, *T*, 10)

Resemblance is similarity, repetition, in quality; contiguity is similarity, conjunction, in time and place. Associations of ideas unite, they do not divide, do not present difference and heterogeneity as difference and heterogeneity. Knowledge, truth, ideas, and experience all work to unite against the unaccountability of heterogeneity. Cause and effect, we know, the one principle in Hume that might address differences as well as similarities, is customary and constant conjunction. As are abstract ideas. "A particular idea becomes general by being annexed to a general term; that is, to a term which, from a customary conjunction, has a relation to many other particular ideas, and readily recalls them in the imagination" (Hume, *T*, 22).

This leads directly to Hume's theory of experience, entirely framed within the epistemological project as knowledge and the possibility of truth.

It is therefore by experience only that we can infer the existence of one object from that of another. The nature of experience is this. We remember to have had frequent instances of the existence of one species of objects; and also remember, that the individuals of another species of objects have always attended them, and have existed in a regular order of contiguity and succession with regard to them. (Hume, *T,* 87)

The idea of cause and effect is derived from experience, which informs us, that such particular objects, in all past instances, have been constantly conjoined with each other: and as an object similar to one of these is supposed to be immediately present in its impression, we thence presume on the existence of one similar to its usual attendant. (p. 89)

The nature of experience is the repetition of memory joined with the memory of repetitions, of regularity and constant conjunction, double and triple repetitions, repetitions of repetitions. Human nature bears a propensity beyond almost any limit toward repetition and its repetition.

This principle is Custom or Habit. For wherever the repetition of any particular act or operation produces a propensity to renew the same act or operation, without being impelled by any reasoning or process of the understanding; we always say, that this propensity is the effect of Custom. By employing that word, we pretend not to have given the ultimate reason of such a propensity. We only point out a principle of human nature, which is universally acknowledged, and which is well known by its effects. (Hume, *EHU,* 43)

This universal principle of repetition joins an equally universal principle of variation in human life and experience. What of their conjunction, constant or irregular? And what of memories of irregularity and inconstancy, not to mention unrepeated memories and memories of loss? What of memories of surprise and unexpectedness? Irregularity and inconstancy in experience and memory may be interpreted to remain within the epistemological project, the truth of being and saying. Truth is irregular as well as regular. Where Hume treats truth as something repeatable, reproducible, repetitive and to be repeated again, we might seek a truth in and of irregularity and variation. Still, this quest belongs to the project of truth, its being and saying. The losses, disasters, of memory, its disruption of epistemic and its own authority, lead us to other places, interrupt the project of truth.

I would not leave Hume without two additional considerations. One is how far his principles of repetition take him, to the point where falsity may be preferable to a truth that disallows repetition. For in two famous instances concerning necessity, liberty, and miracles, Hume disallows any truth that might disrupt repetition. The most famous, or infamous, consequence of Hume's equation of truth with repetition is that despite the "skeptical" nature of his conclusions, they allow for a set of rules to foster reason's grip on disorderly experience. I quote in very small part.

> Since, therefore, it is possible for all objects to become causes or effects to each other, it may be proper to fix some general rules by which we may know when they really are so.
> 1. The cause and effect must be contiguous in space and time. . . .
> 3. There must be a constant union betwixt the cause and effect. It is chiefly this quality that constitutes the relation.
> 4. The same cause always produces the same effect, and the same effect never arises but from the same cause. . . .
> 5. There is another principle which hangs upon this, viz. that where several different objects produce the same effect, it must be by means of some quality which we discover to be common amongst them. For as like effects imply like causes, we must always ascribe the causation to the circumstance wherein we discover the resemblance. . . . (Hume, *T,* 173–75)

This last principle allows for something other than constant conjunction, something in common, between cause and effect, something that undercuts too narrow a reading of Hume's idea of repetition. But it offers another repetition. Knowledge of what is not repeated, not common, different between one and the other, difference as heterogeneity, profusion, variety, variability, all repeatedly fail to offer themselves as truth.

Necessity is nothing but constant conjunction and uniformity in past experience. What force can it have beyond moving the mind in customary and repetitive ways? What authority? Immense authority in Hume, beyond any limitation. For he understands liberty as necessity and necessity as repetition.

> If we examine the operations of body, and the production of effects from their causes, we shall find that all our faculties can never carry us farther in our knowledge of this relation, than barely to observe, that particular objects are constantly conjoined together, and that the mind is carried, by a customary transition, from the appearance of one to the belief of the other. . . . Necessity, according to the sense, in which it is here taken, has never yet been rejected, nor can ever, I think, be rejected by any philosopher. (Hume, *EHU,* 85–86)

It is worth noting that Spinoza, for whom everything is necessary, a necessity at least as great, perhaps far beyond Hume's, does not understand necessity as repetition, constancy and conjunction, but as infinite variety. Necessity may never have been rejected, but repetition is not all there is. Yet it becomes normative in Hume: not necessity but uniformity.

what is meant by liberty, when applied to voluntary actions? We cannot surely mean, that actions have so little connexion with motives, inclinations, and circumstances, that one does not follow with a certain degree of uniformity from the other, and that one affords no inference by which we can conclude the existence of the other. For these are plain and acknowledged matters of fact. By liberty, then, we can only mean a power of acting or not acting, according to the determinations of the will . . . (Hume, *EHU*, 87–88)

Necessity may be defined two ways, conformably to the two definitions of cause, of which it makes an essential part. It consists either in the constant conjunction of like objects, or in the inference of the understanding from one object to another. Now necessity, in both these senses, (which, indeed, are, at bottom, the same) has universally, though tacitly, in the schools, in the pulpit, and in common life, been allowed to belong to the will of man; and no one has ever pretended to deny, that we can draw inferences concerning human actions, and that those inferences are founded on the experienced union of like actions, with like motives, inclinations, and circumstances. (pp. 89–90)

So far, Hume's assertion is that human experience is filled with necessity and repetition, with constant conjunction, "a certain degree of uniformity" compatible perhaps with variation and unlikeness. Yet likeness, repetition, and conformity are normative, essential to ethical life.

The only proper object of hatred or vengeance, is a person or creature, endowed with thought and consciousness; and when any criminal or injurious actions excite that passion, it is only by their relation to the person, or connexion with him. . . . According to the principle, therefore, which denies necessity, and consequently causes, a man is as pure and untainted, after having committed the most horrid crime, as at the first moment of his birth, nor is his character any wise concerned in his actions; since they are not derived from it, and the wickedness of the one can never be used as a proof of the depravity of the other. (Hume, *EHU*, 90–91)

This immensely appealing argument that we cannot engage in moral judgments in a world without necessity is qualified by the understanding that necessity is repetition and conformity, "the experienced union of like actions, with like motives, inclinations, and circumstances." In this way, being and its truth exercise authority over ethical judgment in the form of rule.

CHAPTER 8

Miraculous Authority

The extreme conclusion of Hume's equation of truth with repetition emerges in his critique of miracles. A miracle, should it occur, cannot be granted rational authority, cannot bear truth's authority.

> A miracle is a violation of the laws of nature; and as a firm and unalterable experience has established these laws, the proof against a miracle, from the very nature of the fact, is as entire as any argument from experience can possibly be imagined. . . . There must, therefore, be an uniform experience against every miraculous event, otherwise the event would not merit that appellation. And as a uniform experience amounts to a proof, there is here a direct and full proof, from the nature of the fact, against the existence of any miracle; nor can such a proof be destroyed, or the miracle rendered credible, but by an opposite proof, which is superior. (Hume, *EHU,* 104–5)

A convincing and plausible argument that the claims to truth of every miracle exceed any possible authority, that the excessive authority of the Church undermines the authority claimed for any miracle, an argument against undue epistemic authority, becomes an argument with supreme authority. Only what is repeated can carry truth's authority.

> The plain consequence is (and it is a general maxim worthy of our attention), 'That no testimony is sufficient to establish a miracle, unless the testimony be of such a kind, that its falsehood would be more miraculous, than the fact, which it endeavours to establish . . . ' . . . If the falsehood of his testimony would be more miraculous, than the event which he relates; then, and not till then, can he pretend to command my belief or opinion. (Hume, *EHU,* 105–6)

Nevertheless, however plausible, the principle that repetition might enhance authority, that truth might benefit from repetition, cannot be allowed

125

to become the principle, in any epistemology, that only what is repeated is
true, nor that only what is repeated can be known to be true. What is never
repeated, what interrupts the gathering of being and saying, must have its
truth. To deny this is rank injustice, forbidden in the name of the good.

This reading of Hume's *Enquiry*, dwelling on excessive repetition,
expresses one side of his thought, recurrent and pervasive, not so much
offset by any contrary, but interrupted by a supplementation. The supplementation, onto which I am about to enter, belongs to repetition in ways
reminiscent of Derrida's principle of iterability. I have spoken of it in relation to the one exception Hume allows to the principle that ideas copy
impressions. If they do, they do so pervaded with endless departures. With
liberty and necessity and the following discussion of miracles, Hume's idea
of repetition reaches an extreme, demanding an interruption that opens
onto utmost thoughts of deviation and departure.

All this is framed with thoughts of authority and community, reminding us repeatedly that in thoughts of reason and its truth what is at stake
is the good, that truth belongs to and is given from the good and reaches
toward sovereignty and community. I noted that the *Enquiry* begins with
figures of combat and war directed against superstition and the easy life of
practice without reflection. Section 8, on liberty and necessity, begins with
somewhat different political figures.

> as the faculties of the mind are supposed to be naturally alike in every
> individual; otherwise nothing could be more fruitless than to reason or
> dispute together; it were impossible, if men affix the same ideas to their
> terms, that they could so long form different opinions of the same subject;
> especially when they communicate their views, and each party turn them-
> selves on all sides, in search of arguments, which may give them the
> victory over their antagonists. (Hume, *EHU,* 75)

> How could politics be a science, if laws and forms of government had not
> a uniform influence upon society? Where would be the foundation of
> morals, if particular characters had no certain or determinate power to
> produce particular sentiments, and if these sentiments had no constant
> operation on actions? (p. 83)

Each of these figures is political, in part if not altogether, in some cases
entirely so. As such, each is questionable in relation to reason and truth,
especially when we consider the source of reason's authority. We assume
that all human beings share equally and alike in all faculties of mind, all
rational abilities—a democratic principle. We have seen something similar
in Descartes. A principle democratic in spirit has worked traditionally to
subordinate strangers who do not reason like us. Locke calls it madness,

this sense that others do not reason like us, and ascribes it to the association of ideas.[1] I take what is at stake to be how we are to live together with
people who do not share our views and values. First, Hume tells us, we
must assume that everyone has the same mental faculties. Otherwise reasoning, argument, and life together based on anything other than force
would be impossible. Politics and morality as such, Hume says, demand
uniformity, as does a science of politics. He does not consider, as Locke
implies, that reason itself exercises and depends on force, takes its world to
be filled in principle with antagonism and war. If people differed too much,
they could not communicate, would never agree. Yet reason itself seeks
triumph, demands victory over its antagonists.

Such a picture presupposes that communication and shared life are
desirable for community and rational discourse. And if they are not found
in experience, by nature, but are still desirable, then they must be enforced.
So we find Hume assuming that reason presupposes and produces community and shared experiences and values, yet also demanding that it do so
where it does not. He does not deeply explore the possibility that life together is filled with infinite variety, to use Spinoza's phrase, so that our
struggle is to avoid conflict and war but still to find ways to create communities, to belong together, where we share nothing else in common, not
reason or human qualities, and do not have to do so. In that way, perhaps,
as in Spinoza again, we can think of belonging to Nature filled with infinite
variety, where we and everything else belong together not as possessing
anything else in common but that variety, joined in heterogeneity by love.
Reason's repetition here is infinite variety. The uniformity demanded of
science is not a standard even for science. Instead, we may hope for a
science of infinite variety reflecting a nature of similar variety. Necessity
here, as for Spinoza, is inseparable from nature's abundance.

Hume knows of this variety, and his relation to it is mixed, divided, on
the desirability of the heterogeneous life. For he refers to Laplanders and
Negroes who have "no notion of the relish of wine" (Hume, *EHU*, 22) as if
they did not have other, equally worthwhile pleasures, and he demands a
standard of taste in the same breath that he denies that one is possible,
insists on a standard of victory in taste.[2] He insists repeatedly on a universality beyond any possibility of imagining. I have noted several above; several others precede the section on liberty and necessity.[3] Six additional
references are made in this one section on liberty and necessity to what is
universally acknowledged to be true of human and natural necessity, in
every case suggesting obliquely that nothing of the sort is universally acknowledged by any human beings, European or other, that some human
beings think otherwise on all these subjects, and that they are to be dis-
missed as mad, unreasonable, or superstitious. In the same breath in which

Hume claims universality, insists on universality, he acknowledges heterogeneity, and demands that those who do not agree with us be defeated in
the war for reason's sovereignty. "Mankind are so much the same, in all
times and places, that history informs us of nothing new or strange in this
particular. Its chief use is only to discover the constant and universal principles of human nature . . ." (Hume, *EHU*, 78). He cannot resist insisting on
agreement. And he cannot resist demanding triumph, but the repeated
gesture testifies, as it must, to the impossibility of victory, to recognition
that nature composes an abundance each of whose parts contains infinite
variety, and a belonging together of all those parts and individuals that does
not presuppose shared identity or repetition. All that repeats is this belonging together, a gathering of interruptions.

Hume claims unvarying universality as to both what everyone believes
and what they do, yet must also acknowledge diversity (Hume, *EHU*, 79)
and irregularity (p. 80), ascribed to secret causes. His argument concerning
liberty is an argument from necessity, transcribed into uniformity. We cannot think of human actions except under necessity, would be unable to
praise or blame others without necessity. Liberty and necessity both are
requisite to the possibility of ethical judgment, and both pertain to human
beings. In consequence, liberty and necessity are not opposed. Within his
ongoing discourse of conflict and opposition, Hume takes two traditionally
opposing concepts and denies their opposition.

He suggests that liberty and necessity are inseparable, that we can
think of liberty only within necessity, and that necessity, at least in human
life, presupposes liberty. But he defines liberty in relation to the will, as
"power of acting or not acting according to the determinations of the will"
(Hume, *EHU*, 88), restricting it to human beings. If he interpreted it more
in relation to the *conatus*, a power of acting pertaining to every thing, then
to be would be to act according to necessity and at the same time to strive
according to the *conatus* or desire beyond finite limits. Nothing can be, can
be thought of, without liberty and necessity together, alternatives and settle-
ments, indeterminations and determinations. Whitehead speaks of this as
The Category of Freedom and Determination: "whatever is determinable is
determined, but . . . there is always a remainder" (Whitehead, PR, 27–28),
interrupting the assembling.

With this sense of reciprocity and complementarity, understanding
freedom and necessity not as the same but each as the other's other, supple-
ment and excess, where every determination calls for and presupposes excess, we may return to Hume's own excessive zeal for uniformity within
what I am suggesting is a far-reaching sense of heterogeneity. The thought
and concern for uniformity implicates infinite variety. The thought and
concern for necessity implicates indetermination and alternatives, possibilities. The thought and concern for uniformity and repetition implicates

variation. The thought and concern for variety implicates uniformity. All these movements express iterability. To be, to mean, is to repeat, but every repetition is different, exceeds itself. Every gathering is an interruption. Variety and alternatives coexist inseparably with uniformity and necessity, where this coexistence is not identity between identity and difference nor their difference, but excess. All this excessive circulation concerns the authority of necessity in Hume's understanding of uniformity. It leads to the possibility that truth and untruth are inseparable, truth's authority and its interruption, given from the good.

Hume's zeal for uniformity leads him to reject the possibility of singular events that depart from the uniformity of experience. In the nature of this singularity and the rarity of a miraculous event, all the evidence, a complete disproof, falls against its singularity. This is clear with passages that open this chapter.

The obstinacy of a thought that a singular event that violated the uniformity of nature could not be accepted as true even when true is so perverse that it would contaminate our entire idea of truth, with two qualifications. One is that despite what Hume says explicitly, that the proof against an extraordinary event is always complete, he speaks repeatedly of such exceptional events in speaking repeatedly of uniformity. He testifies, that is, to variety and singularity.

The second qualification is that Hume speaks in this section repeatedly of authority. And perhaps it is authority that we should take to be in question, the Church's authority. The truth of miracles is a question of Church authority, not a question of truth devoid of authority. In other words, the thought of truth, in Hume, is a thought that belongs to the good because it presents itself as demanding, imposing, concerning, or undermining authority. The *Enquiry Concerning Human Understanding* contains thirty-five references to authority, several of which I have noted: one each in sections 2, 4, 5, and 6, surrounded by other political references; then 8 in section 7, on necessary connection (described in terms of "weight and authority" [Hume, *EHU*, 114] in section 10 in miracles); joined with several references to the power of the state. With section 10, on miracles, Hume's references to authority dramatically increase, with 17 references in section 10 and 4 additional references in sections 11 and 12. Epistemic authority passes into and is joined overtly with political and religious authority, and Hume's critique of superstition becomes a political event. I offer a few examples from section 10.

A man delirious, or noted for falsehood and villainy, has no manner of authority with us. (Hume, *EHU*, 102)

The very same principle of experience, which gives us a certain degree of assurance in the testimony of witnesses, gives us also, in this case, another degree of assurance against the fact, which they endeavour to establish;

from which contradiction there necessarily arises a counterpoise, and mutual destruction of belief and authority. (pp. 103–4)

I should not believe such a story were it told me by Cato; was a proverbial saying in Rome, even during the lifetime of that philosophical patriot. The incredibility of a fact, it was allowed, might invalidate so great an authority. (p. 104)

I may add as a fourth reason, which diminishes the authority of prodigies, that there is not testimony for any, even those which have not been expressly detected, that is not opposed by an infinite number of witnesses; so that not only the miracle destroys the credit of testimony, but the testimony destroys itself. (p. 110)

It is experience only, which gives authority to human testimony; and it is the same experience, which assures us of the laws of nature. (p. 115)

This last quotation speaks directly to the subject of truth in Hume, which I undertook to examine in the light of the epistemological project, understood to have been invested beyond all possible recompense in reason's authority. Reason possesses that authority, in Hume, because experience gives authority, institutes the only authority there can be. With the qualification that in his skeptical mood, experience's authority is very weak, the debate concerns the authority of the Church, of every established religion, which would claim authority both by history and power and in truth. Against the thought of a truth that imposes authority, we may think of truth without authority, in this way giving up the epistemological project, responding to Foucault's insistence that the political question is truth itself, always a question of authority. We give up the adversarial sense of reason, which must triumph victoriously if it is to gain its authority. If it is possible for us to do so. We may think of miracles, including that of truth, without authority.

Bataille speaks of abundance as general economy, of general economy beyond restricted economy, including the miracle of truth beyond the usefulness of truth, touching the excess and abundance of desire. The miracle, including the miracle of being and truth, recalls Plato's sense of wonder.

Beyond need, the object of desire is, *humanly,* the *miracle;* it is sovereign life, beyond the necessary that suffering defines. This *miraculous* element *which delights us* may be simply the brilliance of the sun, which on a spring morning transfigures a desolate street. (Bataille, *AS,* 3, 200)

May we not say of death that in it, in a sense, we discover the negative analogue of a miracle, something we find all the harder to believe as death strikes down the one we love, the one who is close to us, something we could not believe, *if it, if death were not there.* (pp. 206–7)

We may be touched by extraordinary events, unfamiliar and strange touches, nature's wonderful abundance, anywhere and at any time. I include the touch of truth within a history of a truth given wholly over to familiarity and repetition. Hume's understanding of the miraculous, unrepeated, perhaps unrepeatable, event is unsurpassed, filled with such resistance to its authority as to withdraw from its miraculous glory. Abundance shows itself as miraculous interruption, in infinite exposure and debt, unframing every framing, unauthorizing every authority.

It is time to depart from the epistemological project and its framing. Many scientists still believe that only what meets canonical standards of experimental confirmation can be held to be true—not just established or known—and everything else should be rejected. Against this is the current recognition that alternative medical therapies are worth exploring and even implementing if their risks are small and what they promise is large, that with tribal peoples disappearing with their knowledges at an accelerating rate, it would be willful ignorance not to seek to acquire such knowledge even if it does not meet canonical standards of confirmation. Important truths can be lost if they are disqualified by repetitive standards of confirmation.

All this circulates within the epistemological project, seeking to define the methods for acceptable epistemic authority, disqualifying all other candidates. Important consequences arise within this project for knowledge and truth. But other important implications concern the way we may think of experience and truth in much larger contexts of human life and natural events and things. I return to Spinoza's understanding of a nature of infinite variety, return to variety and heterogeneity in relation to truth. Ari's truth will never belong to the epistemological project though Ari may be seized within that project as an object of scientific truth, and he belongs to nature in its variety. Bats, and fleas, and other creatures, live and experience together. I return to Hume's idea of experience in memory of bats' experiences.

Experience in Hume is constant conjunction and repetition, with memory restricted to copying and repeating. Yet behind or interwoven throughout this repeated repetition is a far-reaching sense of the multiplicity and contingency of human experience and its environments. Ideas are copies of impressions. Cause and effect are constant conjunction. Custom is the great guide to human life, repetition and more repetition. All these repetitions and copies are contingent possibilities in an experience and world that always outstrips them, far beyond the differences that permeate every repetition. If Hume neglects difference, if within the epistemological project he dwells on repetition, it is in part because contingency and uncertainty so deeply pervade his sense of the experience that barely makes do with custom. If Hume overemphasizes the assurance and success of custom, if he establishes standards of taste and judgment that reflect the superiority of higher civilizations over lower forms, it is within a profound sense of the inadequacy of all such measures. In a deep and pervasive way, Hume is skeptical of all the assurances with which European reason imposes its authority—still imposing custom's authority. What Hume says of his darkest skepticism sets the tone for the limits of all the practices he invests with authority.

He interrupts the hold of truth, speaks of the alternation between skepticism and dogmatism in the voice of authority, the voice of the king, reminding us that reason's truth requires authorization, demands authority, recalls something beyond itself for its authority.

> Reason first appears in possession of the throne, prescribing laws, and imposing maxims, with an absolute sway and authority. Her enemy, therefore, is obliged to take shelter under her protection, and by making use of rational arguments to prove the fallaciousness and imbecility of reason, produces, in a manner, a patent under her hand and seal. This patent has at first an authority, proportioned to the present and immediate authority of reason, from which it is derived. But as it is supposed to be contradictory to reason, it gradually diminishes the force of that governing power and its own at the same time; till at last they both vanish away into nothing, by a regular and just diminution. (Hume, *T,* 186)

This passage, and those that follow, reflect Hume's awareness of something largely unknown elsewhere in the Western tradition, even in Hobbes, the dark and terrifying side of this authority, reason's truth. Reason cannot establish its own authority, cannot authorize its authority, and yet, in Hume, this authority offers more to life than truth. Life is the value, recalling Nietzsche, granting the only possibility of instituting authority, including truth's and reason's authority. Truth does not carry its own authority, as if to possess the truth were to be king. As if truth were a possession. As if to be king did not call for skepticism.

> I am ready to reject all belief and reasoning, and can look upon no opinion even as more probable or likely than another. . . . I . . . begin to fancy myself in the most deplorable condition imaginable, environed with the deepest darkness, and utterly deprived of the use of every member and faculty. . . .
>
> These are the sentiments of my spleen and indolence; and indeed I must confess, that philosophy has nothing to oppose to them, and expects a victory more from the returns of a serious good-humoured disposition, than from the force of reason and conviction. In all the incidents of life, we ought still to preserve our scepticism. If we believe that fire warms, or water refreshes, it is only because it costs us too much pains to think otherwise. (Hume, *T,* 268–70)

The skepticism, the sense of reason's inadequacy, produces a dark despair, doubled by the realization that nothing in reason or nature can produce certainty against this pessimism, and that to live as other people do, to make merry, is to give oneself over to uncertainty while we have a strong propensity to do otherwise.

On this reading, emphasizing the skeptical and contingent side of knowledge and truth revealed here at its darkest moments, but extending them to every appearance of custom and repetition, we may read Hume not as glorying in repetition but as finding nothing else, nothing but custom, nothing better than going on as we have gone on in the past. Truth here is not an achievement in which we may take pride, no presentation of the ultimate nature of being gathered in saying, but a contingent, evanescent trace of the movements of life that allow us to live against life's dangers. If we take allowing us to live, acting like other people in the common affairs of life, as ethical—and how else can we take it?—then it is the ethical demands of life that bring us to truth where reason is impotent. Here truth belongs to the good, given in its contingency, uncertainty, and mobility, regulated—too much perhaps—by repetition and social conditions.

Again, we are led by recalling the gift of the good to think of truth without authority. I conclude this chapter with two references to such a truth, both indebted to Hume. One is Dewey's account of inquiry as the local and transitory transformation of a situation from indeterminateness to determinateness, the other Whitehead's account of truth as conformation in relation to beauty. First Dewey:

> *Inquiry is the controlled or directed transformation of an indeterminate situation into one that is so determinate in its constituent distinctions and relations as to convert the elements of the original situation into a unified whole.* (Dewey, *L*, 105–5)

Truth is the controlled outcome of inquiry, local and instrumental. As soon as an inquiry ends, with its truth, new inquiries emerge. Inquiry endlessly interrupts itself.

> What is already known, what is accepted as truth, is of immense importance; inquiry could not proceed a step without it. But it is held subject to use, and is at the mercy of the discoveries which it makes possible. It has to be adjusted to the latter and not the latter to it. When things are defined as instruments, their value and validity reside in what proceeds from them; consequences not antecedents supply meaning and verity. Truths already possessed may have practical or moral certainty, but logically they never lose a hypothetic quality. They are true *if* . . . (Dewey, *EN*, 154–55)

With qualifications concerning control and determinateness in relation to inquiry, and to a unified whole in relation to situations, Dewey's is a thoroughly local theory of truth in which truth never gains overarching authority, but is always subject, still locally and temporally, to consequences and outcomes, to future experience. This subjection expresses Dewey's understanding of the gifts of the good. The circulation of goods is always present in Dewey's thought wherever he thinks of life and experience.

> Because intelligence is critical method applied to goods of belief, appreciation and conduct, so as to construct, freer and more secure goods, turning assent and assertion into free communication of shareable meanings, turning feeling into ordered and liberal sense, turning reaction into response, it is the reasonable object of our deepest faith and loyalty, the stay and support of all reasonable hopes. (Dewey, *EN*, 436–37)

Again, with qualifications concerning security, communication, and shared meanings, all of which come at a price that Dewey does not think we should pay, all one-sided at the expense of creativity and adaptability: "there is in the unformed activities of childhood and youth the possibilities of a better life for the community as well as for individuals here and there" (Dewey, *HNC*, 99). Plasticity and custom are both given to every individual, and from their interaction, promoting goods and evils, truth and knowledge come to pass, locally and instrumentally. Instrumentality, the heart of Dewey's pragmatic thought, expresses the desire, the will, that gives truth forth.

The thought in Dewey closest to that undertaken in the project here is that things are had before they are known. "They are things *had* before they are things cognized" (Dewey, *EN*, 21). They are had in what he calls immediate or qualitative experience, preceding reflection, an understanding bearing affinity with phenomenology. But they are had in an experience filled with goods given before truth, interrupting truth and knowledge, something that holds the authority of truth in abeyance, reminiscent of Nietzsche's critique of metaphysics.

> When the claim of meanings to truth enters in, then truth is indeed preeminent. But this fact is often confused with the idea that truth has a claim to enter everywhere; that it has monopolistic jurisdiction. Poetic meanings, moral meanings, a large part of the goods of life are matters of richness and freedom of meanings, rather than of truth; a large part of our life is carried on in a realm of meanings to which truth and falsity as such are irrelevant. (Dewey, *EN*, 410–11)
>
> one may doubt . . . whether these popular valuations and opposite values on which the metaphysicians put their seal, are not perhaps merely fore-

ground estimates, only provisional perspectives, perhaps even from some nook perhaps from below, frog perspectives, as it were, to borrow an expression painters use. For all the value that the true, the truthful, the selfless may deserve, it would still be possible that a higher and more fundamental value for life might have to be ascribed to deception, selfishness, and lust. . . . Maybe! (Nietzsche, *BGE,* #2)

What the good brings forth as its gift, given to truth and meaning and life, is Maybe!, reminding us of Aristotle's hesitation.[4] With this Maybe!, recognized by Nietzsche and Dewey, we can bring the authority of truth to question. Maybe!

I touch on Whitehead briefly for a different sense of resistance to the authority of truth. For Whitehead, truth does not stand alone, but stands next to beauty. "Truth and Beauty are the great regulative properties in virtue of which Appearance justifies itself to the immediate decision of the experient subject" (Whitehead, *AI,* 309)—a line strongly reminiscent of the thought that truth does not stand alone but must be justified in an experience, a decision, given from the good. Even so, Whitehead restricts truth to reproduction, as perhaps Dewey restricts it to determinateness, in a context of creativity and indeterminateness. "Truth is the conformation of Appearance to Reality" (p. 309). Its value is then doubly limited, by the justification of which Whitehead speaks and the limited value of conformation. For "Beauty is a wider, and more fundamental, notion than Truth" (p. 341); more important, perhaps:

> Good and evil lie in depths and distances below and beyond appearance. They solely concern inter-relations within the real world. The real world is good when it is beautiful. (p. 345)

> The nature of evil is that the characters of things are mutually obstructive. Thus the depths of life require a process of selection. (Whitehead, *PR,* 340)

Good and evil belong to the world, to its reality, not perhaps—I suggest this hesitantly in relation to Whitehead—in virtue of being and its truth, but in reverse, where beauty and goodness lie in the depths of things from which truth and being emerge, at least coexistent with them, resisting the privilege of truth's authority. For if "It belongs to the goodness of the world, that its settled order should deal tenderly with the faint discordant light of the dawn of another age" (Whitehead, *PR,* 339), truth belongs to that settled order, subservient to Creativity, where " 'Creativity' is the principle of *novelty*" (p. 21), fulfilled in intensity of feeling (p. 27), for every actual entity including God (p. 105), returning us to beauty. I understand this beauty, this intensity of feeling, to express "an ideal peculiar to each particular actual entity" (p. 84). Whitehead calls this notion "Platonic" (p. 84). I understand it to return us to the good, reminding us of wonder, of the miracle of being and being's truth, reminiscent of Nietzsche's understanding that truth—metaphysical or any other truth—calls forth the question, with a Maybe!, of the authority of truth, a never-ending question given from life, or experience, or reality, all intensities and beauties. The justification for truth comes from the juncture of beauty and the good where these cannot be distinguished, where no principle of separation holds, where all binary oppositions dissolve into nature's wondrous beauty.

With this interruption, Ari returns us to Carlo Sini to embark upon a rethinking of the authority of truth from within its utmost critique, beginning with Hegel passing through Heidegger to beyond, where we find ourselves today.

CHAPTER 9

Moving Truth

After Hume, our flight toward truth rejoins Sini's way, touching down on Hegel, flying over Kant, reminding us of Aristotle's belief that bats are blinded by the sun, reiterated in Sini's belief that we and bats are blind to what is most true: "like the bat, the understanding is blind to those things that by nature are the most self-evident" (Sini, *IT,* 40). Except that bats can hear and smell and touch, and may know a truth unknowable to those who can see only by the light of the sun. Bat truth remains unheard in Sini and, perhaps, in Hegel, who knew better. But we have overflown Kant, who begins the Hegelian movement toward truth as he began many others in the very thought against which Hegel strives.

For truth is "accordance *[Übereinstimmung]*" (Kant, *CPR,* 48) between knowledge and object, except that such an accordance or agreement offers no universal criterion with respect to the content of knowledge: "a sufficient, and at the same time universal, test of truth cannot be found" (Kant, *CPR,* 49). Instead, we have the "negative condition of all truth" (p. 49), "the universal and necessary laws of the understanding [which] in these very laws present us with criteria of truth" (p. 49). Accordance opens onto an infinite movement from infinite inadequacy. Truth is put into play, put into history, placed on an infinite journey framed by reason's excesses.

> Human reason has this peculiar fate that in one species of its knowledge it is burdened by questions which, as prescribed by the very nature of reason itself, it is not able to ignore, but which, as transcending all its powers, it is also not able to answer. (Kant, *CPR [NKS],* 7)

Reason and its truth are driven beyond themselves to unreason and untruth. This movement is political—more deeply, epistemological‖metaphysical‖architectural‖ethical‖political—reminding us of Descartes but reaching beyond. Kant repeatedly speaks of reason in architectural and political terms, describing reason's sovereignty. Of metaphysics:

137

> Her government under the administration of the *dogmatists*, was at first *despotic*. But inasmuch as the legislation still bore traces of the ancient barbarism, her empire gradually through intestine wars gave way to complete anarchy; and the *sceptics*, a species of nomads, despising all settled modes of life, broke up from time to time all civil society. (Kant, *CPR [NKS]*, 8)

This resistance to anarchy and insistence on political stability carries through to the famous figure of the Tower of Babel, another description of anarchy, politics joined with architecture, linked first in *Genesis*.[1]

> We have found, indeed, that although we had purposed to build for ourselves a tower which should reach to Heaven, the supply of materials sufficed merely for a habitation, which was spacious enough for all terrestrial purposes, and high enough to enable us to survey the level plain of experience, but that the bold undertaking designed necessarily failed for want of materials—not to mention the confusion of tongues, which gave rise to endless disputes among the laborers on the plan of the edifice, and at last scattered them over all the world, each to erect a separate building for himself, according to his own plans and his own inclinations. (Kant, *CPR*, 397)

With two additions, we may understand Kant's account of reason's truth to bear political|ethical|architectural gravity, gathered together, weighing upon the epistemological project. For to establish reason's limits, to define once and for all the limits of reason's truth, is to lay to rest forever every question of the good. "But, above all, there is the inestimable benefit, that all objections to morality and religion will be for ever silenced . . . " (Kant, *CPR [NKS]*, 30). As if that were possible, as if they did not remain contested spheres.

I gather up that other striking figure of the *Critique of Pure Reason*, extended its full length:

> We have now not only traversed the region of the pure understanding, and carefully surveyed every part of it, but we have also measured it, and assigned to everything therein its proper place. But this land is an island, and inclosed by nature herself within unchangeable limits. It is the land of truth (an attractive word), surrounded by a wide and stormy ocean, the region of illusion, where many a fog-bank, many an iceberg, seems to the mariner, on his voyage of discovery, a new country, and while constantly deluding him with vain hopes, engages him in dangerous adventures, from which he never can desist, and which yet he never can bring to a termination. . . . it will not be without advantage if we cast our eyes upon the chart of the land that we are about to leave, and to ask ourselves, firstly, whether we cannot rest perfectly contented with what it contains,

or whether we must not of necessity be contented with it, if we can find nowhere else a solid foundation to build upon; and, secondly, by what title we possess this land itself, and how we hold it secure against all hostile claims? (Kant, *CPR,* 156)

This island over which we impose authority, by traversing, measuring, and surveying it, putting everything in its proper place, finding it enclosed by unchangeable limits, is the land of truth. Whether or not truth is accordance, agreement, whether or not we can find criteria for the content of truth or only for its formal conditions, the land of truth is an island, fully surveyed, measured, and traversed, with everything put in place. This truth is defined, delimited, properly and unchangeably, by absolute limits open to measure, oversight, and surveyal. Yet it is to be thought, in Kant, only in relation to another truth, not named as truth but surely true, of danger, adventure, and endless circulation. The land of truth is completely circumscribed, surrounded by another circumscription that opens onto wild abundance. Still truth. The description is entirely political, holding the walls of the city secure against the endless encroachments of dangerous adventures upon which we cannot avoid embarking. The state can never make itself secure against its limits, against nature itself.

I read this passage as political, ethical|political|architectural|territorial. Kant's account of the land of truth, recalling Hume, is dominated by political figures: danger, adventure, authority, safety, not to mention owning title to the land and holding it secure against all hostile claims. What hostile claims might impose themselves here on truth? Why think of truth in adversarial terms? Why think that truth must be held secure, requires safety? We may be reminded that Kant speaks of safety also in the *Critique of Judgment,* in relation to the sublime:

> Bold, overhanging, and as it were threatening rocks; . . . volcanoes in all their violence of destruction; hurricanes with their track of devastation; the boundless ocean in a state of tumult; . . . But the sight of them is the more attractive, the more fearful it is, provided only that we are in security . . . (Kant, *CJ,* 100)

The stakes of the epistemological-critical project seem to be safety and security, holding the limits of truth and experience firm—though if they are unchangeable, there is nothing to hold onto, nothing to resist. The wide ocean appears on the one hand to represent the fearfulness of what is outside the walls of the state, beyond the reach of sovereign power, on the other to lure us with its attractions.

I take Kant to speak of truth, the land of truth, possible experience, in political terms, in terms of authority, force, and safety. The peaceful neutrality of truth falls into a maelstrom of power and force, calling for walls to resist hostilities. As we may imagine that the formation of the nation state provided arguments justifying clashing armies to build a sovereign power, monarchic or democratic, within which we may come to safety, science's truth builds its authority upon another war, still repelling invaders, bringing us to security. And as we may wonder if state sovereignty imposed by force in the name of safety might be too great to justify, we may wonder if the rule of science and science's reason might be too strong to justify.

For though he chose not to travel in the flesh, Kant surely knew that his world was built by countless explorers who chose adventure over safety, suggesting two opposing possibilities: the lack of authority of safety and security, the possibility that adventure is more fulfilling than authoritarian rule; and the appropriation of the most adventurous nomadic wandering by authoritarian state powers. Kant surely knew that the state, the edifice of which he speaks, was the result of instituted slavery, that European explorers, who in braving the terrible dangers of hurricanes and volcanoes, brought about a terrible worldwide traffic in human beings. What slavery, we might wonder, goes along with authoritarian truth? What violence lies at the heart of reason?

Kant openly exposes us to the deepest truth of his entire project, and to mine here, that the truth whose limits we seek to define is governed by authority and force, political concerns. We are to be contented *(zufrieden)* with the land of truth. And what if we were not? If it is necessary, inescapable, entirely governed by natural law, then what matter if we are contented? Why must we be made to desire what we have no choice but to accept? And how can any answer be given that does not respond to the call of the good? Kant knows that truth demands force and authority. And all authority is political authority, including truth's and reason's authority. For what we exclude is nomadic truth, a knowledge that strives for truth, driven by desire, that does not seek to impose its authority on other desires.

If the authority of knowledge and truth can be separated from them, nomadically, then the question of their authority is political. And if the authority of knowledge and truth cannot be separated from them, then the question of their authority is political. They come from the good in relation to the possibility that they may lack authority, even where that authority is inescapable.

I find this recognition, however obliquely, where Kant speaks of "use" *(Gebrauch)*, the transcendental use of a concept, restricted to possible experience, an ethical term. *Gebrauch* belongs to custom and propriety, takes us back to *ethos* in Greek. It becomes *Brauch* in Heidegger, though in relation to knowledge, understanding, and truth it is denied ethical weight by Kant and Heidegger. Kant speaks of ethics and morality distinct from the territory of the understanding, from its use. At this juncture we find the authority of truth to be given as ethical authority.

With this recognition of the ethical|political|theological dimensions of truth in Kant, I rejoin Sini and Ari in their journey toward Hegel. The truth that arrives with Hegel, Sini tells us, is the destruction of judgment (Sini, *IT*, chap. 5). This takes place, Sini says, in the *Encyclopaedia Logic*, where Hegel dismisses thinking determinately what is as an early and incomplete thought, placed in endless movement. "But truth is always infinite, and cannot be expressed or presented to consciousness in finite terms" (Hegel, *EL*, §28, 62). The endless movement is described in the *Phenomenology of Spirit* as development. "The truth is the whole. The whole, however, is merely the essential nature reaching its completeness through the process of its own development" (Hegel, *PM*, 81). Truth is process, development, movement, not accordance or agreement. Or if it is agreement, it is an agreement that moves, not held static in judgment. I would say, against Sini's suggestion that with Hegel truth falls out of judgment, that with Hegel judgment embarks on an endless journey toward and in truth. Together they compose the circulation I understand as given from the good. I examine Hegel's understanding.

For the moment I remain with the *Encyclopaedia Logic*, joined by Ari who reminds us that Hegel continues to divide humans from the animals, less in terms of thought and its truth than in terms of religion, and perhaps religious truth (Hegel, *EL*, 4–5). Of animals and their kinds, Hegel has some striking things to say in his *Encyclopaedia Logic*.

> Now, the animal, *qua* animal, cannot be shown; nothing can be pointed out excepting some special animal. Animal, *qua* animal, does not exist: it is merely the universal nature of the individual animals, whilst each existing animal is a more concretely defined and particularised thing. But . . . Take away from the dog its animality, and it becomes impossible to say what it is. All things have a permanent inward nature, as well as an outward existence. They live and die, arise and pass away; but their essential and universal part is the kind; and this means much more than something *common* to them all. (§24, p. 47).

The animal, perhaps the human, can be what it is only as a kind, a universal, which is more than something common. The kind is more than the common truth of the individual, or of all the individuals together. The kind touches something infinite, perhaps beyond being, exceeding the being of individuals together. In the kind, something of the good gives its truth. Identity arrives with universal authority.

At this point, crossing the question of truth at a strange angle, the question of kinds arises, the truth of the individual as kind, the good for the individual as kind. Hegel sacrifices the individual to the kind, at least for animals, denying individual animals their truth, at least any truth worth considering. The kind reaches toward and touches the universal.

> Man is a thinker, and is universal: but he is a thinker only because he feels his own universality. The animal too is by implication universal, but the universal is not consciously felt by it to be universal: it feels only the individual.... For the animal all this never goes beyond an individual thing. (Hegel, *EL*, §24, 47)

In one and the same thought Hegel subordinates the individual and the animal to the universal, authorizing their kinds. Humans and animals both are in their truth in kind. I have journeyed this far with Ari, with bats and other creatures, to agree that truth belongs to kinds, but to add that kinds are given from the good, given truth and authority as kinds, betraying the good in the subordination of some kinds to others, not just individuals but kinds. I postpone for just a moment the thought that the universality of the kind is less a truth of being than a gift of the good. I add that Hegel does not appear to wonder if to think consciously of the universal might be to destroy it, if consciousness were always finite and the universal were infinite. Nor does he think as far as I hope to of universality as unlimit rather than as totality, as All. We are on the verge of the thought of the play, the movement and excess, of limit and unlimit around kinds, sites of the good, supplementing singularity. I think again of touch, touching kinds. I think of touch and kinds interrupting the gathering of being.

On one reading, nothing interrupts the gathering of being in Hegel, nothing interrupts the production of truth, the process of its movement, certainly not the dialectic, understood as the essence of that movement. Hegel surpasses the agreement of subject and object, always interrupted, in an accordance beyond interruption, leading again to kinds. And death.

> In common life truth means the agreement of an object with our conception of it.... In the philosophical sense of the word, on the other hand, truth may be described, in general abstract terms, as the agreement of a thought-content with itself.... All finite things involve an untruth: they have a notion and an existence, but their existence does not meet the requirements of the notion. For this reason they must perish, and then the incompatibility between their notion and their existence becomes manifest. It is in the kind that the individual animal has its notion: and the kind liberates itself from this individuality by death. (Hegel, *EL*, §24, 51–52)

The death of what, we ask, the individual or kind? For the kind may also perish, marking the limits of its own infinity. Without the individual, the kind is abstract, devoid of determinateness in being, in its untruth; without the kind, the individual is in its untruth. Truth and untruth circulate in the space between finite and infinite, individual and kind, a space that Hegel associates with truth and untruth, but which I associate with gifts from the good. I repudiate the privilege of death, but I cannot think of death and loss without thinking of our memories of them and our responsibilities toward them.

Nor indeed can Hegel, for he speaks of "the different forms of ascertaining truth" in the context of the "Fall of Man" (Hegel, *EL*, §24, 52–53), reminding us again of *Genesis*. His narrative of this fall traces "the universal bearings of knowledge upon the spiritual life" where "The spiritual is distinguished from the natural, and more especially from the animal, life" (p. 54), where humans reaffirmed their authority over nature in the name of their spiritual distinction. The truth of humans, becoming Spirit, is a truth of political authority, from Fall to Master, both recalling the good.

Truth is not agreement between idea and object, between two different things, but absolute unity in the idea itself.

> The Idea is truth in itself and for itself,—the absolute unity of the notion and objectivity....
>
> The definition, which declares the Absolute to be the Idea, is itself absolute. All former definitions come back to this. The Idea is the Truth: for Truth is the correspondence of objectivity with the notion.... Every individual being is some one aspect of the Idea ... (Hegel, *EL*, §213, 352)

This language of truth as absolute unity subordinates it to being, the unity of being and the subjection of each individual thing to the Idea, which gathers all things up into itself for its truth and theirs. As if the Absolute were the night in which truth were always the same, black or white. With multiple qualifications: for the Idea is nothing, abstract without the individual things; truth is nothing without error; and the gathering is an endless journey, described as given from the Good under the form of illusion.

> The Good, the absolutely Good, is eternally accomplishing itself in the world: and the result is that it needs not wait upon us, but is already by implication, as well as in full actuality, accomplished. This is the illusion under which we live.... Error or other-being, when superseded, is still a necessary dynamic element of truth: for truth can only be where it makes itself its own result. (Hegel, *EL*, §212, 352)

Despite Sini's reading of truth as the destruction of judgment, the Idea returns to judgment.

> The Idea is the infinite judgment, of which the terms are severally the independent totality ... (Hegel, *EL*, §214, 357)

> The Idea is essentially a process, because its identity is the absolute
> and free identity of the notion, only in so far as it is absolute negativity
> and for that reason dialectical. (§215, p. 357)

The good is forever accomplishing itself in the world, forever accomplished and forever accomplishing. This conjunction gives rise to another reading, speaks against an end for which the Idea strives, against the teleology of the good. The good imposes no goal or end that would measure its means because every means is the accomplishment of that end, however infinite. These enigmatic words may be resolved in non-enigmatic ways, for example: (1) giving precedence to the full actuality accomplished, albeit through an endless process; (2) giving precedence to the process which as endless is all there is, absolute totality and finality. We may instead resolve these enigmatic words enigmatically, (3) giving precedence to neither accomplishing nor accomplishment, leaving the enigma as the full and absolute story of being, the good, and truth, given as the fullness of being, enigmatic rather than complete. Truth is inseparable from error and otherbeing because it remains in the endless movement between them, gathering them up in their identity and difference, not to unify them but to interrupt them in the identity and difference of identity and difference.

> We must be careful, when we say that the ground is the unity of
> identity and difference, not to understand by this unity an abstract
> identity. . . . To avoid this misconception we may say that the ground,
> besides being the unity, is also the difference of identity and difference.
> (Hegel, *EL*, §121, 224–25)

All these readings, with many others, remain within the gathering of being where we find truth. The truth of being is either the result, the process, or the result and process together in their identity and difference, and the result and process together of identity and difference, and their difference, and their identity. Here truth is untruth, inseparable from its other, within the reign of being. Truth is inseparable from untruth because the result includes untruth, because it is the process of the dialectical movement of truth together with untruth, or because truth is untruth and untruth is untruth, where that claim is both its truth and its untruth, expressed in dialectical movement. All with endless qualifications.

Where in all this movement is the good? This question may allow for the same possibilities again: the good is the truth; the good is truth's untruth; the idea is truth and good together, in their unity and their distinctness. The play of abstraction and concreteness demands an endless play of identity and difference, truth and good, science and ethics, spirit and nature. Yet we may ask this question not to repeat the endless and ambigu-

ous movement of identity and difference, the process of being, but to interrupt its movement—to interrupt but by no means to halt the movement,
as if we could. The Absolute is the endless and unlimited movement of
Being through all its limits. I find another reading in Hegel, the possibility
that the Absolute endlessly and unlimitedly interrupts its endless and unlimited movement. The good interrupts the gathering of truth into being
by presenting truth, together with untruth and error and more, as a call,
given from the good, touching others in their kinds, beyond the gathering
of individuals into universality as if without remainder. The good remains
the remainder of being, outside or otherwise than being, in being and
truth. The good as Absolute interrupts the gathering within the gathering,
interrupts but does not halt the dialectic. There is where truth is untruth.

Unless the unity of identity and difference is interrupted by difference,
unless the absolute and infinite variety of nature interrupts the gathering
of all things together, unless the endless accomplishment is endless interruption, it knows nothing of the good. The good is the endless interruption
of the gathering of being in the name of that from which gathering calls.
Untruth is the endless interruption of truth, resisting its authority. If we
add that it is essential to truth, that truth includes its untruth as interruption, we understand it as given from the good.

I do not find this reading of Hegel in Sini. And I do not find it in this
form in Levinas, though he offers the good as interruption. I will discuss
Levinas in detail. I add here only that he resists the gathering of being and
truth in the name of singularity. I resist it in the name of the good, in
memory of kinds. For the moment, however, I remain with Sini, reading
Hegel, echoing Ari's demands to be heard, to belong to truth and being,
interrupting the rule of humanity, not because Ari is less than or more than
human, but against the standard of humanity, against any absolute and
final standard, including Absolute Spirit. The good that is always accomplishing, always being accomplished, always accomplished, can set no
standard.

Sini takes the place of truth to lie in the disjunctive syllogism—if
truth has a place. He reads such a place in Hegel's words: "Accordingly the
Syllogism is the essential ground of whatever is true: and at the present
stage the definition of the Absolute is that it is the Syllogism, or stating the
principle in a proposition: Everything is a Syllogism" (Hegel, *EL,* §181, 314;
Sini, *IT,* 23). I have noted other words of Hegel, and I would emphasize that
he is speaking here of the Absolute at a particular stage before the notion.
Without this understanding, without emphasis upon truth as process, we
have no alternative to reading Hegel as unifying all identities and differences, truths and untruths, into reason without residue, without interruption. "In the *Science of Logic,* Hegel reaches the culmination of what we

could call the total logification of the world (in Peirce's terms, its total semiotization). Hegel shows the complete articulation of being (in genera and species, Plato would say) and thus its identification with rational thinking, without residue" (Sini, *IT,* 28). Including bats and other creatures, I would say, while denying their truth. And all within a " 'process' (the 'progressive unfolding of the truth,' for Aristotle)" (Sini, *IT,* 29).

Again, given the different readings I have articulated, on the one hand the Absolute unifies all finite things in their truth; on the other, in Sini's words, the movement of this unification destroys itself. "By this path, 'traditional metaphysics' in reaching its fulfillment plunges decisively into the abyss of its own dissolution" (Sini, *IT,* 32).

> The entire experience of consciousness, of which every moment is together sublated and preserved, made true in the totality of the process, takes shape then as the science itself. Self-consciousness contains here all its moments just as the disjunctive syllogism contained in itself its species and particularizations—unmediated being and truth of infinite mediation. (p. 39)

Sini's reading of Hegel chooses decisively on the question of interruption.

> For Hegel, to think is to carry out the total mediation of the existing, that is, to transform the existing into an interpreted (a *mediated*) and thinking into an interpretant (a *mediating*). . . . Everything is, thus, always already an "interpreted being" of which one must exhibit the producing middle, the interpreting concept. The whole reality is contained in reason. (Sini, *IT,* 45)

He does so in the interest of saying, returning us to language and the triangle of being, truth, and saying.

> In the final analysis, "concrete" Hegelian thinking says that the world is so because it *has become* so, as it is; and that finally, in the light of absolute knowledge, we discover that it could not have become other than exactly what it is. This thinking, in other words, says that about the world and its truth there *really* is nothing to say. (p. 46)

Putting saying aside, if I may do so in relation to Sini, I will consider in the rest of this chapter a reading of Hegel's thought as interruption in full awareness that it damages the dialectic irretrievably. Or put another way, I recognize that Hegel's language works against this reading, but it also calls it forth. We saw this double movement above where if we were not to read the difference of identity and difference as the unity of identity and difference again we would have to read it as interruption. The moment the Absolute and nature's infinite variety are understood as gathered up in their truth into the truth of being, nature, or God without interruption, nothing is left of the good. The good is that which gives forth truth in its untruth, gathering as interruption, work and its unworking. It is all too easy to read Hegel as mediating difference and mediating mediation without a thought of interruption, without understanding the dialectic as endless interruption, reading the dialectic as imposing rather than resisting its supreme authority. Perhaps he came so close to interruption without quite naming it as resistance to the dialectic because he did not know how to think of interruption in truth. Perhaps we do not know that either, under the privilege of being and being's truth. We must beware of the dialectic's authority, where it impedes the circulation.

The journey of Spirit toward Absolute Knowledge and its truth is told in *The Phenomenology of Spirit*. It is told repeatedly as an endless journey in the light of its systematic fulfillment if not completion. "The systematic development of truth in scientific form can alone be the true shape in which truth exists" (Hegel, *PM,* 70). I cannot forbear a brief interruption calling attention to the word "shape," foreshadowing the "spiritual shapes" *(Geistern)* with which Hegel closes the *Phenomenology,* where Spirit empties itself into time, posing the possibility that the scientific form might be empty were it to be consummated. For he goes on to emphasize the becoming and process as strongly as might be imagined.

> True reality is merely this process of reinstating self-identity, of reflecting into its own self and from its other, and is not an original and primal unity as such, not an immediate unity as such. It is the process of its own becoming, the circle which presupposes its end as its purpose, and has its end for its beginning; it becomes concrete and actual only by being carried out, and by the end it involves. (Hegel, *PM,* 80–81)

Truth is unmistakably reality, truth and being together, and a togetherness of process and end, process with end. This is a gathering of being. Yet it is process "merely," suggesting that the gathering does not preclude interruption, includes and demands interruption, moving on from wherever it finds itself, opening any circle that threatens to close upon its becoming. The dialectic interrupts any possibility of fulfilling the becoming of truth. It also interrupts the whole that allows for the thought of gathering.

> The truth is the whole. The whole, however, is merely the essential nature reaching its completeness through the process of its own development. Of the Absolute it must be said that it is essentially a result, that

only at the end is it what it is in very truth; and just in that consists its
nature, which is to be actual, subject, or self-becoming, self-development.
(Hegel, *PM,* 81–82)

Hegel certainly speaks of reaching the result, completeness, says that only
at the end is the whole in its truth. The whole, however, is "merely" the
process of its development, and it never leaves, never overcomes, its development, but remains within the process. I read this as suggesting that
truth is the whole as end, but that the end is brought about in endless
interruption, so that the truth includes its interruption, demands its can-
cellation, never succeeds in gathering the movement into something which
overcomes interruption. All this is spoken of in the language of being. And
that is where we remain for a while. I would recall the good, to which we
will come after a few more interruptions.

What if we take the whole to be the process, and take the process to
never end? Yet never-ending, of itself, though it constitutes no whole, and
resists totality, presents us with an infinite that never remembers or tries
to remember where it has been, that never interrupts itself. It fails to
gather into totality within the project of gathering. Instead, what if truth
were the process, and the whole, where the whole was the process and its
truth together, presenting us with the good infinite, the image of a circle,
but a circle that does not close by closing off the process, which does not
end, and which remembers forgetting, knows loss? Hegel speaks of this
doubling repeatedly, where the repetition does not close the circle. "For the
real subject-matter is not exhausted in its purpose, but in working the
matter out; nor is the mere result attained the concrete whole itself, but
the result along with the process of arriving at it" (Hegel, *PM,* 69). The
working out never ends, continues to demand work, but the truth resides
in the result worked out together with the process. The circle does not
close but returns to recall where it has been, repeated and repeating, in a
figure of an infinite that cannot become finite.

> Each of the parts of philosophy is a philosophical whole, a circle rounded
> and complete in itself. In each of these parts, however, the philosophical
> Idea is found in a particular specificality of medium. The single circle,
> because it is a real totality, bursts through the limits imposed by its
> special medium, and gives rise to a wider circle. The whole of philosophy
> in this way resembles a circle of circles. The Idea appears in each single
> circle, but, at the same time, the whole Idea is constituted by the system
> of these peculiar phases, and each is a necessary member of the
> organisation. (Hegel, *EL,* 24–25)

The Idea, with its truth, composes a circle rounded and complete. Yet
the Idea and its truth burst through the limits of that whole, giving rise to

a wider circle. The process of bursting, exceeding, overcoming limits, continues, in every case producing a circle that rounds itself to bursting—an inclusion I suggest might involve an endless multiplicity of circles, where bursting continues to put truth in play, interrupting its movement. The production of truth as science includes the necessity of its own production, including the impossibility of laying either that production or its necessity to rest. Every rest collapses the gathering in which truth is truth.

I would then read claims to system as one side of the circularity that defines truth. "The systematic development of truth in scientific form can alone be the true shape in which truth exists"; "the temporal process would thus bring out and lay bare the necessity of it, may, more, would at the same time be carrying out that very aim itself" (Hegel, *PM*, 70–71), where the carrying out belongs in its movement and bursting forth to truth, to the Idea, including truth's other, falsity and untruth. Science cannot produce its truth except understood as production.

> science, the crowning glory of a spiritual world, is not found complete in its initial stages. . . . It is a whole which, after running its course and laying bare all its content, returns again to itself; it is the resultant abstract notion of the whole. (Hegel, *PM*, 76)

> science, in the very fact that it comes on the scene, is itself a phenomenon; its "coming on the scene" is not yet itself carried out in all the length and breadth of its truth. (p. 134)

If that length and breadth can be carried out, once and for all. For the end is abstract, and gains concreteness only "when those previous shapes and forms . . . are developed anew again" (p. 76). Further, it is Dionysian as well as Apollinian.

> The truth is thus the bacchanalian revel, where not a member is sober; and because every member no sooner becomes detached than it *eo ipso* collapses straightway, the revel is just as much a state of transparent unbroken calm. (Hegel, *PM*, 105)

The circle of circles turns back to begin again, in a different way, bursting through the limits of the circles in which it began, in an infinite, unlimited, unending movement, the bacchanalian revel, which without the calm would be merely unending rather than a crowning glory, the glory of truth, infinitely and endlessly torn apart. "It only wins to its truth when it finds itself utterly torn asunder" (Hegel, *PM*, 93), interrupted by death.

Hegel speaks of death; I would speak of falsity, untruth, disaster. Truth comes where Spirit is torn asunder in falsehood and death. Yet this dividedness does not remain intact, unchanged, in the tearing and the process, but undergoes another interruption.

> Difference itself continues to be an immediate element within truth as such, in the form of the principle of negation, in the form of the activity of Self. All the same, we cannot for that reason say that falsehood is a moment or forms even a constituent part of truth.... falsehood is not, *qua* false, any longer a moment of truth. (Hegel, *PM*, 99)

If this is read as converting falsity and untruth to truth, as ending the bursting through, then difference is tamed and the process in which truth wins itself from itself ends, ending interruption. It may instead be read as suggesting that even the binary opposition of truth and falsehood undergoes interruption with the arrival of truth, an arrival that insists on an end within itself that ceaselessly arrives and never ceases to arrive, as end.

Here truth is inseparable from untruth, but untruth is not "falsehood" in the movement of truth, not contradiction, but difference, otherness, variation, movement, heterogeneity, interruption, and more, where none of these can be stabilized in its truth. Truth arrives in the movement of others, where these remain, and depart, in their own truth and untruth. In the language of being, truth is the endless movement of being to its others, beings to their others, truth to its others, untruth, falsehood, difference, heterogeneity, depending on the circle in which we are circling, at which moment.

On one of those circles, Hegel insists that truth close itself into being.

> Consciousness furnishes its own criterion in itself, and the inquiry will thereby be a comparison of itself with its own self; for the distinction, just made, falls inside itself.... Thus in what consciousness inside itself declares to be the essence of truth we have the standard which itself sets up, and by which we are to measure its knowledge. (Hegel, *PM*, 140).

Yet it can do so only by including its others within itself. From the standpoint of the good, we may ask whether consciousness does so by imposing its authority on them or whether their authority interrupts, resists, the authority of consciousness, whether being's authority contains resistance within itself to itself. I say this comes from the good because all questions of authority acknowledge something from the good. Being gains its authority from the good.

Something of this understanding shows in Hegel, for the language of being and truth, given as process, becoming development, movement and end together, passes into relation to the good in a movement we might not have anticipated from the standpoint of the Absolute. For as soon as science—speculative philosophy—arrives on the scene (Hegel, *PM*, 115), it is joined by freedom and authority, joined where difference and heterogeneity meet untruth.

> The first instinctive reaction on the part of knowing, when offered something that was unfamiliar, is usually to resist it. It seeks by that means to save freedom and native insight, to secure its own inherent authority—against alien authority—for that is the way anything apprehended for the first time appears. (Hegel, *PM*, 116)

Anything different is always apprehended for the first time in resistance to authority, acknowledging that its truth is given from the good, caught up in questioning authority, epistemic, political, ethical authority, all in the name of freedom, interrupting authority's rule. Here truth belongs, in this resistance, to freedom of authority, profoundly ethical|political. With this understanding we can also understand that falsehood in relation to truth and difference in relation to the same are always questions of authority, of the good. Hegel introduces the good into the very heart of the movement of truth.

With this thought, with Ari we resume the movement of the good as truth.

CHAPTER 10

True Being

Sini's journey in gathering moves through several families of truth: accordance, freedom, and mystery, all linked with Heidegger and *alētheia*, passing onward to enchantment, Sini's depiction of the darkness of truth, still under the reign of being. I trace this movement in this chapter, from correspondence to enchantment, linking truth with being and saying, in preparation for undertaking the ethical movement I associate with the gift of truth, given from the good, evident in truth's authority. In anticipation, I suggest that the gathering of truth together with being and saying, despite the deepest mystery and brightest enchantment, reduces the abundance of the earth to saying, resisting the profusion of its gifts and heterogeneity.

Sini restricts his discussion of Heidegger almost entirely to "On the Essence of Truth" *("Vom Wesen der Wahrheit").* I will follow Sini's lead, with brief references to *Being and Time* and "The Origin of the Work of Art." I have discussed other works of Heidegger on truth in other places.

Heidegger takes up the question from the first of the essence of truth: "the one thing that in general distinguishes every 'truth' as truth" (Heidegger, *OET,* 117). I would recall Kant's denial that we can find "a sufficient, and at the same time universal, test of truth" (Kant, *CPR,* 49), suggesting perhaps that truth has no essence, that no thing distinguishes truth from untruth, not even a negative condition. Heidegger owes so great a debt to Kant, we may wonder why he does not acknowledge this debt, that truth as *alētheia* has no criterion and no essence, that the essence of truth is no essence. In the same way, perhaps, "Truth, in its nature, is un-truth" (Heidegger, *OWA,* 54).

I hold this thought in abeyance for a while to trace Sini's journey, retracing Heidegger's movement from "The Usual Concept of Truth" (Heidegger, *OET,* 118) to "the goal which should be posted for man in and for his history. We want the actual 'truth'" (p. 118). I hold the actual truth in abeyance for a while.

153

The "usual" concept of truth is accordance, agreement: "A statement is true if what it means and says is in accordance with the matter about which the statement is made" (Heidegger, *OET,* 119). This is the famous correspondence of which Aristotle is said to speak, which sent Ari on his journey toward bat truth, a truth excluded from this correspondence between being and saying. To this accordance Heidegger adds that truth is actuality and falsity appearance. "The true is the actual. . . . False gold . . . is merely a semblance" (Heidegger, *OET,* 119). Here, in Sini's words, "truth is the thing in *accordance* with itself" (Sini, *IT,* 49). In the first case, however, in relation to judgment, "Truth and falsehood, however, pertain also and first of all to our 'judgments' on beings" (Sini, *IT,* 49). We find the reign of being and saying over truth, marked in judgment's sovereignty, expressed explicitly and forcefully without the least acknowledgment of their authority and rule. In accordance, being rules over appearance and language. And yet, where we think of the coming forth of language and appearance in the Open, that they might open the possibility of truth, nothing echoes of the dangers of truth's or judgment's authority.

Where "truth is the correspondence of knowledge to the matter" (Heidegger, *OET,* 120), the correspondence is subordination and subjection. This truth, of truth's inordinate authority, is an ethical thought, comes from the good. Heidegger acknowledges it obliquely in relation to God: "it implies the Christian theological belief that . . . a matter, as created, is only insofar as it corresponds to the idea preconceived in the . . . mind of God" (p. 120), where the capacity for truth is "a capacity bestowed upon man by God" (p. 120), reminiscent of Eden, where God gives man dominion over all natural things. We may ask, in explicit political terms, is man ruler of all things for man's sake, man over women, humanity over plants and animals, supreme authority, or are all these things placed in the care of human beings as in the care of God? If the latter, if God's care of, love for, human beings is for their sake, and God's eye is on the sparrow as well as human beings, on all things, in love and care and truth, then the truth of all those things is given not by God's authority but by God's love and care. Against the subjection and subordination of all things to truth, including Ari and other living creatures, we may think of truth in love and care, given from the good as "cherishment." I hold this thought in abeyance for a while.

From the first, being emerges together with its truth in an unmistakably ethical relation, a relation that has not historically been acknowledged to be ethical within the Western view of truth as accordance, agreement, or correspondence: subordinating truth to being, saying to being's truth. From the first, where the subject is thrown down under, subjected to, the authority of the rule of being, or God, truth belongs to subjects not as rulers but as subordinates, ruled by something higher, dominated by the Same. Heidegger speaks of the supreme act of this highest rule still in relation to accordance: "a worldly reason which supplies the law for itself" (Heidegger, *OET,* 121), another political rendering of truth. For the possibility that reason might give the law to truth is an expression of its ethical freedom. Agreement is within the rule of law, demanding freedom for its truth.

Indeed, *"The essence of truth is freedom"* (Heidegger, *OET,* 125). Heidegger arrives at this essence by a movement around accordance, speaking of "accordance in various senses" (p. 122), including the observation that something "completely dissimilar, the statement" (p. 123) can correspond to the thing only in virtue of a relation already present, in virtue of their comportment *(Verhalten)* (p. 124). "Comportment stands open to beings. Every open relatedness is a comportment" (p. 124). This opening from which accordance emerges, the original possibility of truth, is free, is possible, "Only if this pregiving has already entered freely into an open region" (p. 125); "The openness of comportment as the inner condition of the possibility of correctness is grounded in freedom" (p. 125). What Heidegger does not say, what I cannot avoid saying here, is that freedom is ethical, given from the good. Indeed, we might wish to say that freedom is the good, that the good was named as freedom after Kant, between Kant and Heidegger, in Fichte, Schelling, and Hegel. Perhaps. It is a freedom that, for all these men, opens from humanity outward toward beings. "Man's open stance varies depending on the kind of beings and the way of comportment" (Heidegger, *OET,* 124). To whom, we may ask, does freedom belong? Is it bound to "Man's" comportment, or might it circulate among others? Could the freedom of truth belong to things themselves in their relations?

Here we come to Heidegger's most liberating thought, a far-reaching thought of the good though he does not acknowledge the good in truth. Nor does Sini, who understands freedom as another dominion. "Simply put, freedom is not a property of man, one of its possessions;" (Sini, *IT,* 57)— not a property at all, we might say, not a possession—"on the contrary, it is man possessed by truth" (p. 57). If man's appearance in the world is framed by the question of authority—humanity's and God's—then that appearance is given from and linked to the good. And if freedom's appearance in the world is framed by whether freedom is owned or possessed, then that appearance is given from and linked with the good. Property and possession are ethical|political, linked with authority and use. They recall us to the good.

The freedom of which Heidegger speaks, not a possession, impossible to own, and which I take to be given from the good, is *sein lassen,* letting things be. "Freedom now reveals itself as letting beings be" (Heidegger, *OET,* 127). This is not indifference or neglect (Heidegger, *OET,* 127), but engagement, a practical, ethical term. "To let be is to engage oneself with beings" (p. 127), a relation I would suggest is ethical from the first, to be concerned with the good of others. Heidegger speaks of it in the voice of being. "To let be—that is, to let beings be as the beings which they are— means to engage oneself with the open region and its openness into which every being comes to stand, bringing that openness, as it were, along with itself" (p. 127). Perhaps the letting-be, the letting-being, rather than the engagement or care, takes us from the good to saying as if we had forgotten the good. Perhaps the letting—*lassen*—is not a relation to being, not even beings' being, but to and with and from the good. Perhaps the possibility of letting-happen, come forth, is a gift from the good, recalling nature's abundance.

Heidegger speaks of freedom, which I understand in proximity to the good. But he also speaks of *Brauch*, usage, another neighbor of the good, not least in relation to Anaximander, whose fragment lies at the heart of the good. For where the fragment is translated into English in terms of the ordinance of time and injustice, Heidegger speaks of *Brauch* and *Un-Fugs:* "*entlang dem Brauch; gehören nämlich lassen sie Fug somit auch Ruch eines dem anderen (im Vorwinden) des Un-Fugs*" (Heidegger, *AF*, 57). The world of time, in which we live, perhaps of truth, is usage, *Brauch*, an ethical term, if it does not quite reach to injustice and the good. I would recall *Gebrauch* in Kant, transcendental use, and Dewey's pragmatist truth, given over to use as value. Truth circulates in proximity to *Brauch*.

Heidegger speaks repeatedly of Being, as if letting-be were governed by the rule of Being. He speaks of authority without naming authority. Yet what he says takes us to the good without the name. "Letting-be, i.e., freedom is intrinsically exposing, ek-sisting" (Heidegger, *OET*, 128). I will devote an entire chapter to exposure, Levinas's term that speaks of interrupting the reign of being, given to us from the good. I pause, with Ari, at ek-sistence, recalling ek-stasis, Sallis says in his translator's note on the same page. Being is ek-static, standing outside itself, interrupted. Where it stands, outside, I say is among the gifts of the good. The good is the outside of being, not as if there *is* or *might be* an outside of being, nor being's other, but otherwise than being *(autrement qu'être)*, another thought from Levinas I will defer to another chapter. Exposure to what is other to being but not under being's authority, resisting that authority, is the thought of the good.

Freedom is so close to the good that we might imagine that we might touch it in letting things be except for the rule of being and their truth. Yet instead of reaching toward the good, Heidegger recoils back into beings' truth, into "exposure to the disclosedness of beings" (Heidegger, *OET*, 128), where disclosedness as freedom knows nothing of the good, though it is unthinkable except as exposure. Exposure, in Levinas, is to the face. I understand it in relation to the skin, to touch. Letting-be is touching things with care, caring for them, in our care. "Prior to all this," Heidegger says, "freedom is engagement in the disclosure of beings as such" (p. 128). How, without exposure to things in their inexhaustible freedom, from our care for them, can we undertake to know them and their truth? If truth is freedom, then the freedom of things, of bats and rocks, of prairies and seas, touches them and others with their truth.

Heidegger speaks with a certain obliviousness to this freedom in truth when he tells us that "Freedom, understood as letting beings be, is the fulfillment and consummation of the essence of truth in the sense of the disclosure of beings" (Heidegger, *OET,* 129). Given from the good, truth allows no fulfillment or consummation. Moreover, "because truth is in essence freedom, historical man can, in letting beings be, also *not* let beings be the beings which they are and as they are" (p. 130). All the freedom of which Heidegger speaks belongs to man, however historical, thereby bringing truth together with untruth. Given from the good, instead, freedom belongs to things everywhere, where they touch each other in inexhaustible exposure, always outside themselves, away from their identities and essences toward others, otherwise. The proximity of truth is to the good, its displacement and interruption, not to untruth. Here untruth is another truth, a repetition of being. It does not interrupt the reign of being, resists nature's heterogeneous abundance.

Sini's route in truth moves from accordance to freedom to mystery, all Heideggerian movements, toward enchantment, Sini's revelation of the mystery of truth. These movements are worth retracing in Heidegger before we take up the magical echoes of enchantment in Sini, with a few digressions. For Heidegger repeats the privileging movement of freedom in truth, the movement we have seen that authorizes the superiority of humanity and the human spirit in relation to the gift, always the human gift, of language, never given to others, other beings, things, or creatures, with paws, fangs, or claws, or blowing in the wind. For in the same breath in which he speaks of *phusis*, of nature and "Being as a whole" (Heidegger, *OET,* 129), Heidegger evokes history with authority. "Only ek-sistent man is historical. 'Nature' has no history" (p. 129). And this despite refusing the authority of man as subject, of freedom as property, still in the language of possession. "Man does not 'possess' freedom as a property. At best, the converse holds: freedom, ek-sistent, disclosive Da-sein, possesses man" (p. 129), apparently man alone. "'Truth' is not a feature of correct propositions which are asserted of an 'object' by a human 'subject' and then 'are valid' somewhere, in what sphere we know not; rather, truth is disclosure of beings. . . . Therefore man *is* in the manner of ek-sistence" (p. 129). Apparently, man alone stands outside himself in Being. *Himself.* Alone.

Mystery arrives for humanity in truth's untruth, spoken of first in relation to freedom and history, thereafter in relation to Being as a whole. "Letting-be is intrinsically at the same time a concealing" (p. 132).

> The concealment of beings as a whole, untruth proper, is older than every openedness of this or that being. It is also older than letting-be itself which in disclosing already holds concealed and comports itself toward concealing. What conserves letting-be in this relatedness to concealing? Nothing less than the concealing of what is concealed as whole, of beings as such, i.e., the mystery, not a particular mystery regarding this or that, but rather the one mystery . . . (Heidegger, *OET,* 132).

I add three thoughts, one Lyotard's, that the Forgotten, the mystery, is not Being's being or truth but the Law. What is forgotten is the good, or the gift from the good, or the giving, given everywhere, in every place, not just to human beings. The mystery of being as a whole—I reject every sense of this whole except in refusing any authoritative and total place, the sense of everywhere as anywhere—concerns the gift that belongs to beings in relation to which they may be, may be let-be, may emerge in a truth that responds to the giving, their giving, the giving of them to us, to themselves, and to others.

This is the second thought I add to the mystery, from Heidegger, already noted. The mystery is neither Being nor Being's truth, but the giving, a giving that touches and withdraws, a giving beyond the gift of Being.

> In the beginning of Western thinking, Being is thought, but not the 'It gives' as such. The latter withdraws in favor of the gift which It gives. That gift is thought and conceptualized from then on exclusively as Being with regard to beings.
> A giving which gives only its gift, but in the giving holds itself back and withdraws, such a giving we call sending. (Heidegger, *TB,* 8)

The giving is conceived as the gift of Being and its truth, but continues to withdraw in a sending that presents a call, that touches things and emerges in their touching others, being touched by others. The mystery is the giving, sending, of and from the good. The giving—not what is given—is abundance *(Fülle),* fullness, plenishment of the earth.

The third thought I add, then, is that the giving and its mystery resist the demand to choose in the name of Being and truth. In the name of the gift, Heidegger appears to suggest that we follow Being and its truth and give up correspondence truth for unveiling. *Alētheia* wins out over adequation in the name of the gift. But not the giving, which knows nothing of winning and losing. Unveiling is not better than, superior to, closer to the truth of truth, than adequation. General economy, giving and abundance, are not closer to the heart of being than restricted economy. The truth, in its mystery, is everywhere in abundance. The truth of truth is giving in abundance.

Heidegger speaks of the one mystery as the non-essence of truth: "The proper non-essence of truth is the mystery" (Heidegger, *OET,* 133). Here the non-essence and untruth of truth express something primordial, not paradoxical, something gathered, not otherwise: "the still unexperienced domain of the truth of Being (not merely of beings)" (p. 133). Here, perhaps, we can see the rule of truth in being. For despite the giving, sending, and freedom of the mystery, Heidegger's thought is of the truth of Being, still unexperienced, giving absolute priority to Being's truth. And this despite the associated thought that the thinking of Being, and consequently Being's truth, names the gift rather than the giving, transforms the giving into the gift, does not give the "It." I would think of the It as the good, always giving, giving being, and truth, and beings, touching in its giving, interrupting in its sending. The withholding and withdrawing of and in the gift I understand as the mystery, not of the domain of the truth of being, but of the good that gives and interrupts and waits for a response. Touch and responsibility echo the good.

Heidegger's line of thought proceeds from the truth of Being, still unexperienced, to errancy, given in flight from the mystery. "Man's flight from the mystery toward what is readily available, onward from one current thing to the next, passing the mystery by—this is *erring*" (Heidegger, *OET,* 135). Erring and errancy continue to echo the dominion of truth, if in reverse. The flight recalls creatures who fly more than human beings—bats and birds and flying insects—who fly from the mystery, in the light and echo of the mystery, given in the charge of the good. Heidegger never for a moment considers that although the flight toward what is ready to hand is something he condemns, dwelling in the mystery evokes questions of authority, critique, and possibilities, all together with freedom given from the good. He does not seem to recall Socrates' insistence that truth and knowledge come from the good, not from being, that they are gifts that evoke response and responsibility, touch us with a call, us and others, every thing, including bats and birds and insects, resisting all authority. To the contrary, Heidegger understands Plato to remain within the reign of Being in the name of metaphysics. "The thinking of Being, from which such questioning [the question of the *Being* of beings] primordially originates, has since Plato been understood as 'philosophy' and later received the title 'metaphysics'" (Heidegger, *OET,* 137).

Truth remains together with untruth in error, for Heidegger, retaining its dominion as truth.

> Errancy is the essential counter-essence to the primordial essence of truth. Errancy opens itself up as the open region for every opposite to essential truth. Errancy is the open site for and ground of *error*. Error is not just an isolated mistake but rather the realm (the domain) of the history of those entanglements in which all kinds of erring get interwoven. (Heidegger, *OET,* 136)

All kinds of erring; all kinds of evil; all kinds of beings, things, and kinds, all in the skins, surfaces, entanglements of their touches and responses. Truth and error are given as responsiveness, as interruption and exposure. Without exposure to things, our exposure to them and their exposure to us and to each other, without an infinite touch of exposure to things beyond any accounting, interrupting every measure, the demand of truth, the will, desire, yearning, and call of truth, cannot be given. The will to truth presupposes exposure, the touch of the good.

Heidegger concludes his essay on the essence of truth with another ethical|political figure, translated as lightening sheltering: *lichtendes Bergen.* The sheltering, also a place of safety and salvation, reminding us of Kant who speaks of encountering the sublime in a place of safety, is ethical and political, suggests a peaceful realm in which we are safe, perhaps at home, with little recognition of the historic dimensions in which some people have been placed at risk in the name of truth, little sense of what Foucault might mean in claiming that the political question "is truth itself." In the name of truth, in the name of a régime of truth, some kinds of human beings, some kinds of other creatures and things, are dominated. Truth is an institution of domination and oppression. It belongs to the authorization of rule, belongs to power. Including *alētheia.* Perhaps.

No doubt we may read Heidegger's sense of *Bergen* as a call to peace. "Truth signifies sheltering that lightens as the basic characteristic of Being" (Heidegger, *OET,* 140). To do so, however, is to understand that this peace rests with the good, calls forth a political concern to which truth offers response. It is also to understand that we may seek peace while resisting a shelter in whose name countless human beings and other creatures have been sacrificed and used, resisting every idea of truth that orders the world from high to low. Something of the historical dimension of human political life remains within every thought of truth that demands incessant critique. Sheltering resists critique, forgets that building and dwelling slow the circulation. Safety demands reserve, stocking up the future.

Heidegger's emphasis in *Being and Time,* in relation to truth, is quite different, never quite reaches the mystery, bears suspect traces of the good. Untruth retains a much more powerful sense of historicality. For *"Dasein is 'in the truth'* " (Heidegger, *BT,* 263); *"Because Dasein is essentially falling, its state of Being is such that it is in 'untruth'* " (p. 264). Even so, this sense of fallen *(verfallen)* is that of sin, the primordial Christian fall, filled with ethical significance. Untruth, if not truth, belongs to the good, bears the weight of falling from if not given from the good. Heidegger calls this falling ontological and primordial, a relation to Being. Yet he continues his account in ethical terms, in relation to care *(Sorge)* (pp. 358–82) and guilt *(Schuld)* (pp. 328–35). *"Being-guilty does not first result from an indebtedness [Verschuldung], but that, on the contrary, indebtedness becomes possible only 'on the basis' of a primordial Being-guilty"* (p. 329), a surpassingly Christian thought, related to original sin. We might wish to remind Heidegger of Anaximander, for whom being bears a debt toward injustice, demanding restitution, borne by every being, every thing, not *Dasein* alone, not just human beings.

Even so, we might follow Heidegger's thought a bit further to wonder what it might mean to imagine that we are guilty for being in the truth, primordially guilty in truth and untruth. Truth here is not a neutral, autonomous state of Being, covered or uncovered; nor is the mystery. The mystery evokes the gods in an ethical|political|theological juncture; truth is given from the gods, comes from the good, comes from and demands endless response. That is what the primordiality demands.

With this powerful sense of the suggested but unnamed good in Heidegger's understanding of truth, weighed down by guilt, by debt, perhaps by God, in any case given from the good, demanding endless responses from us and others, the endless responsiveness we associate with nature's abundance, with *phusis* and *poiēsis*, we can see something of the way in which sheltering works to halt the movement of the gift in the name of truth, historical or otherwise, gathers the gift in its place, imposes destiny on truth without acknowledging the endless interruptions of the good. The spirit of man continues to rule in Heidegger against all the openings he evokes toward nature. And in Sini.

For I return to conclude our journey with Sini, taking up the challenge given by Ari, demanding that we pursue bat truth. We pass from the mystery, filled with forgetting, especially forgetting the law, the good, oblivious to debts and guilt, to enchantment, which seems to know nothing of the good or the debt, deaf to the songs of bats. Truth and error come from the experience of the world as en-chantment, the song of the earth.

> the *event* itself . . . is not experienced at all as mystery. . . . What is its sense? *It is experienced as en-chantment.* Its sense is enchantment.
>
> The en-chantment *knows* nothing of truth and error. For the enchantment, there is neither 'wonder' nor will to knowledge (and nothing to know), no *alētheia* (revelation of the concealed), no *lēthe* (concealment of the revealed). (Sini, *IT,* 148)

Nor nothing of the good, of shelter, guilt, and debt. Nor of nature, of the abundance of *phusis* in which we move, to which we respond, which is filled with responsiveness and touch everywhere, even where we are not. Enchantment suggests a music in all things, the song of the good, yet continues to belong to the gaze and to us. "In the sense of 'chants-in,' *i.e.,* it becomes sign and word. *In what* does that 'in' occur? Obviously 'in' the Response, 'in' that response that we 'are.' Enchantment of moon for the look of moon" (Sini, *IT,* 148).

Sign, word, look, us, all fall down under the Same, again. "The enchantment, instead, is precisely the experience of the Sameness of the Other" (Sini, *IT,* 148). Ari screams his rage, as if he can be experienced as the same when he is so different, without destroying that difference, in its truth, responsive to the good. He demands infinite exposure. He insists on interrupting the human rule of truth.

Especially, he rages at the *look* of moon when he does not see, at the *sign* and *symbol* of moon when he cannot write or speak, but knows, and cares, and touches things, other bats and things, wherever he is.

> For en-chantment, to participate means to be a part, to take part, to assume *the* part, in every sense and above all in the sense of being a part, finite and perfect, as *symbolon*. In our example, it means: to be part *of* moon, to take part *in it*, to take on its countenance. For this reason, as we said, the child's looking is *made of moon.* (Sini, *IT,* 149)

But not Ari's look, or not look but ring, under the moon, and sky, and sun. Yet Sini touches the good despite the least granting its touch, touches it without saying or knowing it, except obliquely.

> Only in en-chantment does the *finiteness* of experience, already vindicated in the course of our journey, present itself finally complete and "perfect," because the enchantment, what en-chants, are *beings themselves* (in our example the moon, the world in countenance of moon). (Sini, *IT,* 150)

Sini's journey presents the finiteness of experience, our human experience, as complete and perfect as if the journey might come to an end with beings showing themselves in their face, their countenance and look, to us. Ari, who sees nothing but knows much, clicks and squeaks of his own enchantment, of the magic and beauty of song. Ari celebrates the truth—another truth, perhaps—of beings themselves in their abundance, heterogeneous, multiple, profuse truths that emerge in the responsiveness of things within themselves and to one another in their looks, and sounds, and songs, celebrating excess beyond law. Ari's enchantment rings the anarchy of truth. Not lawlessness without truth, but the law beyond beings themselves of truth, given from the good, as the magic of sound and music and song. We have heard the echoes, felt the touch, of the good in truth in recalling the interruption of *technē*'s truth in *mimēsis* and *poiēsis,* remembering the music of the cicadas, given beyond the rule of truth, echoing in its song.[1]

Sini approaches this anarchy of music and song, the release of the limits and boundaries of looks and sight in sound, and recoils.

> This enchantment [of equilibrium] is the moment, or the point, at which the dancer, dancing, is drawn to the margins of the Chorus, to its extreme edge. From here, he can "see" his companions dancing and the dance which, while still dancing, he "is." That is, he can see the very provenance of his dancing and of his seeing *himself* as dance and dancer. The "dance" is a thing of the gods. (Sini, *IT,* 150).

What would dancing be without music? Does the dancer see or feel the presence of other dancers, feel their breath and touch when unseen? The dance speaks, or sings, of bodies touching, of things touching each other in their materiality, still touched by the gods. The chorus sings while dancing, dances while singing, for we can imagine singing without bodies no better than we can imagine dancing without bodies. Or painting. But looks have always led us to imagine disembodied images, truths given to minds without the fleshy touch of bodies, squeezing truths between their membranes, suckers, tentacles, and groins. Enchantment sets in play—here the play of music, performance of song, celebration of events in material spaces and places—the circulation of things around us and each other, a circulation that would not stop were all human beings to vanish from the universe. When all human beings die—all!—enchantment and truth will not die with them. For in no sense given from the good are humans All.

Sini speaks of Penelope waiting. What enables her to wait, I would say, is the touch of enchantment from memories of passion and loss, deeply pervading her body and soul, pervading her world. Sini describes this somewhat differently. "What Penelope experiences, what she does not withdraw from, is the fact whereby the symbolic event of passion, its enchantment, is not separable from the befalling and falling of the sign (but is the Same)" (Sini, *IT,* 151). Penelope waits, I would say, in the absence of the Same, surrounded by endless journeys, the circulation of countless movements, given from the good. She represents the good that gives where nothing remains the same. That enchantment, the ringing music of endless movements and circulations, the general economy of all things, beyond the limits of any rule, any calculation, any restricted economy. If Odysseus travels in general economy, Penelope waits in her restricted economy, knowing its excesses beyond any limits. What she needs, what we need, is to know that general economy circulates as thoroughly in equilibrium and stability as in open journey, that the home is filled with enchantment, that women touch the good where they are, beyond any limits or rules. Held in bondage, women and slaves touch the good, exceeding any limits, circulating in general economy. Throughout the nature of which Diotima speaks, "of wondrous beauty," journeys and excesses are restricted almost everywhere in the world to men, held in thrall by men, as if women do not dance, are not enchanted, or if they are can be recognized as magical only by men. Still they dance, know the enchantments of their gifts, open the indefiniteness of the dyads of their touch.

At this point Ari reminds us that her name is short for Ariadne, who spun her thread, reminding us of Arachne and the spider's web. Bats and spiders, male and female, demand their truth in the name of the good.

Sini concludes with a gesture I take to repeat this recognition, reassigning the truth of enchantment to men, without acknowledgment, lacking every reverse gesture.

> Many times, in the past, the greatest thinkers have been able to *say* the ecstatic enchantment of the mystery; they have been able to translate into words the enchantment of their passion, of their desire for knowledge, attracted by the mystery of the world that made them, in fact, philosophers (Sini, *IT,* 153).

The "greatest thinkers" have always been men, not women, in the West and elsewhere, because women have been relegated to the home, as if the home and hearth lack enchantment and ek-stasy, lack the good. The world begins at the limits of the home, begins an endless journey driven by inexhaustible desire to know, when in one's place are endless truths and unlimited passions and desires. Sini speaks of the task and achievement of philosophy—Western philosophy—to say the enchantment of the passion for truth, speaks of philosophy and finally of science, neglecting the possibility that art, including music, painting, and poetry, and more, all *mimēsis,* bear the weight of the gift of the good and nature's wondrous beauty. In the name of truth we forget too much of the good, disregard too many gifts of the gods.

If truth sings of the enchantment of things, of the world and of our passions, it sings everywhere in the beauties and wonders of things touching each other, everywhere, in every place and thing. The magic of enchantment reaches beyond the neutrality of being and the world, beyond their surface and depth, to what calls forth, or reaches toward, or touches every limit with excess. The profusion, multiplicity, heterogeneity, and inexhaustibility of things is not more things, more beings, not more and more being, but interrupts the assembling of being under the rule of *legein,* interrupts the establishment of sovereignty and authority. Truth, bearing supreme authority for the *logos*, under the sovereignty of Western reason, closes the circle of enchantment under reason's speculation without interruption by desire and passion, from the good. Truth bears nothing of the gifts that give it its truth. Interruption is this nothing.

Here we may read Heidegger's understanding that truth is freedom as interrupting Sini's journey. I return to *sein lassen,* resisting the authority of *Sein*, of Being. Truth is *lassen*, understood as response, responsibility to the gift of the good, a responsiveness that interrupts rather than reimposes the authority of being. Freedom here is not caprice, or willing, or choosing, but giving in response to gifts given from the good, resisting the gathering and its authority. What is given has been named in the West as Being, as if that name, once gathered, bore infinite authority, the authority of God. The giving does not come from Being, named as the gift, but from something that interrupts that name, something that does not stabilize even as enchantment, but sings and celebrates the magic of the good beyond any being, and Being itself, the beyond of truth from which truth emerges, in memory of that beyond—nowhere in being, no other place than being. Freedom, in its excesses, speaks of the inexhaustibility of the good. That is the place\nonplace of truth. In every place; its nonplace.

Calling for an interruption, in anticipation:

> The maternal-feminine remains the *place separated from "its" own place* [*lieu séparé de « son » lieu:* "his" or "its" place], deprived of "its" [*« son »*] place. She is or ceaselessly becomes the place of the other who cannot separate himself from it. Without her knowing or willing it, she is then threatening because of what she lacks: a "proper" place. She would have to re-envelop herself with herself, and do so at least twice: as a woman and as a mother. Which would presuppose a change in the whole economy of space-time. (Irigaray, *ESD*, 10–11)

Or of bodies and souls, angels and intermediary movements.

> The angel is that which unceasingly *passes through the envelope(s)* or *container(s)*, goes from one side to the other, reworking every deadline, changing every decision, thwarting all repetition. Angels destroy the monstrous, that which hampers the possibility of a new age; they come to herald the arrival of a new birth, a new morning. (Irigaray, *ESD*, 15)

> A remaking of immanence and transcendence, notably through this *threshold* which has never been examined as such: the female sex. The threshold that gives access to the *mucous*. Beyond classical oppositions of love and hate, liquid and ice—a threshold that is always *half-open*. (p. 18)

All in relation to truth, truth's enchantment, in the name of woman.

> Supposing truth is a woman—what then? (Nietzsche, *BGE*, Pref.).
>
> From the beginning, nothing has been more alien, repugnant, and hostile to woman than truth—her great art is the lie, her highest concern is mere appearance and beauty (#232).
>
> Why do women, our women, lie so poorly? (Irigaray, *ML*, 78)

The enchantment of *The* Woman. Woman as truth.

Yet I must not leave Heidegger steeped in enchantment without the names he gives to its abundance, to abundance and gifts. Letting-be can be understood only in relation to giving and abundance, to what is given to us in order that we may respond. I fear that Sini does not respect this giving, this enchanted gift, from the good. Despite never openly acknowledging that it is so, and despite betraying it to tyranny, Heidegger seems to me to give something of this giving of the good.

CHAPTER 11

Woman's Truth

"Supposing truth is a woman—what then?" (Nietzsche, *BGE*, Pref.).
Truth, and life, are . . . women! *Vita femina. Veritas femina.* Two thoughts
touch where we do not expect them, where we may not want them to
touch, opening up new juxtapositions: truth and woman; life and woman.
With two additions. One is that these neutered ideas of life and truth,
especially the idea of truth—for what kind of life could we imagine humans
might have without women?—have always touched women obliquely, have
always in their neutrality touched upon gender and sexual difference. For
women have always worn the veil while truth unveils. Truth unveils woman
as object of desire, veiled by reason's neutrality. And of life, we say, to thine
self be true, against the masks, the veils of women, and great men.

The other addition is that truth and life and woman all belong to other
pairings, touch other places, which we may suppose are brought into proximity by the proximity of truth and life with women. For truth circulates
with untruth, whether in proximity or opposition; life circulates with death,
again in proximity or opposition; and women with men, if not always or
everywhere, in opposition and proximity. And perhaps, as the will to truth
suggests to Nietzsche, together with the desire for untruth, for deception
and lies, the value for life may be more lie than truth, the value for life may
be death, and the value for men may be women. What then of the good for
women? Or spiders, birds, and bats.

More to the point perhaps, the opposition, separation, and distinction,
the territoriality of truth and untruth, life and death, men and women, are
undermined in their proximity. "How *could* anything originate out of its
opposite? for example, truth or error? or the will to truth out of the will to
deception? or selfless deeds out of selfishness? or the pure and sunlike gaze
of the sage out of lust?" (Nietzsche, *BGE*, #2). Leading to one of Nietzsche's
most far-reaching claims concerning truth and life, though not here, women.

The fundamental faith of the metaphysicians *is the faith in opposite values.*

For one may doubt, first, whether there are any opposites at all, and secondly whether these popular valuations and opposite values on which the metaphysicians put their seal, are not perhaps merely foreground estimates, only provisional perspectives, perhaps even from some nook, perhaps from below, frog perspectives, as it were, to borrow an expression painters use. For all the value that the true, the truthful, the selfless may deserve, it would still be possible that a higher and more fundamental value for life might have to be ascribed to deception, selfishness, and lust. . . . Maybe! (Nietzsche, *BGE*, #2)

If there are no opposites at all, what of Nietzsche's comments on women, as if they were the opposite of men? What of frogs, as if the opposite of humans?

Nietzsche says many hateful things of women. Among the worst is his disdain for any consciousness of the rights of women, if that is what he means in speaking of "woman as such," women as women: "Woman wants to become self-reliant—and for that reason she is beginning to enlighten men about 'woman as such': *this* is one of the worst developments of the general *uglification* of Europe" (Nietzsche, BGE, #232). Yet perhaps we can read this disdain as directed at men as well as women, men more than women, including Germans, perhaps, with supreme Nietzschean irony.

So far enlightenment of this sort was fortunately man's affair, man's lot— we remained "among ourselves" in this; and whatever women write about "woman," we may in the end reserve a healthy suspicion whether woman really *wants* enlightenment about herself—whether she *can* will it . . .

. . . From the beginning, nothing has been more alien, repugnant, and hostile to woman than truth—her great art is the lie, her highest concern is mere appearance and beauty. . . .

Finally, I pose the question: has ever a woman conceded profundity to a woman's head, or justice to a woman's heart? (Nietzsche, *BGE*, #232)

Yet Nietzsche repeatedly acknowledges, deeply and profoundly, how thoroughly the idea of woman is owned by men, reminding us that "any theory of the subject has always been appropriated by the 'masculine' " (Irigaray, *SOW*, 133).

Will and willingness.—Someone took a youth to a sage and said: "Look, he is being corrupted by women." The sage shook his head and smiled. "It is men," said he, "that corrupt women; and all the failings of women should be atoned by and improved in men. For it is man who creates for himself the image of woman, and woman forms herself according to this image."

"You are too kindhearted about women," said one of those present; "you do not know them." The sage replied: "Will is the manner of men; willingness that of women. That is the law of the sexes—truly, a hard law for women. All of humanity is innocent of its existence; but women are doubly innocent. Who could have oil and kindness enough for them?"

"Damn oil! Damn kindness!" someone else shouted out of the crowd; "women need to be educated better!"—"Men need to be educated better," said the sage and beckoned to the youth to follow him.—The youth, however, did not follow him. (Nietzsche, *GS*, #68)

I hope to explore the possibility that untruth is always appropriated by truth, that life is always appropriated by death, under the shadow of the masculine subject. Here we may reach the proximity and juxtaposition of truth and life and woman. I do so by following the track of the sea to Irigaray, in intermediary movement.

We might say that Irigaray's interest lies in woman more than truth, that if she speaks of the truth of woman, it is woman she seeks, not truth, as if we might find woman without finding truth. And we might say the reverse of Nietzsche, who speaks of woman to speak of truth, and the truth of truth, however profoundly he inverts the truth of truth. We find both of these sayings under water in Irigaray, where neither bats nor spiders live, but octopuses, shrimp, and squid. I say "under water" because she is *Marine Lover of Friedrich Nietzsche* who, "Speaking of Immemorial Waters," speaks in and from the sea. "Is there any greater rapture than the sea?" (Irigaray, *ML,* 13); "endless rapture awaits whoever trusts the sea" (p. 13); against the worship of the sun on the highest mountain (p. 15). But I was speaking of women, who speak with "veiled lips" (p. 77).

To write that "from the very first nothing is more foreign . . . to woman than truth," and then that "her great art is falsehood, her chief concern is appearance and beauty" is surely to say the same thing twice, with the exception that one word has been forgotten the second time, the word *foreign*.

Neither falsehood nor appearance and beauty are "foreign" to truth. They are proper to it, if not its accessories and its underside. (p. 77)

Perhaps it is in the name of women that men hope to strip truth bare. For "Man needs an instrument to touch himself with: a hand, a woman, or some substitute" (Irigaray, *VF*, 232). But "Woman is neither open nor closed. She is indefinite, in-finite, *form is never complete in her*" (p. 229).

We are concerned with truth, here with the juxtaposition of women and truth, exploring the possibility, the suggestion, that truth is a woman. And woman? Women? Supposing woman is truth, or true, or whatever. We are led to the thought of strangeness, to what is strange and foreign. I pause for a brief interruption.

Foreigner: a choked up rage deep down in my throat, a black angel clouding transparency, opaque, unfathomable spur. The image of hatred and of the other, a foreigner is neither the romantic victim of our clannish indolence nor the intruder responsible for all the ills of the polis. Neither the apocalypse on the move nor the instant adversary to be eliminated for the sake of appeasing the group. Strangely, the foreigner lives within us: he is the hidden face of our identity, the space that wrecks our abode, the time in which understanding and affinity founder. . . .

Can the "foreigner," who was the "enemy" in primitive societies, disappear from modern societies? (Kristeva, *SO*, 1)

If truth is the stranger, foreigner, alien to women, do women hate truth or do they reveal the possibility that truth might cease to be the enemy—if it, or women, were ever enemies, toward each other, toward men. "Although femaleness has taken it/them [beauty and appearance] as part of her forms, although she cannot do without it/them if she is to pass for what is: the truth" (Irigaray, *ML*, 77). For the moment, Irigaray speaks of truth as "what is," speaks of being, together with beauty and appearance, though we may recall the angels, always on the move in intermediary movements, circulating in general economy beyond the hold of being and truth, echoing the good, "endlessly reopening the enclosure of the universe, of universes, identities, the unfolding of actions, of history" (Irigaray, *ESD*, 15).[1] I take the good to be this endless reopening, interrupting the gathering of being as Diotima and Irigaray interrupt the assembling of men. And Nietzsche, a strange man, a stranger. The strangeness of truth interrupts the rule of the state dividing those who belong from strangers.

If truth is a woman, then it and she endlessly interrupt the assembling of its/their limits, revealing the stranger within. Why should we imagine that falsehood is foreign, strange, to truth? Why not its intermediary movement, its angel? Under water.

But this is Nietzsche, if under water. For truth without error is like man without woman, not an impoverished man or impotent master, but unthinkable, impossible, beyond thought or desire. Without women there would be no men. Truth cannot be thought of or desired without error. This is a Dionysian thought.

Thus, if error becomes the "truth" of pleasure, the "idea" become woman. Woman becomes the possibility of a "different" idea, which amounts to a store of strength. "The eternal feminine" moves away, goes into exile in another representation: that will find pathos in the crucifixion of Christ, that scion of Dionysos. (Irigaray, *ML*, 79).

I do think adorning herself is part of the Eternal-Feminine? . . . From the beginning, nothing has been more alien, repugnant, and hostile to woman than truth—her great art is the lie, her highest concern is mere appearance and beauty. Let us men confess it: we honor and love precisely *this* art and *this* instinct in woman—we who have a hard time and for our relief like to associate with beings under whose hands, eyes, and tender follies our seriousness, our gravity and profundity almost appear to us like folly. (Nietzsche, *BGE*, #232)

Something of adornment and hostility to truth deserves honor against its seriousness, gravity, and profundity. Here I would speak not of women but of music, or of women and music together. I would recall the *Stabat Mater*, which in its music echoes a different truth, perhaps a woman's truth, a woman's relation to the good, perhaps repeating the story of Christ.[2] This thought of music and women opens onto a nature without qualities, of wondrous beauty.

> What alone can be our doctrine? That no one gives man his qualities—neither God, nor society, nor his parents and ancestors, nor he himself. . . . No one is responsible for man's being there at all, for his being such-and-such, or for his being in these circumstances or in this environment. . . . It is absurd to wish to devolve one's essence on some end or other. (Nietzsche, *TI*, 500)[3]

Man is without qualities. Or is it woman? Music, and woman, express the arbitrariness of things, the Dionysian, while we continue to hope to define man around a single point of desire, under Apollo's rule.

Irigaray brings us repeatedly face to face with castration, said in our time to be the defining quality of men. Women are nothing but castration, a wound.

> Castration stems/sublates from the giving of the self into the making the self "out to be." . . . Castration? Wasn't that, precisely, the gesture of repetition which gave the key to the whole stage set by the same? . . .
>
> Castration would be merely some simulacrum—with nothing added on—unless the other has nothing, and is not lent what she doesn't have, what she would have been allowed only to take care of. . . .
>
> Given up more and more to "foreignness" now that castration has been taken over by the master's desire, the-act-of-castrating recircumscribes the practice of the game from some kind of outside. But it is forgotten in castration.
>
> Or, sometimes, circumcision. Now the Jewish operation, despite what is cut away, lies in the realm of the sign. (Irigaray, *ML*, 80–81)

Reminding us of Jews. How shall we relate Nietzsche's wonderful insights into truth with his hatefulness toward women and his anti-Semitism—

reminding us of Heidegger and Hitler? Nietzsche joins women and Jews around the mask, one might say, in opening up the deceptions in truth, as such, wounds in truth.

> As for the *Jews*, the people who possess the art of adaptability par excellence, this train of thought suggests immediately that one might see them virtually as a world-historical arrangement for the production of actors, a veritable breeding ground for actors. And it really is high time to ask: What good actor today is *not*—a Jew? The Jew as a born "man of letters," as the true master of the European press, also exercises his power by virtue of his histrionic gifts; for the man of letters is essentially an actor: He plays the "expert," the "specialist."
>
> Finally, *women*. Reflect on the whole history of women: do they not *have* to be first of all and above all else actresses? . . .
>
> Woman is so artistic. (Nietzsche, *GS*, #361)

Matching in its concluding structure the extended passage quoted at length by Irigaray:

> *Vita femina.*—For seeing the ultimate beauties of a work, no knowledge or good will is sufficient; this requires the rarest of lucky accidents: The clouds that veil these peaks have to lift for once so that we see them glowing in the sun. Not only do we have to stand in precisely the right spot in order to see this, but the unveiling must have been accomplished by our own soul because it needed some external expression and parable, as if it were a matter of having something to hold on to and retain control of itself. But it is so rare for all of this to coincide that I am inclined to believe that the highest peaks of everything good, whether it be a work, a deed, humanity, or nature, have so far remained concealed and veiled from the great majority and even from the best human beings. But what does unveil itself for us, *unveils itself for us once only.*
>
> . . . I mean to say that the world is overfull of beautiful things but nevertheless poor, very poor when it comes to beautiful moments and unveilings of these things. But perhaps this is the most powerful magic of life: it is covered by a veil interwoven with gold, a veil of beautiful possibilities, sparkling with promise, resistance, bashfulness, mockery, pity, and seduction. Yes, life is a woman. (Nietzsche, *GS*, #339; quoted in Irigaray, *ML*, 92–93)

Woman is so artistic. Life is a woman. Truth is woman is artist is Jew is lie is love. Perhaps. Leading to another interruption. And others.

Suppose truth were a bat, or spider, or frog, an animal rather than a woman or man—what then? Suppose truth were a woman and woman were not man—what then? Suppose truth were not what we take it to be, were never what we take it to be, in a certain way were precisely that it is never what we take it to be without qualification, misdirection, untruth, ornamentation, *mimēsis*, or whatever—what then? Woman, Irigaray says, is not what man takes her to be, but is not something else, other, that she might be taken to be instead, but remains fluid and indeterminate. Perhaps like truth, or bats, or bodies. We do not know what bodies can do. Or truth. Or women. Or frogs. Or, for that matter, men. But it seems that we think we know, suppose ourselves to know, demand that we know. "He [that is, She] whom I suppose to know, I love" (Lacan, *GJW*, 139); in other words, "Who or what the other is, I never know. But the other who is forever unknowable is the one who differs from me sexually" (Irigaray, *ESD*, 13). Or animally. In its, or her, truth, Arachne's, Ariadne's, truth.

One may doubt whether there are any opposites. Even reading that "Whatever is profound loves masks; what is most profound even hates image and parable. Might not nothing less than the opposite be the proper disguise for the shame of a god?" (Nietzsche, *BGE*, #40), suggesting that opposites are masks obscuring the shame of a god, the masks of truth. Here masks are truth; truth is masked. Including the disguises of the gods. And women, or spiders and bats? What then of the opposition of men and women, humans and bats?

> To go wrong on the fundamental problem of "man and woman," to deny the most abysmal antagonism between them and the necessity of an eternal hostile tension, to dream perhaps of equal rights, equal education, equal claims and obligations—that is a *typical* sign of shallowness, and a thinker who has proved shallow in this dangerous place—shallow in his instinct—may be considered altogether suspicious, even more—betrayed, exposed: probably he will be too "short" for all fundamental problems of life, of the life yet to come, too, and incapable of attaining *any* depth. A man, on the other hand, who has depth, in his spirit as well as in his desires, including that depth of benevolence which is capable of severity and hardness and easily mistaken for them, must always think about women as *Orientals* do: he must conceive of woman as a possession, as property that can be locked, as something predestined for service and achieving her perfection in that. (Nietzsche, *BGE*, #238)

Nietzsche assaults women, equality, enlightenment, all in the name of a depth that takes woman as a possession, recalling to our mind that men— I mean here human beings, but I hope to include spiders, frogs, and bats— are taken by that deep and holy capitalist economy as possessions, commodities, predestined for use, perfect in that and requiring, demanding, no more. And animals are owned by men, living possessions, as if no more, bearing no more truth. The truth of woman is, for Marx, capitalism's truth. Why should we doubt that truth to be Nietzsche's truth? Why should we suppose that it is what he means by depth?

Capitalism creates commodities out of human beings in the ideality of use. Men exchange women. Perhaps property and exchange go back to time immemorial, even where we find divine gifts. "Man has created woman— out of what? Out of a rib of his god—of his 'ideal' " (Nietzsche, *TI*, 468). I have no interest—or very little—in defending Nietzsche against being savaged as he seems to savage women. I am more interested in following the supposition that whatever we or Nietzsche might say of woman, truth is a woman; whatever we might say of spiders, bats, or rocks, truth is a spider, or a bat, or rock. Truth, we may say, is sometimes shallow, sometimes profound. The most likely reading of our retraversal of truth with Sini and Ari, up to Heidegger, through Hegel and Nietzsche, is to turn from shallow correspondence truth to deep and mysterious truth, enchanted truth. Demanding our resistance. Leading back to women. "Women are considered profound. Why? Because one never fathoms their depths. Women aren't even shallow" (p. 470). Perhaps truth is neither profound nor shallow, like women and frogs. And Germans.

> The Germans—once they were called the people of thinkers: do they think at all today? The Germans are now bored with the spirit, the Germans now mistrust the spirit; politics swallows up all serious concern for really spiritual matters. *Deutschland, Deutschland über alles*—I fear that was the end of German philosophy. (p. 506)

And we—men?—who think that we, or truth, or God, is profound, we too aren't even shallow. We suppose that truth is a woman to cancel the vertical dimension in which we erect that phallic tower to God, always falling short. *Deutschland, Deutschland über alles;* Man's rule, everywhere. "[A]lthough we had purposed to build for ourselves a tower which should reach to Heaven, the supply of materials sufficed merely for a habitation" (Kant, *CPR,* 397); one image of truth, man standing upright imposing sovereign truth, resisting proliferation and fragmentation. "[A]nd at last scattered them over all the world, each to erect a separate building for himself, according to his own plans and his own inclinations" (p. 397). If truth is a woman, the human realm knows neither overarching truth nor sovereign rule.

I return to the extended passages from which I undertook this brief interruption, return to *vita femina,* life as a woman, reminding us of Jews, another European repression, veiling and unveiling, asking us to remember the ghettoization of Jews and the domestication of women. Both passages end with corresponding figures. "Woman is so artistic"; "Yes, life is a woman." To which woman responds (I postpone a Jewish response for just a moment):

> The possible that is reserved, the modesty that is bashful, the seduction that is elusive and promises—resistingly, mockingly, pityingly—to give itself: life as a woman.

> The return of what is repressed, while she is kept in repression. Beneath a veil interwoven with gold. (Irigaray, *ML*, 93)

Woman, and perhaps Jew, mark the repression, all the while remaining repressed. We will remember the gas chambers, the murder and destruction of Jewish people, so that we may become liberated. It is absolutely necessary to do so and impossible. Liberation means forgetting. Woman, as truth, evokes the veiling, the repressing, forgetting of truth, the forgotten untruth at the heart of truth, reminding us of the miracle of truth, which will unveil itself for us once only. And women, who demand their truth, or bats and frogs, who claim a truth that is not already claimed within the veiling, the veils that men employ to cover their shame—diverted to cover women's pudendum as if that were man's shame—women remain subjected to endless repetition.

> For it is precisely repetition that prevents her from returning. Repetition embroiders the gold veil that covers beauty. Perhaps indeed this is the greatest charm of life. . . . Which is as much as to say that suspense has more attractions than pleasure. That it has become pleasure: the expectation, desirable in mastery, of gods who will not return again. (Irigaray, *ML*, 93)

All keeping women in subjection to the abyss that surrounds the masculine subject. And its truth. In the name of truth, men insist on being "on top," a striking sexual figure: "Those who feel 'I possess Truth'—how many possessions would they not abandon in order to save this feeling! What would they not throw overboard to stay 'on top'—which means, *above* the others who lack 'the Truth'"! (Nietzsche, *GS*, #13). Or even above those who have or are in the truth, if they are women, or bats.

Suppose truth were ambiguous, indeterminate, forever contested—what then? What of the following, within another violence toward women, here women who deserve better but who have throughout European and other history been destroyed as witches?

> *Skeptics.*—I am afraid that old women are more skeptical in their most secret heart of hearts than any man: they consider the superficiality of existence its essence, and all virtue and profundity is to them merely a veil over this 'truth,' a very welcome veil over a pudendum—in other words, a matter of decency and shame, and no more than that. (Nietzsche, *GS*, #64)

Suppose this veil covered the desire for a truth that could not work except as veiled? That is, suppose skepticism marked a certain truth of truth—what then? For like an old woman, Nietzsche produces ultimate skepticism. "*Ultimate skepsis.*—What are man's truths ultimately? Merely his *irrefutable* errors" (Nietzsche, *GS*, #265). Or even refutable errors, properly veiled, claiming nobility. Do women know nobility in this sense? If their greatest art is falsehood? How if women are never in power can they be anything but skeptical of sovereignty, including truth's authority?

Perhaps we are to believe that nobility knows nothing of shame and weakness, all in the name of derogating women.

> *Devotion.*—There are noble women who are afflicted with a certain pov-
> erty of the spirit, and they know no better way to *express* their deepest
> devotion than to offer their virtue and shame. They own nothing higher.
> Often this present is accepted without establishing as profound an obligation
> as the donors had assumed. A very melancholy story! (Nietzsche, *GS*, #65)

> *The strength of the weak.*—All women are subtle in exaggerating
> their weaknesses; they are inventive when it comes to weaknesses in order
> to appear as utterly fragile ornaments who are hurt even by a speck of
> dust. Their existence is supposed to make men feel clumsy, and guilty on
> that score. Thus they defend themselves against the strong and "the law
> of the jungle." (#66)

The noble man—no longer German; if he never was German—knows nothing of weakness or shame, but exists on the highest mountain. Without women or Jews. Women ornament themselves, wear veils; Jews are actors, even when they mawkishly moralize. "In the last analysis he [Schopenhauer] was a Jew (all Jews become mawkish when they moralize). . . . No, the Germans of today are no pessimists. And Schopenhauer was a pessimist, to say it once more, as a good European and *not* as a German.—" (Nietzsche, *GS*, #357). Yet if Jews are actors, and do not nobly and authentically bring us face to face with truth, not even their truth or ours, still we may suppose that truth is an actor, or Jew, or woman.

> *On the problem of the actor.*—The problem of the actor has troubled
> me for the longest time. I felt unsure (and sometimes still do) whether it
> is not only from this angle that one can get at the dangerous concept of
> the "artist"—a concept that has so far been treated with unpardonable
> generosity. Falseness with a good conscience; the delight in simulation
> exploding as a power . . . ; the inner craving for a role and mask, for
> *appearance*; an excess of the capacity for all kinds of adaptations that can
> no longer be satisfied in the service of the most immediate and narrowest
> utility—all of this is perhaps not *only* peculiar to the actor? (Nietzsche,
> *GS*, #361)

Leading us back to the Dionysian. Perhaps Apollinian appearance is mawkish, while Dionysian deception knows the masks of truth. Perhaps women and Jews are both strangers to a European truth that demands a home, a domicile. Perhaps Jews and women and gypsies—all nomads, perhaps, despite interring women in their domiciles, the forcible entombment of women, slaves, and truth without a place.

Suppose truth were nomadic—what then?

> We who are homeless are too manifold and mixed racially and in our descent, being "modern men," and consequently do not feel tempted to participate in the mendacious racial self-admiration and racial indecency that parades in Germany today as a sign of a German way of thinking and that is doubly false and obscene among the people of the "historical sense." We are, in one word—and let this be our word of honor—good Europeans, the heirs of Europe . . . (Nietzsche, *GS*, #377)

In other words, suppose truth were European, not German; perhaps of the world, not European; perhaps of the earth, not human; and more. What if all these exalted gestures toward universality were not to produce a common truth, but proceeded from habitations scattered nomadically throughout the earth?

All these suppositions, returning to a heinous view of women.

> Woman wants to be taken and accepted as a possession, wants to be absorbed into the concept of possession, possessed. Consequently, she wants someone who *takes*, who does not give himself or give himself away; on the contrary, he is supposed to become richer in "himself"—through the accretion of strength, happiness, and faith given him by the woman who gives herself. Woman gives herself away, man acquires more—I do not see how one can get around this natural opposition by means of social contracts or with the best will in the world to be just, desirable as it may be not to remind oneself constantly how harsh, terrible, enigmatic, and immoral this antagonism is. For love, thought of in its entirety as great and full, is nature, and being nature it is in all eternity something "immoral." (Nietzsche, *GS*, #363)

Perhaps the same may be said of truth. Indeed, if Nietzsche represents any truth against the Western tradition of truth, it is to insist that truth, and women, cannot be possessed. Men, and women, and truth, and animals, and more, none can be possessed, though they may be forced, coerced, gripped. All things in the earth surpass possession, but we human beings, we men, insist on possessing, owning, controlling, having all things, including women, and truth, and animals. Yet women are not possessed even when they desire to be possessed; nor are frogs and bats and spiders, and truth. Desiring to gain the limits of truth under God does not make it so. Desiring to lift the veil does not make it so. Desiring justice does not make anything just, though it may remind us, those of us who are skeptics, that we hope to resist injustice. Yet that resistance does not make it so, does not eliminate injustice. To the contrary. It institutes other injustices. The pursuit of truth institutes untruth. The pursuit of women, by men, institutes another reign of men, forcing women underground. Being, nature, love, woman, and truth, and more, are given from the good. That is how I understand "immoral": in the name of the good resistant to the authority of any morality, including the authority of truth.

That is why women return from the sea, where no régime rules. That is why they return—at least, Irigaray returns—with love, against the rule of opposition and domination, resisting castration. Castration is a figure of delimitation, of a cut, that undercuts abundance, a sign of truth. The sea is a figure of fluidity filled with abundance.

As I conclude this chapter, I remind you that I speak of love and truth in abundance, that Irigaray speaks as Nietzsche's lover from under the sea, who loves him despite his monstrous remarks on women struggling to be themselves, to know their truth, as if held in the grip of being—by what? by whom?

And what, we may ask, has love to do with truth? What has beauty, or art? I have spoken of art and beauty in another volume of this project, though I might speak of them again. Beauty is nature's abundance. Woman also is abundance, the same abundance and something different and more. Reminding us of nature's abundance. Love is toward the earth's abundance, however mad that may be. Truth belongs to, recalls abundance even where it cuts. I have returned to castration. Perhaps we cannot escape. But I hope that we recall abundance, recollect its heterogeneities.

Woman is so artistic.

Life is a woman.

Women and Jews are actors, not castrators. Just a little circumcision. With love. In the name of sexual heterogeneity. In the name of truth.

CHAPTER 12

Fecund Exposure

Where truth is correspondence, as we have met it in Aristotle and many of his Western followers, under the sign of being, it seeks to restore or create the same, gathered under the sign of *legein*: saying or thinking or holding being in hand as if it might be restored, or repeated, or inaugurated again. Where truth is *poiēsis,* or woman, for Heidegger and perhaps for Nietzsche, its relation to the same is disrupted, still under the sign of being, framed as gathering. Here truth evokes, or inaugurates, or institutes; it does not reassemble, or repeat, the play of being. The opening of truth is an opening beyond the restoration of being as truth. The question is, how far? And to where?

How far, O Lord, beyond the gathering of being?

Even for God we may think of truth, God's truth, as its gathering: repeating and knowing the word of God. And this is so even where we take God to be absolutely and enigmatically other, beyond the assembling of being, so that no divine word can be repeated, in time, in being; no divine command or promise can be repeated, where every divine gift is unique and singular. God's word does not gather in being, cannot be said, cannot be held or repeated. God's truth is unrepeatable, in the name of singularity. Here the miracle becomes the miracle of truth, that which cannot be repeated. Not beyond being, unreachable, but given as the truth of the unique and singular. Except, perhaps, to us, who cannot think or speak of such a singularity.

Such a thought can be found in Levinas, who speaks of truth in relation to the Thou, in memory of Buber, as community, reciprocity, alliance: *Verbundenheit.* "*Verbundenheit* characterizes the reciprocity of the I-Thou relation of the dialogue where I commit myself to the Thou just because it is absolutely other. The essence of the 'word' does not initially consist in its objective meaning or descriptive possibilities, but in the response that it elicits" (Levinas, *MBTK,* 68). Truth emerges here, belongs to and within, a relation to the other, the absolutely other, beyond any reach of the same, of repetition or reassembling, beyond the reach of being. Yet it calls for, demands, elicits response, touches us with a gift that calls to us to respond, exposes us to endless responsibility. Truth responds to the touch of the other. Truth emerges here in infinite *exposition|exposure*. I insist on recalling the materiality of touch, the embodiment of response and alliance. This truth does not fade into the empty airiness of a singularity and uniqueness beyond the touch of embodiment. Or, at least, it would seem not to.

Even so, Levinas does not resist the pull of spirit, the infinite attraction of subjectivity, as if the call and gift of the good were known, were possible, only to and for us, in a language that seems to evoke an entirely different movement, toward the other, and countless others, beyond return.

> But is not the diachrony of the inspiration and expiration separated by the instant that belongs to an animality? Would animality be the openness upon the beyond essence? But perhaps animality is only the soul's still being too short of breath. In human breathing, in its everyday equality, perhaps we have to already hear the breathlessness of an inspiration that paralyzes essence, that transpierces it with an inspiration by the other, an inspiration that is already expiration, that "rends the soul"! It is the longest breath there is, spirit. Is man not the living being capable of the longest breath in inspiration, without a stopping point, and in expiration, without return? (Levinas, *OB*, 181–82)

Levinas speaks of the absolute difference in being of human spirit, as if he knows, without the slightest empirical investigation, that animals, together with human animality and materiality, cut short the breath of soul and spirit. He cuts short the reach of animal truth, as if truth and the good were given only to Us, we Humans, the only and true heirs of God, returned to us alone in the name of subjectivity. As if God's gifts were given only to Man, though every thing in every place, including the sparrow, is touched by and falls under the eye of God.

I have begun with the subject, or rather, with the Human Subject, forgetting our journey with Ari|Arachne|Ariadne, with bats and spiders and frogs, male and female and other; and plants and trees and vines, as if truth belonged only to human beings, to us, only to those who can see in the light of the sun, within the assembling of being. I have noted the movement in Levinas where bats are forgotten, and more, despised in the light of the noonday sun, in the gathering of being in the breath of the voice. And this despite the fact that bats speak in other voices, know other truths. Of song and night.

I have begun my discussion of Levinas with an interruption, with the breath that divides the man from the bat, though I might have recalled another breath, recalled where spirit divides the man from the woman, restoring us to our materiality. Irigaray speaks of air.

> In what *is* it? Diaphanous, translucid, transparent. Transcendent? Inter-mediary, fluid medium in contact with itself without obstruction, with certain of its parts following their customs: real or decreed "trues." . . .
> What *is* it in? In air. (Irigaray, *OA,* 11–12; my translation)[1]

I have noted how this materialization of spirit into air passes through the spiritualized threshold thickened by materiality, by mucus.[2] The spiritual-ization of truth becomes materialized, embodied, giving birth to something that had to be born from the beginning of time if there were being, the giving birth in bodies, matter, materiality. Air and mucus resist the emp-tiness of a being that would assemble everything together without remain-der. Air and mucus remind us of the materiality of this remainder, remind us of rest.[3]

I return from this inaugural interruption to recall another thought of truth in Levinas, not forgetful of the other, of heterogeneity, nor of the response to that other in the name of truth, but more expressly in terms of exposure *(exposition)* and fecundity *(fécondité).* I return to think with Levinas of truth as an exposure to the fecundity of others so far beyond the gathering of being in saying that it can appear only as interruption, sus-pending, disturbing, the gathering. Truth is exposure to fecundity, abun-dance, given as interruption, touching us and everything else with something else, otherwise.

If truth belongs to being, the ordering, assembling, or saying of being, bringing to light what is, then the possibility of truth depends on the opening of being to what is other, including what is not. This is Heidegger's account of truth. What makes this opening possible, what allows being to show itself, and to whom, divides Heidegger from Levinas. In part, Levinas's movement restores the subject in its subjectivity, whose infinity interrupts the identity of essence with the possibility of truth. "Substitution is signi-fication. Not a reference from one term to another, as it appears thematized in the said, but substitution as the very subjectivity of a subject, interrup-tion of the irreversible identity of the essence" (Levinas, *OB,* 13). The open-ing comes from Being, Heidegger replies, not from the subject. The opening comes from being's difference, which interrupts the assembling of being itself. Levinas names the origin of the opening and interruption that allows being to appear in its truth, names it subject, subjectivity, God or Man. We might respond that being is no name, has no name, does not gather. Yet both Heidegger and Levinas understand the possibility of truth as some-thing that absolutely privileges humanity *by an abyss of essence.* I under-stand the gift of the good, the gift of truth, as endless resistance to, interruption of, the privilege and authority of being. The good interrupts every absolute privilege, including its own.

Perhaps the most striking of all portrayals of this interruption, essential to the very possibility of truth, can be found in Foucault, who tells us that the political question is truth itself, demanding interruption, but who speaks elsewhere of the prose of the world, a world teeming with multiplicity and heterogeneity, where everything resembles, connects with, and interrupts everything else. Together with endless similitude is endless interruption.

> *Convenientia, aemulatio, analogy,* and *sympathy* tell us how the world must fold in upon itself, duplicate itself, reflect itself, or form a chain with itself so that things can resemble one another. They tell us what the paths of similitude are and the directions they take; but not where it is, how one sees it, or by what mark it may be recognized. (Foucault, *OT,* 25–26)

Foucault speaks of the displacement of similitudes by signs and language. Unless reality is displaced within itself, it cannot show itself. The assembling of being, mirrored endlessly in the prose of the world, can present itself as truth only by an interruption that is so minute as to be unrecognizable in being except as interruption.

> Resemblances require a signature, for none of them would ever become observable were it not legibly marked. . . . Every resemblance receives a signature; but this signature is no more than an intermediate form of the same resemblance. As a result, the totality of these marks, sliding over the great circle of similitudes, forms a second circle which would be an exact duplication of the first, point by point, were it not for that tiny degree of displacement which causes the sign of sympathy to reside in an analogy, that of analogy in emulation, that of emulation in convenience, which in turn requires the mark of sympathy for its recognition. (Foucault, *OT,* 28–29)

The mark of truth requires displacement, interruption, so minute and tiny as to take place as a repetition, like the Eternal Return, another tiny interruption of the same that makes an infinite difference.

Levinas gives the name of exposure to this interruption of being, the displacement that allows being to show itself as truth, truth together with untruth. It lies in the responsiveness he describes as belonging to the subject who is called by the gift of the absolute other. Exposure is responsiveness, given as a gift, as a call. I offer a passage that apparently has nothing to do with truth, but which I understand to have everything to do with it.

The intention *toward another,* when it has reached its peak, turns out to belie intentionality. *Toward another* culminates in a *for another,* a suffering for his suffering, without light, that is, without measure, quite different from the purely negative blinding of Fortune which only seems to close her eyes so as to give her riches arbitrarily. Arising at the apex of essence, goodness is *other* than being. (Levinas, *OB,* 18)

The relation of truth of another emerges from a call toward another, a call that becomes for another, caught up in goodness, given from the good. The other touches us, and others, with infinity without measure, given in abundance and fecundity, other than, interrupting the gathering of being. Truth demands such an exposure. I do not repeat intentionality, subjectivity, or humanity. I remind you of Ari and other bats who are said to be blind to truth in the light, who are others for us and who are exposed to others in their truth.

If we wished to speak the language of origins, of what comes before, precedes, if we wished to speak of primordiality, we might say that truth is a response to, presupposes, the heterogeneity of the other, a multiplicity beyond and before any scale or measure. We are called to truth by an archaic beyond measure. And if we are not so called, not open from the first to inexhaustible responsiveness, to endless responsibility, we are not open to truth, but at whatever point we cut it off, cease to be open to truth, cease responding to something beyond the possession of truth. In this sense, interrupting origins, truth is a response to a touch beyond possession, and we can never possess the truth, retain or gather any truth. The truth we hold stops within the assembling of being, responding to something that demands endless interruption. Levinas speaks of this cessation in the abyss of essence as the seduction of being that holds us in its gathering despite the petition, the call, from elsewhere. "If one is deaf to the petition that sounds in questioning and even under the apparent silence of the thought that questions itself, everything in a question will be oriented to truth, and will come from the essence of being" (Levinas, *OB,* 26). The seduction of being for a pure subject. "Truth can consist only in the exposition of being to itself, in self-consciousness" (p. 26). Yet even within this account of truth in being, gathered into itself, we find the inescapable presence of exposure beyond any truth, being inadequate with itself. "Truth can consist only in the exposition of being to itself, in a singular inadequacy with itself which is also an equality, a partition in which the part counts for the whole, is the image of the whole" (p. 61). Or put another way, "Phenomenality, the exhibition of being's essence in truth, is a permanent presupposition of the philosophical tradition of the West" (p. 132). The adequacy of being's truth is presupposed within a singular inadequacy.

Against this gathering in presence, this exhibition of the one for the other in truth, Levinas speaks of responsibility for the sake of the other. "The conjuncture in which a man is responsible for other men, the ethical relationship, which is habitually considered as belonging to a derivative or founded order, has been throughout this work approached as irreducible. It is structured as the-one-for-the-other. It signifies outside of all finality and every system . . ." (Levinas, *OB*, 135). The simplest reading of this irreducibility, Kantian in spirit, is that ethics and truth inhabit two different realms, though they share the same territory. Levinas replies that the one for the other makes it possible for truth to appear, the saying within the said. Speaking of Descartes, of the *cogito* as a responsibility, a touch from the other, not closed or finalized in me alone, he names the condition of truth, present, unnamed in Descartes.

> It is the subjectivity of a man of flesh and blood, more passive in its extradition to the other than the passivity of effects in a causal chain, for it is beyond the unity of apperception of the *I think*, which is actuality itself. It is a being torn up from oneself for another in the giving to the other of the breast out of one's own mouth. (p. 142)

The other, that whose truth would be known, presents itself as demanding a passivity beyond passivity, an infinite letting-be, without which that other's truth cannot exercise a claim on me. The claim of truth is passivity, vulnerability, demanding from the one who responds an infinite responsiveness, giving oneself over to the other, proffered as exposure. Nothing less is demanded of us by truth. It is given as the glory of the Infinite, as inexhaustible exposure and responsibility.

> For subjectivity to signify unreservedly, it would then be necessary that the passivity of its exposure to the other not be immediately inverted into activity, but expose itself in its truth; a passivity of passivity is necessary, and, in the glory of the Infinite ashes from which an act could not be born anew. Saying is this passivity of passivity and this dedication to the other, this sincerity. (Levinas, *OB*, 142–43)

I would leave aside subjectivity, even activity, and with them saying and sincerity. These breathe of subjects who give themselves the task of mastery, where truth demands releasement of mastery, letting-be. Truth demands that we, or others, open up ourselves to countless others, arises in a relation of an opening beyond the possibilities of being. This infinite opening is glory, and we cannot imagine truth without it, a truth that would cut off the opening before its infinity. Yet perhaps we should not presume to begin with subjects, agents, who would master others and whose yearning for mastery must be cut short. Perhaps we should not begin by demanding truth. The gathering of being in truth presupposes that things touch each other, reaching for their truth, in immeasurable glory, given from the good. In relation to others, touching them in their heterogeneity, truth emerges in response, a response that presupposes the infinite and cuts it off. I would think of a call to endless responsiveness without demand.

Levinas speaks of "the glory of the Infinite" as "the anarchic identity of the subject flushed out without being able to slip away" (Levinas, *OB,* 144), expressed as responsibility, as "here I am" (p. 145). I understand this presentness, this "I am," as exposure more than subjectivity, responsibility, or identity, as touch. To know, to be, is first of all to touch, to be exposed to others and to expose oneself to others. Exposure is witness: I am here, exposed to you and others, in endless witness to the immeasurable fecundity in which we are joined, in touch, in the earth. "There is witness, a unique structure, an exception to the rule of being, irreducible to representation, only of the Infinite. The Infinite does not appear to him that bears witness to it. On the contrary the witness belongs to the glory of the Infinite" (Levinas, *OB,* 146). This glory, infinite and abundant belonging, all give forth the possibility of truth. Perhaps more directly, the idea of a found truth, stumbled upon, ready to hand, perhaps as correspondence or something else, maybe enchantment, lights up the world already given. But the call, or responsibility, or touch from which we may say the truth issues forth—the will or demand or call to know, to be in the truth, from which the authority of truth issues forth—is an insistence, a critique, that owes something to an endless exposure. This exposure, to the infinite as Levinas says, is itself without measure and truth respond. Truth responds to something beyond, or other than, the being before us, interrupting its essence and measure. The gathering of being, in its truth, gives itself forth as displacement, otherwise.

The idea of truth, as I understand it, dwells in and responds to a call of an abundance in and beyond being, interrupting, disturbing, and calling for the gathering of being. Truth presupposes both that being can be gathered and responds with interruption to the impossibility of that gathering, to the debt to which that gathering responds, the injustice of things together that cannot allow themselves to be gathered together. Whitehead calls it evil.

> The ultimate evil in the temporal world is deeper than any specific evil. It lies in the fact that the past fades, that time is a "perpetual perishing." . . . The nature of evil is that the characters of things are mutually obstructive. Thus the depths of life require a process of selection. . . . Selection is at once the measure of evil, and the process of its evasion. (Whitehead, *PR,* 340).

The characters of things are mutually obstructive, heterogeneous. The call of being, of things together, reveals the impossibility of gathering them all together without exclusion. As being. As truth. In truth. This recognition is exposure, both the gathering and its impossibility—its evil. It belongs to being as exposure to the heterogeneity that disallows the gathering of being as truth. All given from the good.

Said as truth, in truth, the evil of which Whitehead speaks forbids the possibility of total, gathered, assembled truth. Things cannot be all together in their truth without violence, destruction, obstruction. Yet truth calls from this gathering, and we find ourselves called by things to know them, to touch them, in our exposure to each other. We are exposed to both the appearing or touching or showing of things together, their gathering, and in that gathering, its obstruction, its impossibility. The call is given in the gift. The gift of truth is the gift together of the call to truth, to know, to witness, and its impossibility, enacted as interruption.

Levinas speaks of the paradox of the infinite in the appearance of truth, recalling Kant.

> The ethical is the field outlined by the paradox of an Infinite in relation-ship with the finite without being belied in this relationship. Ethics is the breakup of the originary unity of transcendental apperception, that is, it is the beyond of experience. Witnessed, and not thematized, in the sign given to the other, the Infinite signifies out of responsibility for the other, out of the-one-for-the-other, a subject supporting everything, subject to everything, that is, suffering for everyone, but charged with everything, without having had to decide for this taking charge, which is gloriously amplified in the measure that it is imposed. (Levinas, *OB,* 148).

He speaks in the language of the subject, of subjectivity. Yet witness, as touch and exposure, may be thought without the least vestige of subjectivity. To know, for truth to appear, things as well as humans touch, are exposed to each other, charged by something far exceeding the truth whose measure is imposed. The idea of truth—even as correspondence—glows with the radiance and glory of something other than the thematizing—the measuring and gathering—of truth, rings with nature's cacophony, other-wise. Within the idea of any particular truth is a fecundity and abundance to which truth, and touch, and being bear witness.

In this sense of the abundance given, of the giving and abundance, we may think of witness and exposure as given "before" truth as the injustice and debt to which truth as measure responds. Truth appears in a debt to what far exceeds it in its fecundity and abundance, to which all things in their exposure are witness. Things bear witness to each other beyond the slightest possibility of totality—in Whitehead. I add to Whitehead something more ethical, if that is possible, that in the obstruction things pass away, vanish beyond the possibility of witness. Truth, The Truth, demands and presupposes a recovery that is destroyed beyond repair in every institution of truth. That is its violence. And being's violence. But truth demands that we know, or if we cannot know at least know that we cannot know something of the sacrifices of truth in the impossibility of gathering, collecting, assembling. Truth bears witness to its own disaster. "The witness is a traitor" (Lyotard, *I*, 204). Demanding interruption.

This thought, of witness, truth as witness, touches something beyond objectivity, resists the possibility of the neutrality of truth. The one—or many—who would know truth, the expression and representation of truth, bear witness in this truth to the other, and more, to the other's otherness, beyond any correspondence or adequacy, beyond neutrality. And still others. The neutrality of adequate truth defies the interruption, the infinite exposure and vulnerability, within which truth emerges, the endless debt to truth's injustices, all obscured, obstructed, within truth's neutrality and objectivity. Throughout our previous discussions, from Plato to Descartes and beyond, to Kant, the betrayals of truth, in error, untruth, violence and destruction, the oppressions and exclusions of knowledge and truth, have repeatedly shown themselves as witnesses to the betrayals of truth, to the betrayals of witness. Perhaps authority remains the most violent of all violences, the most treacherous of all betrayals, in witness. For we would hope to know, to witness, a knowledge and truth without authority, always finding that authority rules, excluding and oppressing others. Not just Western reason, or European truth, but truth itself institutes authority, against which truth itself must wage endless war. The war of truth is the betrayal of witness. And still we seek a truth of peace, without authority, seek to witness our own betrayal.

In Levinas, witness becomes prophecy, realized in sincerity. "[T]his responsibility prior to commitment, is precisely the other in the same, inspiration and prophecy, the *passing itself* of the Infinite"; "That the glory of the Infinite is glorified only by the signification of the-one-for-the-other, as sincerity, that in my sincerity the Infinite passes the finite, that the Infinite comes to pass there, is what makes the plot of ethics primary, and what makes language irreducible to an act among acts" (Levinas, *OB*, 150). I resist the deification of the Infinite, as if the Infinite had a name. I resist the privilege of language, reinstituting the privilege of The Human. But the inexhaustible demand and promise of truth, the endless beckoning of nature's abundance and fecundity to which truth is witness and response, that inexhaustibility calls within every place and being for the possibility of truth. The possibility of critique, the untruth in every truth that allows it to come forth as true, is an infinite call to infinite responsiveness, however we may experience our limits. The difference again is that this infinite call is a debt that works against any name of the infinite, against any measure. Including witness and abundance.

In the language of ethics, Levinas speaks of justice, realized in the third party who arises from the one for the other. "In the proximity of the other, all the others than the other obsess me, and already this obsession cries out for justice, demands measure and knowing, is consciousness" (Levinas, *OB*, 158). I understand this justice and measure as truth, one of the measures of justice, of restitution. It emerges, Levinas says, from the one for the other.

> All the others that obsess me in the other do not affect me as examples of the same genus united with my neighbor by resemblance or common nature . . . The others concern me from the first. . . . My relationship with the other as neighbor gives meaning to my relations with all the others. . . . Justice is impossible without the one that renders it finding himself in proximity. (p. 159)

I substitute, or understand here, truth for, truth as justice. The possibility of justice demands proximity—infinite exposure and vulnerability to the abundance and fecundity of the other. And so with truth. The possibility, the meaning, of truth demands infinite exposure and vulnerability to the abundance and fecundity of others. All in the infinite and endless response to others and their heterogeneity. All in the endless and inexhaustible response to the infinite abundance of heterogeneity.

I call this responsiveness "exposure," after Levinas, adjacent both to responsibility and to proximity. The call of the good, realized as truth, demands—calls for, beckons, yearns toward—inexhaustible proximity, exposure to what would be known as true beyond any adequacy or correspondence, beyond magic, mystery, and enchantment, if these measure instituted truth. I speak of a truth that lies enframed in critique, touched by incessant untruth, where the task, the responsibility, and the authority of truth insist on unceasing proximity and openness to untruth. I do not mean vigilance against untruth, the destruction of error, though many have understood truth as such a vigilance, caught up in endless war. Yet even within this vigilance, taken as an obligation, is an opennness and alertness beyond any reach of adequacy or correspondence, beyond any institution. And beyond this vigilance, however infinite or inexhaustible, is the critique of the exclusions and violences of vigilance, the cost to human and other lives, to the earth, of a vigilance that would destroy to know, to bring into truth. And beyond this beyond, however inexhaustible, there circulates another critique, witness to the exclusion and destruction of every critique. The witness is a traitor. Exposure is the precondition of this witness together with its betrayal.

What—if we may speak of "what"—we are exposed to in exposure, as witness, in truth, or justice, or any instituted good, is first, the earth, the giving of the good; then second, its abundance, the general, excessive economy of goods in circulation beyond any measure, including the measure of truth. Levinas speaks of fecundity, a relation to time.

> Both my own and non-mine, a possibility of myself but also a possibility of the other, of the Beloved *[l'Aimée]*, my future does not enter into the logical essence of the possible. The relation with such a future, irreducible to the power over possibles, we shall call fecundity. (Levinas, *TI*, 267)
>
> Infinite being, that is, every recommencing being—which could not bypass subjectivity, for it could not recommence without it—is produced in the guise of fecundity. (p. 268)
>
> In fecundity the I transcends the world of light—not to dissolve into the anonymity of the *there is,* but in order to go further than the light, to go *elsewhere [ailleurs].* (p. 268)

Fecundity is contrasted with being as subjectivity, resisting the assembling of being within the ek-static dehiscence of totality. Levinas resists the assembling of being as difference in Heidegger in the name of the "power of the subject" (Levinas, *TI*, 267). Myself, my subjectivity, my *I* all give fecundity its otherness, against the anonymity of the *there is,* the *es gibt,* the gift and the good. Fecundity is held against the anonymity of being in the name of myself and the Other, the other subject.

Yet this purported anonymity, given as the gift from the good, is all we have with which to speak against the anonymity of being, to speak critically, even when we speak from where we are, we subjects, if we will speak of the betrayal at the heart of subjectivity. The subject, as witness, betrays; the subject is a traitor. Not the only traitor, not the worst, or best, or measurable on a comparable scale. But the subject—rather, The Subject—betrays the gift of being, always in a relation of mastery or non-mastery, mastery's resistance: vulnerability and passivity.

If we were to speak of touch, together with heterogeneity and abundance, we might understand fecundity to know nothing at its heart of subjectivity, with the subject's betrayals, to express the openness of a future and its possibilities and heterogeneities without the slightest sense of power over them, mastery in them. To speak of power and mastery is always to speak of a subject, however obliquely, an autonomous subject who rules and masters and controls, whose future is mastery and its betrayal. We may resist such mastery in ethical terms, an ethics, given from the good, which knows nothing of mastery or of subjects, but circulates in trust and touch.

If we were to speak of touch in intimacy, the proximity and vulnerability of touch, of love and intimacy, we might understand fecundity to know nothing at its heart of subjectivity but something of abundance and its call, given from the good. "Intimacy is not expressed by a *thing* except on one condition: that this *thing* be essentially the opposite of a *thing,* the opposite of a product, of a commodity—a consumption and a sacrifice" (Bataille, *AS,* 1, 132). Bataille contrasts thing and subject. In the name of sacrifice, thing and subject express intimacy, along with truth, the intimacy of truth, as cursed. Fecundity and abundance are cursed in truth by the intimacy of touch, and show themselves as interruptions given by the intimacy of touch.

The infinite, recommencing being expresses fecundity and abundance in intimacy and love, where things touch each other, and still others. I call the abundance inexhaustibility. I call the touch cherishment. It is not more of the same—or less, or other. It can be named as the Eternal Return, more of the same with a vengeance, so much the same as to demolish its authority. It is not the assembling or reassembling of being but the very possibility of that assembling, bearing witness and the authority to witness, to see and to gather being in its place, realized as interruption. If being assembles, or we assemble it, if it gathers in the touch of things together, the one steps forth from it as witness or authority, demanding and imposing privilege, if only that of the gaze, to gaze and see, to be gazed upon, from a space of touch and circulation. The abundance and fecundity of circulation is the temporality of witness and prophecy, realized as interruption.

Heidegger speaks of abundance *(Fülle);* Levinas speaks of fecundity *(la fécondité).* In their contrast and relation, we find that one or the other lacks something of abundance or fecundity, in Being's giving or the subject's proximity. Heidegger's abundance knows too little of the good. Levinas's fecundity knows too little of its own betrayal. I prefer to speak of general and restricted economy, borrowing from and augmenting Bataille.[4] Restricted economy is where work is done, understood by Bataille in terms of use (Bataille, *AS,* 1, 59). Yet there is also useless expenditure. General economy is this extravagance. Bataille speaks of general economy in a binary relation, as if we might choose to accumulate or to squander. And in another binary, if we choose to spend, we may choose to do so "gloriously or catastrophically" (1, 21). General economy is a surplus of wealth, energy, or forces that must be spent.

I understand all "musts" to belong to restricted economy. If we must spend or die, accumulate or die, spend or be destroyed, we are under the rule of limits, of life and death. General economy as I understand it is not restricted economy, but in the sense of otherwise, something very different from, resistant to and interrupting restriction and limit, belonging to unlimit, otherwise, immeasure. Abundance is not too much of this or that, too much energy to spend, but perhaps not energy at all, perhaps nothing. Paraphrasing Bataille, abundance, like sovereignty, is NOTHING. "The main thing is always the same: sovereignty is NOTHING" (Bataille, *AS*, 3, 430). Sovereignty, which Bataille says is nothing, is the consumption demanded by general economy, which I say is nothing.[5]

This nothing is abundance, fecundity, general economy. As nothing, it interrupts the reign of being, endlessly instituting something. As nothing it reminds us of the debt, the obligation, the touch of the other, otherwise, beyond. In truth, it reminds us of the debt evoked by knowledge, to know beyond any limits, to exercise truth's authority. We are reminded of the earth's abundance, or fecundity, the endless circulation of things and goods in general economy. But truth is always instituted in restricted economy. General economy, abundance, is accursed *(maudite)*, the curse I call sacrifice. Humanity, truth, every kind, is "nature transfigured by the *curse*" (Bataille, *AS*, 1, 78), by exclusion and taboo. The witness betrays, every witness, truth betrays, is cursed. Yet every restricted economy touches general economy. It touches it with excess, excess authority, excess objectivity, excess neutrality. It imposes a régime on truth, which always circulates in general economy except where it is brought to a stop, in a régime of restricted economy.

The curse is the contaminated side of general economy. We can do no work, can create no culture, cannot live, propagate, care for ourselves and others, cannot even care for the earth and its kinds, without sacrifice, exclusion, disaster. Growth and accumulation is sacrifice. Restricted economies are economies of growth and sacrifice. Exposure is infinite sensitivity to the curse, to what is, what might have been, and what has been destroyed. The curse, like the witness's betrayal, is the visible mark of the good.

We may hope to speak against the restrictions of truth in restricted economy, hope that the idea of truth itself might work against restrictions, always to fall into restrictions. To witness is to betray. Truth is cursed. Without the curse there is no truth.

That is how far, O Lord, to the next betrayal. In circulation.

Leading back to heterogeneity, to another interruption, where Irigaray criticizes Levinas. For when she asks him, "is there otherness outside of sexual difference?" (Irigaray, *QEL*, 178), she answers:

> The function of the other sex as an alterity irreducible to myself eludes Levinas for at least two reasons:
> He knows nothing of communion in pleasure. . . .
> . . . he substitutes the son for the feminine. (pp. 180–81)

In the face, the gaze of the subject, Levinas does not consider the heterogeneity of the other, feminine subject, or other others. Nor does Irigaray consider other heterogeneities beside the feminine. The witnessing offers up sacrifices to its gaze. The anonymity of ethics, the universality of rules or the abstraction of the Other, endlessly sacrifices something to its installation. Ethics betrays itself, betrays the very movement that calls it forth. That is the betrayal of the witness, to betray the witnessing.

The betrayal of truth is to impose its authority as if infinite and inexhaustible exposure did not divide and resist every authority. The betrayal of truth is to reduce and limit and circumscribe the earth's abundance.

CHAPTER 13

Abundant Truth

As we approach the end of our journey in truth, together with bats and countless natural creatures and things, we might hope to know what truth is, gathering being again under the sign of truth, beings together in truth. That truth, what truth is in truth, has been spoken of throughout our journey, and others, truth in being, the gathering of being in saying: adequacy, correspondence, coherence, mystery and enchantment, in or behind or given to being and saying. *Alētheia* belongs no less to being than does adequation, together with mystery and enchantment. We hope to say the truth of what truth is, in truth, gathered up into being by saying. That truth would be the truth of being, being in truth, gathered, assembled, and instituted in restitution to the good, memory of something in truth for which it is an endless response—not beyond, *au delà,* outside being and truth, but otherwise than, other in, being's other, as and in truth, interrupting the assembling. All in memory of the abundance of the good, which is otherwise forgotten. A memory that interrupts the gathering of being in the name of heterogeneity and abundance. A creative memory that some have known as imagination, others as unforgetting, *anamnēsis.*

And thus we come to a memory of truth as given from the good, forgotten, otherwise: the truth of truth given from the good, interrupting the reign of truth. What, we may ask, have we forgotten, in truth, instituting its rule? What, we may wish to know, might we remember, in truth, within its authority? Both truths in and of being, reassembled and reinstituted—I would say, hostage to being, forgetting the good. But we may also wish to know, or say, or do something else, in memory of forgetting, of the very possibility of forgetting, or remembering, or knowing in truth, which we may not be able to say or know or remember in truth, but in some way reach for, grasp, and touch, exposed to and vulnerable in our exposure, of truth. We might wish to speak of or touch the touching from whose exposure truth allows itself to be gathered, toward which it pays a debt, truth in restitution for the gift of touch, or something else, in abundance.

I speak of this exposure in abundance as plenishment, recalling the forgotten gift from the fecundity of the good which institutes itself as truth, in truth, in being. Plenishment does not strive toward something other than being, nor other than truth, belongs to neither truth nor being, but exceeds them otherwise, cares for the endless abundance of things in memory of disaster, mourning for loss. It is never a possession, never possessed or gathered, where every truth and being offers itself as a possession whose mastery we may hope to claim with authority. For plenishment, possession and mastery are disasters evoked in building the edifice of truth's authority, in making a home, a dwelling, for truth gathered in being. Culture, and cultural authority, are disasters required for work, for gathering. Plenishment is the giving of the possibility of authority that resists its own authority, that interrupts the founding of authority—though as judgment, along with every other judgment, it gives and seeks authority. In this giving of authority we find truth in being. And perhaps we can find no truth, in or out of being, that does not brush up against, touch too much with too much force, the authority of being, that does not insist too much on too much authority. The response in judgment to this excessive force and authority, remembering the good and endless disasters, is plenishment. It begins in cherishment and struggles with the betrayals of sacrifice, the inescapable disasters of identity, essence, and authority. In this triangle of cherishment, sacrifice, and plenishment circulate the gifts from the good, an abundance surpassing any authority and measure. These givings circulate as general economy, instituting the restrictions that slow the general circulation of gifts to become possessions and measures in restricted economies.

I return from plenishment to respond more carefully and caringly to the touch of cherishment. For without things touching each other, exposed to each other in abundance, they cannot open toward each other in their truth, whatever that truth may be taken to be, under whatever restrictions. This exposure in and to abundance is cherishment, marking the abundance of general economy, marked by the care and love and desire and will that dissipate its alleged neutrality. This neutrality, claimed to belong to objective, rational knowledge, claimed also, if perversely, to belong to indifferent nature, the nature whose members cannot know in truth, denies the gift of knowledge and truth from the good, disclaims its own abundance and the fecundity of truth and desire for truth. Yet truth is more than the juxtaposition of one thing to another, but is unmeasurable in exposure and vulnerability, where we are exposed to the embrace of others in the heterogeneity of the touch, the inexhaustibility of others gathered together in the archaic impossibility of gathering we know as sacrifice.

The care and love and desire that belong to cherishment's exposure are at one and the same time and place wills to measure, to work, and excesses surpassing any measure. This will is the endless desire to gather that institutes truth under the sign of being, born in the excess and abundance of desire and the desire for truth. This excess is the boundless desire that surpasses any desire to own in recognizing its own desirability, thereby interrupting the authority of any stopping place for desire, any place to master and possess any thing or its truth, interrupted by fascination and seduction interrupting the limits of desire. In this doubling of the excesses of desire and love, truth emerges in the gathering and displaces itself by interruption, another fascination, another fetishization, inexhaustible yearning for mastery of truth, the fascination of gathering in truth. The possibility of such a gathering is instituted in the possibility of interruption, given from the abundance of the good. This includes all the truths we have touched in our journey, from adequation through *alētheia* through mystery to enchantment.

We come to truth given from the good as cherishment, authorized by sacrifice as the exclusion of authorized truth, the truth whose truth is plenishment. This truth is not the truth grasped in the hand or eye, held or fixed in place as if possessed and owned—though such truths are not to be despised—but the endless promise in such truths to reach beyond themselves, interrupting themselves in every gathering and place, promoting ceaseless questions and inexhaustible critique, witness and interruption, responding to nature's abundance and endless giving from the good. This promise of truth interrupting truth reaches beyond the limits of what is held in place, touched by vulnerability and exposure. Being and its truths, held in place, owned and possessed, always promise and demand something that exceeds the hold of that place. Is this claim to truth true? The question calls for incessant answers, assurances, and adjustments. Is this claim to truth truthfully expressed? Another question demanding countless assurances. The thought of truth opens within an inexhaustible debt borne by witness and exposure, to bring truth forth from falsity, to seek out and overcome error, to link smaller truths together in larger aggregates: the endless pursuit of truths in their restricted places to overcome the restrictions, to establish and criticize truth's authority. Every authority. Each task is inexhaustible, interrupting the measures that truth's work may institute. Each task emerges from the good, given from the good, within the debt and touch of such gifts, called by, responsible to, witness of something more than the possession and place of every truth.

The gift, or giving, of truth emerges as plenishment in a doubly limitless movement, first, the desire or care or love, the cherishment, in each touch of one thing by another, reaching toward the other, and still others, abundant beyond any task or work or place. Each thing or being contains or promises something immeasurable, exceeding the limits of any place, something inexhaustible, always more. The more, the excess, the inexhaustibility of abundance is immeasurable, incalculable, not another, larger, aggregation. Nature's abundance, given from the good in general economy, circulates beyond the limits of great and small, still belonging to restricted economy. Limit gives way everywhere to unlimit in the circulation of general economy. And second, this unlimited movement of truth in which every truth emerges in and together with its untruth, an untruth that institutes an inexhaustible project of witness and critique, is a movement of promise, debt, and restitution, of sacrifice and betrayal. Every limit destroys, violates the promise of another limit, something different, another inexhaustible truth or being in its place, or adjacent. This is Anaximander's understanding, that the ordinance of time—being, its identities and truths—pay restitution for endless injustices, for the exclusions and oppositions that found its identity and truth, in memory of the wounds, the sacrifices, and curses that institute truth. The institution and promulgation of each truth destroys countless other truths. Cherishment is the exposure within every touch, everywhere, to the abundance of things, witness thereby to the violence and injustice of sacrifice. I do not regard cherishment as uniquely human, but find it everywhere in nature, in every touch. Every thing that can respond responds to the truths it finds in others. Every thing touches others in their inexhaustible being and truth. As promise and desire.

The exposure named by cherishment is not teleological, oriented to fulfill tasks, satisfy needs, overcome lacks, though all of these may be understood as restitutions, all come forth in exposure. Before or within every such need and lack is a relation, an exposure, touch, and desire, toward and for the other, touching the other, boundless and inexhaustible in promise and debt, the inexhaustible call of that other which every task and project reduces to limit by exclusion. Cherishment is the endless response to goods in general circulation, the giving of things to each other as goods, from the good. The gift is given from the good, where each thing, measured and finite, is the gift, but as good, as inexhaustible and infinite, circulates in the giving of other things in the inexhaustible exposure of cherishment. Truth emerges in its authority and debt within inexhaustible exposure bearing inexhaustible promises of witness, to criticize itself, to foster and nurture other truths, bringing them forth, to light and sound and touch. The bringing emerges from and within the debt of cherishment. Everywhere in the earth things circulate beyond the limits of every place, giving rise to the possibility of such limits, including the limits of truth.

We sometimes speak of desire as exceeding limit, including the desire for desire. We sometimes speak of love as exceeding limit, disturbing the hold of every limit, including the limits of truth. Yet in the bounds of its limits, truth too exceeds limit, exceeds the limit of every gathered truth. For within every correspondence, every saying of what is in its truth, lie endless and inexhaustible debts and promises, to criticize, to know, to verify, to seek, to remember, endless exposures beyond the measures of truth. Truth is filled with inexhaustible desire in inexhaustible ways, the desire for truth, the desire to control and limit truth, the desire that demands that we go beyond every limit established in truth. All of these, desires and promises, belong to cherishment: exposure to the good everywhere, in every thing, beyond the institution of every limit.

Even so, there are limits to truth, in truth. The excess of cherishment is inexhaustible exposure, but an exposure and touch before the limits of every place, still in general circulation, always in restricted places. To be, to be in truth, is to be limited, in place, within unlimited exposure. To be, in truth, is to exceed every limit and place, as interruption, in a place. The ideality of truth belongs to truth in its very possibility, touching particular places. This marks the inexhaustible abundance of truth we and Ari have noted throughout our journey from Plato to the present, an ideality without which we could not imagine truth, yet one which repeatedly takes oppressive forms, instituting arbitrary and extreme authority, excluding those who do not measure up to this authority. All truths oppress and exclude in their incessant movement—the endless circulation of gifts from the good. But within the oppression and exclusion we can see the ideality of the good.

The ideality of truth and being is cherishment, a double ideality of gathering and saying together with the inexhaustible and unsayable singularity and excess that is never said, never gathered, whose gathering is disaster, destruction, and death. Within truth we know an ideality that allows for and demands endless critique, representing and circulating its ideality, the ideality of truth, always present, as saying, gathering, assembling, and the possibility of critique, always present as error and untruth. Both of these presences show themselves as plenishment. Both may be understood as exposure. Exposure is the immeasurable debt to ideality, exposed as both gathering and disaster. This ideality is cherishment. I think of it as general economy, interrupting every restricted economy.

Cherishment is the general economy and circulation of goods, the movement of desire, filled with intimate movements, gatherings, and interruptions. The full movement is general economy, present everywhere as interruption. The most prevalent form of interruption is the gathering of movement in place, interrupting its endless flow to build a home, to institute a territory. Cherishment demands work to fulfill its ideality, otherwise a circulation without fulfillment. Yet the gathering in place for work and fulfillment is always disaster, always sacrifice. The ideality of cherishment makes disaster unavoidable. Every gathering in place requires limits and walls that exclude and oppress, wound and harm.

Truth is no exception, perhaps the most visible example. Truth is dangerous, risky, demands channels to regulate its hazards. That is its ethical|political truth. Cherishment exceeds every boundary and measure, surrounds us with immeasurable debts and promises. Truth responds to this immeasurable debt and risk with measures, yet contains abundance beyond measure in heart and soul, filled thereby with greater dangers. We have seen this double play of unlimited exposure in our journey from Plato to the present, especially perhaps in Descartes, where science's limitless yearning for truth is matched by a boundless will so to regulate reason as to ensure the starvation of truth. At the expense of bats and other creatures.

Science—Western science—is a wonderful, inexhaustible response to the inexhaustible desire for truth's ideality. Science is one of the ways in which we are immeasurably exposed to the earth's abundance, the teeming abundance of life in every drop, the worlds in every world, the play of forces throughout nature, and more. If we have lost something of the awe we might feel before the Olympian gods, we have gained something of awe before the fecundity of things. It is science's task to reveal something of the earth's abundance as truth. Yet that task has imposed constraints on the scope of science itself, revealed with two dimensions. The ideality of the task to gather and show the world's truths has imposed forceful restrictions on the possibilities of science. Only this method, some say, shows us truth, the ideality of method, of science. One dimension, then, to the ideality of truth leads to the reign of science and scientific truth, instituting its overweening authority, excluding everything that is not science, every possibility of truth that does not conform to the rule of science. The other dimension of the ideality of truth, responsive to the ideality but not the authority of science, recalls the inexhaustible debt that truth imposes on science to seek ever more hidden, forgotten, obscured truths, to pursue the very small and the very large, but especially those truths covered over by science's authority and scientific practices. The earth's abundance promotes the abundance of science and more abundance, more truths than any science, than any institution of sciences, more than science itself can gather in any place. In this extreme sense, science interrupts the gathering of truth in any one place, including that of science's authority. An anarchistic science returns to resist the very rules that grant it authority, not against the truth of science but against the excesses of its authority.[1] An anarchistic science witnesses the curse under which science gains its glory. Nature's anarchy, *tuchē,* demands the gathering that betrays it. The end of science, and art, in Kant and Hegel, betray the abundance of the world.

Science is given by and is responsive to the earth's abundance and truth's ideality, belonging to the general economy of the circulation of goods, gathering and interrupting the gathering as truth. But like every sphere of work, science is also restricted economy, at any moment and in any place, limited and limiting, doing its work by restriction and exclusion, imposing authority, instituting disaster. The circulation of goods and truths is cherishment and sacrifice together, driven by desire to know and to gather the most hidden and forgetful truths, always obscuring and excluding some truths to promote others. Science is plenishment, where cherishment and sacrifice meet, given from the good in the tasks given to science to pursue truth. It is impossible to gather all truths together. Some are incompatible. What Whitehead says of evil is true of truth. "The nature of evil is that the characters of things are mutually obstructive" (Whitehead, *PR,* 340). The nature of truth is that the characters of things are open to gathering within their mutual destruction. In this sense, the ideality of truth recalls its evil. Science's historical failing is not to bear this evil openly in its self-exposure.

This evil is another expression of the gift of truth from the good, a giving within the scope of exclusion and authority that recalls the circulation of goods beyond any such authority and exclusion. The possibility of questioning the evils of truth and truth's authority, of pursuing truth to counter its and other evils, recalls something of the good, not the better or best, but the demands and debts and embraces of things to which we are exposed in order that we may gather them in truth and interrupt that gathering, again in truth, all in response to the good.

Here we may return to Habermas's understanding, after Descartes, mentioned in the Introduction here, of the impossibility of making a normative judgment of truth or goodness or trustworthiness without normative grounds, without an absolute standard. At least, that is what Descartes claims, that I can understand my and other's imperfections only within a standard of perfection ascribed to God. Habermas reinscribes this claim within a set of obligations:

> with a truth claim, obligations to provide grounds,
> with a righteous claim, obligations to provide justification, and
> with a truthfulness claim, obligations to prove trustworthy.
> (Habermas, *CES,* 70)[2]

As it stands, these obligations reinstitute standards, rather like Descartes, standards that define grounds, justification, and trustworthiness. Yet to the question of how we are to criticize such standards, how we might resist too oppressive or exclusive an understanding of reason, we are left stranded

unless we understand the key word in this account to be "obligations."
What Habermas suggests, but expressly denies, is that the good, the law,
something ethical, imposes an immeasurable debt, an inexhaustible obligation, in the very possibility of truth or ethics or science or art that we
might be able to make judgments, that we might provide grounds or jus-
tifications, might fulfill trusts, and these judgments, in their places, respond to an inexhaustible obligation, bear witness to this debt, given from
the good, beyond the restrictions of any judgment. What Habermas suggests, but expressly denies, is that criticism owes an endless debt to exposure, to the touch and opening that reaches toward what has been forgotten.
Even where it cannot be remembered, it bears a debt to recall the loss, the
sacrifice and curse. In order that we may judge by exclusion and authority
we must be able to judge, called to judgment by our exposure to the
hetereogeneous things around us, touched by their abundance, vulnerable
to them. This exposure is the call of the good. This exposure at the heart
of being is the gift of the good. It gives birth to judgment, which presupposes such exposure. It gives birth to the authority of truth, to all authorities, which presuppose that exposure. And it gives birth to resistance to
authority, to the critical judgment, which in its obligations knows no limits. The presence of authority everywhere in our experiences bears witness
to the demands of the good, to the possibility of interrupting the hold of
authority everywhere upon our judgments and responsibilities. The possibility of truth rests upon a debt that bears witness to the curse. The possibility of work, of truth and judgment, demands exclusion within a debt in
memory of inclusion, the debt and care for and toward all things known as
cherishment, given from the good.

I take this debt to be given from the good to work, given as a debt
demanding response, in human worlds instituting responsibility, given to
the gathering of being as truth in saying, to the gathering of being as good
in practice, the gathering of being as trustworthy in judgment. I take this
debt to be given from the good to work, to judgment and representation,
marked as interruption. Habermas's account does not recognize the call of
the good as insurrection, interrupting gathering and assembling. He reas-
sembles judgment within the norms of being. The interruption appears as
an obligation to challenge every norm, every obligation. The interruption
interrupts the authority of norms of measure in order that norms of measure may institute authority.

Something may be added in relation to the tripartite division among
truth, righteousness, and truthfulness, calling for another tripartite division among grounds, justification, and proof of trustworthiness. For either
these compose a triangle in which each reaches toward the others, raising
the question of why and how they are divided, or something other than this

triangle, other than the triangle of faculties found in Kant, interrupts the hold of each vertex so that each can touch the others. If it is true, for example, that truth is autonomous relative to goodness, so that the question of whether truth is good does not override the truth of truth, then that truth, of truth's autonomy, cannot be given from within the autonomy and sovereignty of truth. Rather, it is given from that which gives it measure and authority, from what I call the good though it is not the measure of good that divides it from evil. If truth is autonomous and carries authority, something beyond the measures of autonomy and authority must circulate these as possibilities. Something beyond standards and measure, interrupting their measures and standards, not another measure or norm, allows norms to work, and allows for their critique. The good circulates wildly beyond any norm or measure, interrupting every body of work, displacing every place.

The gathering of being in abundance as truth emerges in inexhaustible debt to seek, to know, to respond beyond every limit, a demand for responsiveness I understand as exposure and name as cherishment in desire. Truth emerges within our exposure to others, within the touch of others upon our skins and senses, and of others touching each other, inexhaustible exposure and desire. Truth calls from within the gift of exposure, within a desire and movement toward things that goes beyond every established limit. Truth gathers in being as the limits that constitute truth's representations, moved by desire and exposure toward a responsiveness that exceeds every limit. I speak of this responsiveness as cherishment. I speak of the constitution of limits as sacrifice, knowing that to limit is always to exclude. Sacrifice presupposes cherishment, that we are touched by, care for, and respond to things at and beyond the limits of every measure. The circulation of goods in this responsiveness beyond measure is general economy. The halting of goods at the limits of work is restricted economy. Every restricted economy circulates in general economy. General economy circulates through the institution of restricted economies. In the language of abundance, cherishment and sacrifice are general and restricted economy.

Where cherishment joins sacrifice as limit and work, where general economy meets restricted economy, we have plenishment, the circulation of gifts from the good. The giving is general economy, given within an inexhaustible debt to respond, an exposure beyond exposure, a responsiveness beyond responsiveness from which responsibility emerges in human worlds. The gifts are gatherings of being in restricted economies, always excluding some gifts in order to gather others, a gathering that gestures toward totality while always excluding some from that gathering. Plenishment is this endless movement of giving gifts within a debt toward the injustices of the exclusions of giving, a debt calling for endless responsiveness toward what has been sacrificed, given from cherishment, and endless memories of what has been forgotten. Plenishment demands endless work and endless interruption, transgressing the limits of its work. Plenishment is witness to the good and to the betrayals of every witness.

Truth is the gathering of being in the exposure of things to each other, always an inexhaustible exposure and debt beyond any given touch, any given limits. I understand the face to face of which Levinas speaks as the relation to the other, the saying of the good, as touch, touching the other in its skin, reaching toward its depths, a touch beyond the revelation of any touch, a touch beyond the limits known as exposure. Plenishment is the impossible union of general and restricted economy, impossible because that union knows no measure. Plenishment is where immeasure touches measure. This limitless touch is the exposure known as truth, gathering and interruption.

We have seen the repeated movement in which the gathering of being in truth calls for saying, understood in Greek as *legein*. With Ari and Ariadne and Arachne, I have resisted the gathering of being as truth in saying, have pursued other gatherings, in flesh and images and sound, in music and touch. Every gathering as truth demands interruption, demands it in its truth. That is the endless debt within truth to resist the authority of every limit while as truth to insist on the authority of limits. The interruption of which I speak here is that which interrupts the authority of language as the saying which gathers being as truth under the name of *legein*.

I return to the gathering of being and saying as truth to speak of saying and speaking in a different way, another interruption, in pursuit of the truth of truth, truth itself, we might say, if truth gathers itself in truth, however strange such a gathering might be. "What is truth itself, that it sometimes comes to pass as art?" (Heidegger, *OWA*, 39), Heidegger asks. I hope, in the name of the good, to resist this gathering of truth itself. We have seen that the gathering of being is given to saying, to language and words, within the rule of humanity. I respond that things touch and reveal each other to each other in their truth, in and out of language, throughout the earth. I understand this touch as gathering, where every gathering is a re-gathering. Truth gathers in a re-gathering; there is always repetition. We might represent this repetition in gathering as representation and work, recalling the denigration of representation in Western thought, as if presupposing an originary presentation against whose measure representation falls short. We might represent this repetition in gathering as *poiēsis* and *mimēsis*, recalling their denigration in Western thought, as if presupposing an originary truth against whose measure *poiēsis* and *mimēsis* might fall short, resisting abundance. We might represent the dyad as truth, its indefiniteness as untruth, the untruth of general economy, again resisting abundance. Yet with Derrida, we may understand every origin to demand repetition, every repetition to be a founding, every natural being or thing to participate in representation and work beyond the authority of humanity and language, every institution to call forth interruption in remembrance of abundance. We may think of representation as the indefinite dyad, measure interrupting itself in the name of the good. And perhaps with Derrida, we may think of truth in painting as well as language, not as an extended saying but as the gathering of being beyond the limits of language, whether saying or said, interrupting the authority of words. I quote enough to convey the flavor, aroma, design, or mood of Derrida's interruption of the gathering of being in truth as saying, interrupted by paint. If "someone, not me, comes and says the words: 'I am interested in the idiom in painting'" (Derrida, *TP*, 1):

> Does he mean that he is interested in the idiom "in painting," in the idiom itself, for its own sake, "in painting" [an expression that is in itself strongly idiomatic; but what is an idiom?]?
>
> That he is interested in the idiomatic expression itself, in the words "in painting"? Interested in words in painting or in the words "in painting"? Or in the words "'in painting'"?
>
> That he is interested in the idiom in painting, i.e., in what pertains to the idiom, the idiomatic trait or style [that which is singular, proper, inimitable] in the domain of painting, or else—another possible translation—in the singularity or the irreducible specificity of pictorial art, of that "language" which painting is supposed to be, etc.?
>
> Which makes, if you count them well, at least four hypotheses; but each one divides again, is grafted and contaminated by all the others, and you would never be finished translating them.
>
> Nor will I. (pp. 1–2)

Nor will I, or you, or us, ever be finished representing them, gathering them, in their truth, resisting the assembling of being in language.

Derrida continues to frame "the truth in painting" as if gathered in language, the language which painting is supposed to be, as if to think of truth in painting as an idiom. He opens his thought of truth in painting as an idiom perhaps to overlook the authority of language imposed wherever we think of idioms, however idiomatically, perhaps to question that authority. I prefer to wonder about the gathering opened by another frame, that of painting, truth "in painting": what of truth and being gathered in painting, or music, or anywhere else but words, as singularity, or repetition, or division, together with grafting and contamination. How many truths, exactly, are we called upon to think or represent or something else in relation to truth in painting or thought or representation or something else? If there is a number, something to be counted, measured, gathered: the in-definiteness of the dyad. If there is a truth of truth.

Of which Derrida has something to say. For these questions of the idiom in painting bear on the truth of truth and on truth and untruth: "[t]ruth of truth still, with the two genitives, but this time the value of adequation has *pushed aside [écarte]* that of unveiling" (Derrida, *TP*, 5). I understand *écarter* to suggest an opening, an intermediary movement, between adequation and unveiling, to resist, perhaps, the demand to choose between them. Does Heidegger, perhaps, insist that we choose between one truth and another, choose *alētheia*, when *alētheia* knows nothing of choice? Is the truth of truth, truth itself, something to find and choose? And in whose or in which name, that of adequation or unveiling? All choice, I have repeatedly suggested, belongs to *technē*, to adequation, resists abundance. All measure belongs to *technē*, including that of the relation between *poiēsis* and *technē*. *Poiēsis* knows nothing of choice and measure, nothing of gathering or the curse, though all its work is riven by the curse. The gathering of truth gathers into a place forgetful of abundance. If the truth of truth is witness to abundance, it cannot gather.

I take the truth of truth, if there be such a truth, to be the curse, framed by blasphemy as the curse, that which forbids all truth to gather, given from the good as sacrifice, in the name of cherishment and abundance. Truth is accursed, the truth of truth is the curse, the disaster from which it is possible for beings to gather, in memory of that which does not gather, the touch and intimacy beyond measure of the good which calls for the gathering of truth. The curse, like the witness's betrayal, is the visible mark of the good. The nature to which we return in the name, I say, of general economy, is nature transfigured by the curse. For us there is no other nature, no other general economy. We cannot relate to nature without memory of the curse, that is, of prohibitions, dominations, oppressions, subjugations. Nature includes all exclusions in memory of the betrayals under which it gathers.

I read Derrida as opening the space of the gathering of representation in its immeasurability. The idiom, the truth, the measure, the gathering of being in painting questions and reaches in the deepest way, not toward another gathering of being in its pictoriality, but toward the limits and unlimits of gathering, of truth, in representation. The gathering of truth in saying, framed now as painting, interrupts the gathering as saying in words, resisting the authority of language, interrupts the gathering of any mea-sured or represented truth, for example, propositional truth, resisting the authority of measure, including that of grammar, syntax, or any other pro-priety. The re-framing of truth in painting interrupts the gathering of truth as if it might reach for totality. Every gathering is an ungathering and a re-gathering, interruption and its interruption, representation and its misrepresentation. Every gathering of being in truth is plenishment, abundance, heterogeneity, and betrayal. As general economy it imposes a debt to circulate goods wildly, excessively, and abundantly beyond any limit. As restricted economy it imposes a debt to re-circulate every good held within any limit under the curse.

I understand representation to move in this divided space of measure and interruption, after Plato's indefinite dyad. I understand it together with judgment as plenishment, as circulating in general and restricted economy. Against all the critiques of representation as restriction, repetition, and exchange I respond, in writing and, I hope, in truth that representation knows no restrictions, escapes from every restriction, while always falling under restriction.[3] In this capture and escape we find truth. Truth together with untruth circulate within the general economy of representation, filled with misrepresentation, interrupting the limits of representation. Truth circulates together with untruth as gifts from the good.

Where Aristotle understands truth as saying what is, we may now understand it as being's gathering in representation, judgment, gathered as what can be represented, where representation is restricted neither to language and other forms of human judgment nor to humanity, but opens being to work in the abundant ways given by general economy, by excessive circulation and desire, by touch, in gathering and interruption, opens being and curses it with exclusion. The political question is truth itself both in the authority invested by each régime in truth, which we must endlessly call into question, and in the movements and displacements truth imposes in imposing its authority. Judgment and representation are identified here, not with humanity, subject, or Ego, nor with the concept, as in Kant, but with the inexhaustible slippage and displacement of every being circulating against itself and its limits, described by Foucault as "that tiny degree of displacement" (Foucault, *OT*, 29) whereby things in their abundance show themselves, give themselves to each other, represent each other as each other, in their being and truth, an abundance of abundance.

It is aptly and deeply expressed by Whitehead as the ways actual entities are for each other, always given from the good, given in freedom and desire. Every actual entity arises in the prehension of other entities, in a representation joined with feeling, touched by other entities. The feeling of a past actual entity is a physical prehension; the feeling of a timeless form, an eternal object, is a conceptual prehension. "Prehensions of actual entities—i.e., prehensions whose data involve actual entities—are termed 'physical prehension'; and prehensions of eternal objects are termed 'conceptual prehensions'" (Whitehead, *PR*, 23). In this way, being is always a gathering of other beings in truth as representation, a gathering as repetition. But repetition is always more than repetition; representation is feeling, valuation, and freedom, recalling the good.

> whatever is a datum for a feeling has a unity as felt. (Whitehead, *PR*, 24)

> The subjective form of a conceptual feeling has the character of a "valuation" . . .
> . . . the importance of the eternal object as felt in the integrated feeling is enhanced, or attenuated. (pp. 240–41)

> that in each concrescence whatever is determinable is determined, but that there is always a remainder for the decision of the subject-superject of that concrescence. (pp. 27–28)

To be is to represent, but representation is feeling, valuation, and freedom. Prehension in Whitehead is at once repetition, freedom, desire, and valuation, all embodied, close to touch and to exposure, to cherishment. In the same way, Creativity, the universal of universals, is the becoming of new entities in their truth as a gathering which is an ungathering and a re-gathering. There is always a remainder in every gathering beyond any gathering.

Whitehead speaks of truth as conformation. "Truth is the conformation of Appearance to Reality" (Whitehead, *AI*, 309). He restricts the gathering of being as truth to repetition. Yet he repeatedly interrupts the authority of this repetition in relation to Beauty, and more. "Truth and Beauty are the great regulative properties in virtue of which Appearance justifies itself to the immediate decision of the experient subject" (p. 309); "Beauty is a wider, and more fundamental, notion than Truth" (p. 341); "the general importance for Truth for the promotion of Beauty is overwhelming" (p. 342). The general importance of beauty is its relation to discord, beyond the reach of truth.

Whitehead does not speak of gifts and plenishment, though he knows of love and sacrifice. His sense of evil is a sense of sacrifice. It is joined with a love close to cherishment with two qualifications: "the love of particular individual things. . . . all personal desire is transferred to the thing loved, as a desire for its perfection" (Whitehead, *AI*, 372). One qualification is that cherishment is response to the ideality and perfection of the other without conflict with desire for oneself, the responsiveness that constitutes one's own ideality. Every gathering of beings bears this inexhaustible debt to ideality, within the one and the other, realized as exposure to the other. The second qualification is that this cherishment and love is for individual things and more, for the kinds they are as well as in their singularity. Beings, others, are what they are in their identities and kinds, gather in their truth and in the inexhaustible debt borne by the kinds of the earth. Every kind gathers in its truth, cursed in kind. Every kind circulates among countless other kinds, in endless possibilities of truth.

We have journeyed, flown, from one end of the earth to the other, from the saying of what is as truth to plenishment in the earth as judgment toward others in the inexhaustibility of their truth and the endless circulation of goods. This gives us Ari|adne's|Arachne's truth. Can we say, in conclusion, something of the disciplining of such a truth, in the name of the good? Can we speak of the truth that continues to gather in the autonomy of the faculties of judgment, given that truth demands that we interrupt that gathering?

I interrupt this general account to offer some guidelines to truth as given from the good, anarchistic guidelines to the gift of truth, expressive of and resistant to their disciplining. These are guidelines to plenishment rewritten in memory of the gathering of truth.[4]

1. We find ourselves individuals who belong to many different kinds, mixed kinds, kinds belonging to other kinds, by birth, by history, by blood, by choice, and by the activities and representations of others. This is our condition, our abundance, the abundance of the earth. We find ourselves surrounded by, touching, working for the sake of many different individuals and kinds, which we constitute by our activities and representations, and by which we and they constitute who we are, as human and as individual. To be is to be individual among kinds, individual in virtue of complex and mobile kindred relations. Our relation to knowledge and truth is a relation to kinds, heterogeneous kinds to which we may belong, other kinds in our proximity to which we know we will never belong. Truth gathers in the limitless abundance of heterogeneous kinds, nature's general economy; truth gathers its authority in restricted economy. Individuals and kinds belong together, circulating in nature's general economy, all included. Individuals and kinds gather under the curse of exclusion.

2. Truth gathers in nature's abundance, given by cherishment. Truth gathers as nature's presence, *parousia*, interrupted by abundance beyond any *parousia*. Nature in its monstrosity and fearsomeness, in its plenitude, calls to us as endless desire to pursue its truth. It follows that everything matters in truth, everything is inexhaustibly, heterogeneously relevant, every individual thing and every kind. Everything matters in truth beyond any gathering of truth. Everything in the earth touches others in inexhaustible ways, in its ways, known and unknown, in the kinds in which it participates. Everything responds to the good beyond any gathering of truth. To revere, to know, the truth of things is to

know that they pursue their own truths and to bear a debt, an obligation, to respond to that pursuit in endless exposure, for their own sake and the sake of others, for the sake of something otherwise, with three qualifications:

3. *(a)* They may not know their own truth, though nothing, no one, else can know it better. The good resists the better and worse of truth. *(b)* Such a truth, one's own proper truth, is multiple, heterogeneous, impure, bound to others face to face, constituted by memberships, practices, representations, and mobilities, heterogeneous beyond any gathering in any place. *(c)* The kinds of the earth, human and other kinds, spiders, frogs, and bats, with their truths, circulate everywhere in nature in fourfold relations: constituted by their members, constituting their members' identities, in virtue of their mobilities and circulations, related heterogeneously; touching each other in every place, exposed to each other as individuals and kinds in multiple, heterogeneous ways, exposed to, touching others for their sake, called by something beyond measure. This heterogeneity of being's abundance shows itself as the monstrosity of kinds, the betrayals of the truth of every individual and kind. One's truth in proximity with others shows itself as monstrosity. It works by authority, gives rise to injustice. Truth's authority gives birth to monsters. The strangeness of truth, wherever it gathers, brings us in endless proximity with strangers. The task of truth bears the task of welcoming strangers.

It follows that:

4. Cherishment gives rise in time to the impossibility of knowing the truth of strange and heterogeneous things together, and to the impossibility of any measure of fulfillment, the impossibility of achieving truth, holding it in place, within the circulation of countless truths in restricted places. This impossibility, sacrifice, knows no rules, demands judgment without criteria, is wounded by endless responsibilities toward the good. This impossibility, sacrifice, knows the calamities of insisting on gathering all truths together, of imposing rules for gathering in different, restricted places. Sacrifice responds with endless responsibility to resist the rules for assembling, to interrupt the gathering. Our responsibility in truth, toward truth, is to gather things together with limitless care in truth joined with limitless resistance to the authority of any gathering. This responsibility, borne by judgment, instituted as representation, brings with it a certain joy enriched by sorrow. The joy of truth is filled with sorrow. The institution of truth and knowledge always betrays knowledge and truth, mourning for endless disasters.

5. Among creatures who can know their truth, they must know it for themselves, exposed to, touching others in abundance, resisting every truthful authority. None can know the truth of another with authority, especially another kind; no one can authorize the truth for another, especially not the heterogeneous truths of other kinds, foreigners and strangers. Imposing the authority of truth on others brings about endless disaster. We impose our understanding of others' truths upon them briefly at best and with boundless caution. We impose our own truth upon the truths of others as sacrifice, as injustice, knowing disaster. Plenishment serves for the most part, if not always, as a letting-be, in being and truth as given from the good, resisting gathering all goods in any place as truth. We can never know in truth the joy possible for another kind, find a joy for ourselves in letting that other kind be in its truth and joy.

6. Nothing can justify the sacrifice of any kind or its truths to others' truth, of any kind, women, children, animals, Jews, not even the HIV/AIDS or smallpox virus. Cherishment demands sacrifice, but can never in the name of the good and nature's abundance of kinds impose on others the destruction, death, of a kind or of its truths, reducing heterogeneity. Such a destruction is profoundly unjust, bears with it responsibility for endless restitution. The sacrifice of an individual, of many individuals, is terrible. But sacrifice is inescapable. Nothing can justify the destruction of a kind or its truth in the march of history. Yet history is the recurrence of such catastrophes. Truth gathers in memories of endless catastrophes.

7. In the places where we compose ourselves and others in proximity, exposed in face and touch, we may know our truths to whatever extent they are knowable and we may hope to know of, grant, the truths of others, touched by others. Especially, we bear a debt to know the weight of our injustices in the struggle for truth. The work of the good is undertaken locally, in proximity and touch, in this sense private. The work of the good disperses in the general economy of goods in circulation, in this sense public. Truth bears this double relation of public and private, circulating in general economy beyond any gathering, gathered repeatedly in place with excessive authority.

8. Truth gathers within a double debt, each unlimited in its exposure: to institute truth beyond the reach of any authority, and to challenge the institution of every authority in the name of truth. Our utmost desire in truth, given from the good, must be to gather truth without authority, a profoundly anarchistic truth whose sovereignty is nothing, whose truth is the curse, whose work is disaster. This desire beyond authority

always institutes sovereign authority, in the name of truth, desiring its own destruction in the promulgation of truth. The desire for truth falls back on itself *(se rabattre sur)*, instituting its own repression, at the same time that it interrupts every authority. The fulfillment of truth without authority takes place through interruption, resisting truth's authority. We may thereby contrast everyday, familiar truths that arise within the endless abundance of the world as if without authority, resistant to interruption, driven by endless desire to gather truth wherever it may be gathered, with disciplinary truths that arise in extreme authority, resistant to abundance, driven by endless desire to gather truth in its sovereignty. Everyday truths, everyday experience, gather in the least authority, gather in nature's abundance. Disciplinary truths reinstate boundaries that impede the circulation, demanding endless interruption. Some of the greatest calamities known to us arise where disciplinary authority imposes authority on everyday, familiar truth which finds itself too subject to too many authorities.

9. Heterogeneity works face to face, in proximity and touch, arising in the wounding and joy of love, in unbounded desire, passing away into the general economy of goods, circulating everywhere. Heterogeneity complicates the identity of every kind in proximity, the indefiniteness and impurity of every truth. What we find in proximity are cherished bodies whose sufferings and joys plenish the earth. Authority, sovereignty, and truth all do their work upon bodies, work through representation upon material and embodied things. Truth gathers in the touch of flesh as desire, reaching beyond itself, exposed in flesh and bodies beyond any limits. The body of truth, desire, circulates in the exposure of embodied touch. The will to truth is the body of truth.

10. Abundant, plenished truth is strange in the double sense that familiar truth is always touched by strangeness and that the gathering of truth gathers friends and strangers together in an ethical|political place. Gathering the good bears the endless debt to gather and to know the impossibility of gathering friends and strangers together in truth. The task, we may say, is to accept strangers and their truths without insisting on their monstrosity. The task is to accept in truth what cannot be gathered. That is the ethical|political task in relation to strangers, human and otherwise, responsive to the abundance of the earth.

Plenishment in the earth gathers abundant gifts from the good in restricted economies against their endless circulation in general economy, the circulating and giving of the good. Among the gifts gathered are truth, beauty, and good, all divided in their places, in restricted, exchange economies, from others: truth from falsehood, beauty from ugliness, good from bad. Yet the gathering and gift reveal that truth requires untruth to be truth, to gather; beauty requires ugliness to gather itself; good and bad are not exclusive. And more: the gathering requires interruption to gather, challenges authority to institute authority, endless relations of truth and untruth, untruth interrupting truth, ugliness interrupting beauty, bad interrupting the measure of good. And more: these and other interruptions all represent, in truth, the gathering of the abundance of the earth, an abundance that cannot be gathered in disciplinary places, in restricted economies, except as interruption, all resisting truth's authority.

The abundance of the earth is nature's inexhaustibility, its general economy. Its work, its representativity, takes place everywhere locally in restricted economies, nature's locality and ergonality. General economy circulates in restricted economies, in particular locales and places, limited by exclusions, instituting disasters. No other places can be established for its circulation. Moreover, gatherings are possible only in virtue of exclusion, imposing sacrifice. In consequence, every witness to general circulation betrays it. In return, every restricted economy circulates in general economy, in the abundance of earth and the wild and excessive circulation of things and kinds. These show themselves, are gathered in their abundance as interruptions. Truth as truth requires interruption, sometimes as untruth, sometimes as truth's others, ugliness and beauty, right and wrong, good and evil. Truth as truth requires these and other interruptions. This is the truth of abundance, gathered as truth, that truth emerges within a debt that it is required endlessly to pay, but cannot pay off. It cannot be truth without that debt, given from the good, whose restitution is betrayal.

Truth is the gathering in restitution within endless gifts given from the good. Without these gifts, nothing could be gathered as truth. Yet the gifts are not the giving, and the giving cannot be gathered as if it were a gift. But it can be gathered as giving, circulating in the name of the good, within exposure, vulnerability, inexhaustible responsiveness, and debt: that is, as cherishment, sacrifice, and plenishment, the earth's abundance.

This abundance is an abundance of givings, restricted and general economies. The specificity of truth—disciplinary truth—constitutes it as a gift. The circulation of truth as gathering, among other gatherings, constitutes it as giving. The play of gifts and giving gathers within the abundance of the earth as its truth: cherishment, sacrifice, and plenishment. Including human beings and others, frogs and bats, in the light of the sun or in the dark.

Notes

General Preface to the Project

1. I recall Socrates' suggestion that knowledge, truth, and, perhaps, being itself all come as gifts from the good, discussed later in this Preface. I also recall Socrates' description of the indefinite dyad, which I associate with the good. Socrates speaks of "a gift of the gods" (16c), that "all things . . . consist of a one and a many"; but we must "come to see not merely that the one we started with is a one and an unlimited many, but also just how many it is"; we are to discern "the total number of forms the thing in question has intermediate between its one and its unlimited number" (16d), an intermediate number I associate with *technē*. "It is only then, when we have done that, that we may let each one of all these intermediate forms pass away into the unlimited and cease bothering about them" (16e). I understand the passing away as the circulation of gifts, and understand the unlimited as the good, demanded by the intermediate number, by all human and natural works. See n. 3. I understand this movement to represent intermediate numbers, all measures, norms, and standards, as intermediary figures in ceaseless circulation. See the Introduction here, pp. 19–26. I understand the good as intermediariness, that which gives forth the possibility of intermediate numbers, of work.

2. I recall three allusions to gifts and giving. One is the "gift of the gods" from *Philebus*, the movement from limit to unlimit touching intermediary numbers, intermediary movements, all understood in terms of general and restricted economy. See n. 3.

The second is Heidegger's portrayal of the "it gives" *(es gibt)* and giving of Being, examined in detail in the Introduction and chap. 7 here, and throughout: "In the beginning of Western thinking, Being is thought, but not the 'It gives' as such. The latter withdraws in favor of the gift which It gives" (Heidegger, *TB*, 8). I understand these words to call attention to the giving more than to the It or to Being, the gift.

In a similar vein, the third allusion is what Hyde says of the giving, the circulation, of the gift:

213

a gift is a thing we do not get by our own efforts. We cannot buy it; we cannot acquire it through an act of will. It is bestowed upon us. (Hyde, *G*, ix)

The only essential is this: *the gift must always move*. There are other forms of property that stand still, that mark a boundary or resist momentum, but the gift keeps going. (p. 4)

I understand the good to give, and understand giving as always moving, circulating, where the works of humanity and nature strive to halt the circulation by imposing limits and exclusions. In this way the thought of the good and giving is a thought of inclusion, beyond the limits of work and *technē*. *Technē* works by limits, exclusions; all choices and boundaries belong to *technē*. The thought of the good is a thought beyond the limits of *technē*.

I understand the circulation as general economy, after Bataille. See n. 3.

3. I think of the work of the good as occupying restricted economies, goods divided from bads, binary oppositions and exclusions, setting prices. I think of the good as interrupting every restricted economy, circulating in the general economy of excess, unlimit, unmeasure. The gift of the good is the general economy of priceless goods that circulate everywhere in restricted economies as work within immeasurable exposure. It works dyadically where things touch each other in restricted economies; it exceeds every measure in the intimacy and abundance of touch.

In this way, the good resists every binary opposition, resists every measure, not as another opposition or measure, and not as another place or thing. The good is not a good, neither good nor bad, nor good and bad, nor neutral, indifferent to good and evil. It is neither transcendent nor immanent, high nor low, inside nor outside, but interrupts the choice of either/or and neither/nor, the hold of the one or the other, the authority of "or," and "and," and "neither," and "both," all belonging to restricted economies. I speak in the name of the good of the exposure borne by every creature and thing within its limits to countless others, and the responsibility they bear to resist the injustices of every limit by a movement interrupting limit. I call this movement the general economy of the good. I think of nature as the general and excessive circulation of goods beyond price exposed to others giving birth to the work they do in restricted, exchange economies.

I pursue the thought of restricted and general economies found in Bataille, *AS*. See my *PE*, chaps. 5 and 6; and my *GB*, chap. 7. I understand the crossing of restricted and general economy as the giving of the good, expressed by Plato in *Philebus* as the indefinite dyad: limit joined with unlimit; limit passing away into unlimit. See my *PE*, chap. 5. I speak here of general economy as abundance, concerned with the restricted economy of truth.

4. I speak of the good in memory of Plato, but where the good provides no measure. I speak of the good interrupting measure rather than of instrumentality and teleology; I think of inclusion rather than of hierarchy and exclusion. I speak of the good remembering desire, think of excesses of love and care, of dyads touching each other intimately in the flesh. I speak of the good rather than of power, think of moving toward and way, of touching, rather than of causation. I speak of

the good rather than of freedom, think of the call of conscience to work, to touch, rather than of movements without limit. I speak of the good rather than of being, think of truth as exposure. I speak of the good rather than of God, think of circulating in general, excessive economy, giving without ground or law. All these renunciations belong to work, to judgment, as we strive to build and control. But something in this striving summons us to know that building requires sacrifice, that judgment calls for endless vigilance. I think of this something as the good, something that calls us to work, makes judgment possible. I speak of the good in memory of disaster.

5. I have spoken of the good, after Anaximander, as injustice, for which all our works are restitutions. See n. 8. Derrida has spoken of it as justice (see Derrida, *FL*). Plato speaks of it repeatedly. Again, the good is not a thing, a measure, it does not divide, does not exclude, but gives all things to us, places them in circulation, exposes us to them, charges us to respond.

6. I speak of sonance in my *RR:* the ring of representation. Levinas speaks of *la gloire de l'Infini* (Levinas, *AÊ*, 230).

7. See n. 8.

8. "Kata to chreōn didonai gar auta dikēn kai tisin allēlois tēs adikias." The entire fragment from Simplicius is canonically translated as: "Into those things from which existing things have their coming into being, their passing away, too, takes place, according to what must be; for they make reparation to one another for their injustice according to the ordinance of time, as he puts it in somewhat poetical language" (Simplicius *Phys.*, 24, 18 [DK 12 B 1]) [Robinson, *EGP*, 34]).

9. So that wherever I speak of ethics and politics I speak of them together as ethical|political, circulating in intimate relation. From the standpoint of the good, no essential boundary holds between ethics and politics.

10. Heidegger speaks of abundance *(Fülle)* (Heidegger, *TB*, 6; *OWA*, 34, 76); Levinas speaks of fecundity (Levinas, *TI*, 267–69): "my future does not enter into the logical essence of the possible. The relation with such a future, irreducible to the power over possibles, we shall call fecundity" (p. 269). I speak of inexhaustibility.

Introduction

1. Expressed, for example, in Tarski's semantic definition that "A sentence is true if it is satisfied by all objects and false otherwise" (Tarski, *SCT*, 25). I understand the relation of satisfaction as gathering saying and being together as truth. I pursue the question of gathering.

2. See here chap. 1, p. 14, for the full quotation.

3. See General Preface to the Project here, n. 9.

4. See my *RR*, chap. 8; *IJ*, chap. 8; and *PE*, chap. 7.

5. See my *GB*, chap. 7, where I speak of general economy as abundance; and my *PE*, chap. 5, where I speak of general economy and the indefinite dyad. I understand abundance to exceed measure in every place, where beings touch each other dyadically, where every measure is interrupted by and exceeded by desire.

6. I speak of these matters in detail in my *GB*, chap. 7. I speak of the relation between general and restricted economy and the indefinite dyad in my *PE*, especially chap. 5.

Chapter One

1. See here General Preface to the Project, p. xii–xiii.

2. I have spoken of the gift of beauty in my *GB*. Much of what I say there of truth is relevant here, though I hope to repeat myself as little as possible.

3. The Jowett translation is the only one of several current translations that addresses the words *phusin kalon* directly, nature's beauty and abundance. I take Jowett to confront the radicality of this passage more directly than the translations by Michael Joyce in Hamilton and Cairns and by W. R. M. Lamb in the Loeb Classical Library edition. Lamb translates *phusin kalon* as beautiful in its nature; Joyce does not translate *phusin* at all.

4. Bataille says that sovereignty is NOTHING. See here chap. 12, p. 191.

5. See my *GB*.

6. See my *IR*.

Chapter Two

1. Figures of age and youth circulate throughout the dialogues. Here Socrates is old, Theaetetus is young. In *Parmenides,* Socrates is young, Parmenides is old. In *Parmenides*, Zeno alludes to age and youth, opening repeated figures of time and experience throughout the dialogue (Plato, *Parmenides*, 136e). See the discussion of time in *Parmenides* in my *RR*, 53–54.

2. Also:

> As soon, then, as an eye and something else whose structure is adjusted to the eye come within range and give birth to the whiteness together with its cognate perception—things that would never have come into existence if either of the two had approached anything else—then it is that, as the vision from the eyes and the whiteness from the thing that joins in giving birth to the color pass in the space between, the eye becomes filled with vision and now sees, and becomes, not vision, but a seeing eye, while the other parent of the color is saturated with whiteness and becomes, on its

side, not whiteness, but a white thing, be it stock or stone or whatever else may chance to be so colored. (Plato, *Theaetetus*, 156de)

3. The passage continues:

And so this pair—Socrates in this condition and the drinking of the wine—produce a different offspring, in the region of the tongue a sensation of sourness, and in the region of the wine a sourness that arises as a movement there. The wine becomes, not sourness, but sour, while I become, not a sensation, but sentient. (Plato, *Theaetetus*, 159e)

No doubt you remember how we put this earlier—that nothing has any being as one thing just by itself, no more has the agent or patient, but, as a consequence of their intercourse with one another, in giving birth to the perceptions and the things perceived, the agents come to be of such and such a quality, and the patients come to be percipient. (182ab)

4. The very idea of truth, philosophical truth, is joined with giving birth, against the grip of being, in the eyes of heaven. For to the philosopher, those for whom birth ceases to move as a gift are ridiculous, a contamination of memory.

When they harp upon birth—some gentleman who can point to seven generations of wealthy ancestors—he thinks that such commendation must come from men of purblind vision, too uneducated to keep their eyes fixed on the whole or to reflect that any man has had countless myriads of ancestors and among them any number of rich men and beggars, kings and slaves, Greeks and barbarians. To pride oneself on a catalogue of twenty-five progenitors going back to Heracles, son of Amphitryon, strikes him as showing a strange pettiness of outlook. He laughs at a man who cannot rid his mind of foolish vanity by reckoning that before Amphitryon there was a twenty-fifth ancestor, and before him a fiftieth, whose fortunes were as luck would have it. But in all these matters the world has the laugh of the philosopher, partly because he seems arrogant, partly because of his helpless ignorance in matters of daily life. (Plato, *Theaetetus*, 174e–175ab)

5. See my *GB*, chap. 2, where I consider the triangle composed of *mimēsis*, truth, and art.

6. See this chapter, n. 1.

7. An immensely difficult passage:

Mistake is impossible in the following cases.
(1) No one can think one thing to be another when he does not perceive either of them, but has the memorial or seal of both of them in his mind; nor can any mistaking of one thing for another occur, when he only knows one, and does not know, and has no impression of the other; nor can he think that one thing which he does not know is another thing which he

does not know, or that what he does not know is what he knows; nor (2) that one thing which he perceives is another thing which he perceives, or that something which he perceives is something which he does not perceive; or that something which he does not perceive is something else which he does not perceive; or that something which he does not perceive is something which he perceives; nor again (3) can he think that something which he knows and perceives, and of which he has the impression coinciding with sense, is something else which he knows and perceives, and of which he has the impression coinciding with sense;—this last case, if possible, is still more inconceivable than the others; nor (4) can he think that something which he knows and perceives, and of which he has the memorial coinciding with sense, is something else which he knows; nor so long as these agree, can he think that a thing which he knows and perceives is another thing which he perceives; or that a thing which he does not know and does not perceive, is the same as another thing which he does not know and does not perceive;—nor again, can he suppose that a thing which he does not know and does not perceive is the same as another thing which he does not know; or that a thing which he does not know and does not perceive is another thing which he does not perceive: —All these utterly and absolutely exclude the possibility of false opinion. (Plato, *Theaetetus*, 192ac)

Summarized by Cornford in a translator's note as follows:

(a) If neither object is now perceived, I cannot mistake an acquaintance for another acquaintance, or confuse him with a stranger, or confuse two strangers.

(b) If perception only is involved, I cannot confuse two things which I see, or an object seen with an object not seen, or two objects neither of which is seen.

(c) Where both knowledge and perception are involved, I cannot confuse two acquaintances both now seen and recognized, or confuse an acquaintance now seen and recognized with an absent acquaintance or with a stranger who is present. And there can be no confusion of two total strangers, whether I now see one of them or not.

I reject Cornford's reading because it is told without memory. In every one of these cases, the thought is unintelligible without memory—for example, in *(a)* of two persons known but not remembered at the moment; in *(b)* where what is not present is not remembered; in *(c)* where something is ready to hand, in the mind, undisplaced by memory. Memory is presence displaced by absence, in ongoing intermediary movement. That is its relation to error.

Chapter Three

1. See my *PE*.

2. See my *PE*, 258–59. See also chap. 10 here, p. 163.

3. On my reading of *Poetics*, discussed in *GB*, chap. 3.

Chapter Four

1. An example:

Now all animals are naturally subject to man. This can be proved in three ways. First, from the order observed by nature; for just as in the generation of things we perceive a certain order of procession of the perfect from the imperfect (thus matter is for the sake of form; and the imperfect form, for the sake of the perfect), so also is there order in the use of natural things; thus the imperfect are for the use of the perfect; as the plants make use of the earth for their nourishment, and animals make use of plants, and man makes use of both plants and animals. Therefore it is in keeping with the order of nature, that man should be master over animals. (Aquinas, *ST*, Part 1, Q96)

2. "But then if I look out of the window and see men crossing the square, as I just happen to have done, I normally say that I see the men themselves. . . . Yet do I see any more than hats and coats which could conceal automatons?" (Descartes, *M*, 2, 21).

3. Perhaps the first Congress of the United States had such thoughts in mind in restricting naturalization to those "aliens being free white persons" (Cose, *NS*, 11). Race, species, kind determined who shared our political and rational traditions.

4. I read the exchange between Socrates and Thrasymachus in Book I of Plato's *Republic* as representing this relation between reason and authority. Socrates rules over Thrasymachus by force, the superior force of reason's truth, giving reason authority and Socrates power over Thrasymachus, who protests as clearly as he can that he has been beaten by numbers, not by truth itself. "Revel in your discourse, he said, without fear, for I shall not oppose you, so as not to offend your partisans here" (Plato, *Republic*, 352b). But he has said the truth of reason's truth, that it rests on force, exercises and demands authority, an authority that neither reason nor truth can possess except as gifts from the good.

You think, do you, that it was with malice aforethought and trying to get the better of you unfairly that I asked that question?

I don't think it, I know it, he said, and you won't make anything by it, for you won't get the better of me by stealth and, failing stealth, you are not of the force to beat me in debate. (Plato, *Republic*, 341ab)

Thrasymachus knows that beating exercises force, and that Socrates' authority requires a might that reason does not own if Socrates does.

5. I will not go into Foucault's discussion of the ways in which Descartes puts madness away from himself (Foucault, *FD*), nor Derrida's discussion in response of "madness itself" (Derrida, *CHM*). I am concerned with something close to madness in Descartes, which he does not put away from himself, yet cannot accept in reason.

6. See also: "since I now wished to devote myself solely to the search for truth, I thought it necessary to do the very opposite and reject as if absolutely false

everything in which I could imagine the least doubt, in order to see if I was left believing anything that was entirely indubitable (Descartes, *DM*, 126); and in summary: "I will now shut my eyes, stop my ears, and withdraw all my senses. I will eliminate from my thoughts all images of bodily things, or rather, since this is hardly possible, I will regard all such images as vacuous, false and worthless" (Descartes, *M*, 3, 24).

7. Continuing:

> Again, ancient cities which have gradually grown from mere villages into large towns are usually ill-proportioned, compared with those orderly towns which planners lay out as they fancy on level ground. Looking at the buildings of the former individually, you will often find as much art in them, if not more, than in those of the latter; but in view of their arrangement—a tall one here, a small one there—and the way they make the streets crooked and irregular, you would say it is chance, rather than the will of men using reason, that placed them so. And when you consider that there have always been certain officials whose job is to see that private buildings embellish public places, you will understand how difficult it is to make something perfect by working only on what others have produced. Again, I thought, peoples who have grown gradually from a half-savage to a civilized state, and have made their laws only in so far as they were forced to by the inconvenience of crimes and quarrels, could not be so well governed as those who from the beginning of their society have observed the basic laws laid down by some wise law-giver. Similarly, it is quite certain that the constitution of the true religion, whose articles have been made by God alone, must be incomparably better ordered than all the others. (Descartes, *DM*, 116)

8. Some of Bourdin's objections:

> Other systems of house-building lay down very firm foundations such as stone blocks, bricks, quarried stones, and numerous other materials of this sort, and by using these as a base they are able to make their buildings as high as they wish. But your method is quite different, since it aims to construct something not from something but from nothing. It demolishes, digs up and rejects all old foundations without exception; it requires the will to be turned in completely the opposite direction, and to avoid the impression that it has no wings, it puts on artificial wings of wax and lays down new foundations which are the complete opposite of the old ones. (Descartes, *OR*, Obj. 7, 369)

> Here, then, are the chief ways in which your method cuts its own throat or cuts off all hope of producing a building. (1) You do not know whether there is sand or rock beneath the topsoil, and hence you can place no more confidence in the rock (that is, if you do ever manage to stand on

rock) than you can place in sand. Hence everything is doubtful and shaky and your very walls are unstable. I shall not produce any examples; you may yourself proceed to run through the storehouse of your memory, and if you find anything which is not infected with this rot, then bring it out, and I shall congratulate you. (2) Until I find firm ground which I know for certain does not have shifting sand beneath it or any goblins who may undermine it, I must reject everything and consider all building materials as suspect. Or at any rate—to revert to the ordinary and traditional architectural technique—we must first of all determine whether there are any materials which should not be rejected, and if so what they are; and we must instruct our diggers to keep these materials in their trenches. So everything is doubtful, just as we found under point (1), and hence there is nothing which is of the slightest use for constructing a building. (3) If there is anything that could possibly be shifted, even slightly, then we must turn our will in completely the opposite direction and believe that it has already collapsed; indeed we must believe that it is necessary to re-excavate, and use the empty trench as our foundation. But this cuts off every pathway which could lead to successful building. (p. 371)

Descartes replies that he did not cut himself off from building, accusing his critic of madness, entirely overlooking that the criticism is not that he might build something but that his method is mad, overblown, unlike the building of a house as much as that house is like his tower to heaven.

> Here none of the bricklayer's complaints against the architect are more ridiculous than the complaints which my critic has devised against me. In rejecting what is doubtful I no more cut myself off from knowledge of the truth than the architect's excavation precluded the subsequent building of the chapel, as is shown by all the truths I was able to demonstrate later on. At the very least my critic should have tried to point out something false or uncertain in my demonstrations; but since he does not do so, and is incapable of doing so, we must accept that he is suffering from an inexcusable delusion. (Descartes, *OR*, Rep. 7, 372)

9. See also:

> To avoid being deceived I look round carefully and decide to accept only things of the kind which provide no possible scope whatever for that rascally demon to impose on me, no matter how hard he tries—the kinds of fact that not even I can make myself refuse to acknowledge, or bring myself to deny. So I reflect and turn things over and over in my mind until some fact of this sort occurs to me; and when I come across it I use it as an Archimedean point on which to construct other truths, and in this way I arrive step by step at further facts that are wholly certain and thoroughly scrutinized. (Descartes, *OR*, Rep. 7, 313)

Chapter Five

1. This is Spinoza's language. See here chap. 6.

2. See here chap. 4, n. 5.

3. See also:

In order to make our knowledge complete, every single thing relating to our undertaking must be surveyed in a continuous and wholly uninterrupted sweep of thought, and be included in a sufficient and well-ordered enumeration.

So I shall run through them several times in a continuous movement of the imagination, simultaneously intuiting one relation and passing on to the next, until I have learnt to pass from the first to the last so swiftly that memory is left with practically no role to play, and I seem to intuit the whole thing at once. In this way our memory is relieved, the sluggishness of our intelligence redressed, and its capacity in some way enlarged. (Descartes, *RDM*, 25)

4. See also:

when the mind understands, it in some way turns towards itself and inspects one of the ideas which are within it; but when it imagines, it turns towards the body and looks at something in the body which conforms to an idea understood by the mind or perceived by the senses. I can, as I say, easily understand that this is how imagination comes about, if the body exists; and since there is no other equally suitable way of explaining imagination that comes to mind, I can make a probable conjecture that the body exists. But this is only a probability; and despite a careful and comprehensive investigation, I do not yet see how the distinct idea of corporeal nature which I find in my imagination can provide any basis for a necessary inference that some body exists. (Descartes, *M*, 6, 51)

It may provide no basis for any necessary inference, in the sense that such an inference depends on thought alone. But it may be a necessary inference, in quite another sense, for mind to make if it is to know anything: that it belongs to a body, imagines through that body, perceives, conceives, and remembers, all imprinted on the body through which the mind recovers what it knows, loses and recovers experience and life as memory and imagination.

Chapter Six

1. Projected as *The Gift of Touch: Embodying the Good.*

Chapter Seven

1. See my *IR*, chap. 7, for an extended reading of Book I.

2. See chap. 4, n. 4, p. 219.

Chapter Eight

1. Those who differ from us are mad in the extravagance of their reasonings and opinions.

> There is scarce any one that does not observe some thing that seems odd to him, and is in itself really extravagant in the opinions, reasonings, and actions of other men. . . .
>
> I shall be pardoned for calling it by so harsh a name as madness, when it is considered, that opposition to reason deserves that name, and is really madness; and there is scarce a man so free from it, but that if he should always, on all occasions, argue or do as in some cases he constantly does, would not be thought fitter for Bedlam than civil conversation. I do not here mean when he is under the power of an unruly passion, but in the steady calm course of his life. (Locke, *E*, 527–28)

I emphasize this last point in Locke, that it is not just when overcome with uncontainable passions, but when calmly differing with us that we regard others in their thoughts as mad, unreasonable. Reason's authority becomes excessive here to the point of coercion. Locke goes on to offer a horrific example.

> The death of a child, that was the daily delight of his mother's eyes, and joy of her soul, rends from her heart the whole comfort of her life, and gives her all the torment imaginable: Use the consolations of reason in this case, and you were as good preach ease to one on the rack, and hope to allay, by rational discourses, the pain of his joints tearing asunder. Till time has by disuse separated the sense of that enjoyment, and its loss, from the idea of the child returning to her memory, all representations, though ever so reasonable, are in vain; and therefore some in whom the union between these ideas is never dissolved, spend their lives in mourning, and carry an incurable sorrow to their graves. (Locke, *E*, 532)

Indeed, reason cannot prevail against such grief. But is it mad? And is it better that we should hope that a mother might forget the death of her child, might overcome her incurable sorrow?

I associate this desire in Locke with Hume's desire for agreement, repetition, and communication, all good things indeed except where they are taken to excess and where they forbid the excesses of others.

2. Hume's words:

> The great variety of Taste, as well as of opinion, which prevails in the world, is too obvious not to have fallen under every one's observation. . . .
>
> As this variety of taste is obvious to the most careless enquirer; so will it be found, on examination, to be still greater in reality than in appearance. The sentiments of men often differ with regard to beauty and deformity of all kinds, even while their general discourse is the same. (Hume, *OST*, 78)

> It is natural for us to seek a *Standard of Taste;* a rule, by which the various sentiments of men may be reconciled; at least, a decision, afforded, confirming one sentiment, and condemning another. (p. 80)

Triumph and condemnation are central thoughts to Hume in one of his voices. I am at this moment exploring another.

3. For example:

> It is universally allowed that matter, in all its operations, is actuated by a necessary force, and that every natural effect is so precisely determined by the energy of its cause, that no other effect, in such particular circumstances, could possibly have resulted from it. (Hume, *EHU*, 76)

> It is universally acknowledged, that there is a great uniformity among the actions of men, in all nations and ages, and that human nature remains still the same, in its principles and operations. (p. 77)

> So readily and universally do we acknowledge a uniformity in human motives and actions as well as in the operations of body. (p. 79)

> Thus it appears, not only that the conjunction between motives and voluntary actions is as regular and uniform, as that between the cause and effect in any part of nature; but also that this regular conjunction has been universally acknowledged among mankind, and has never been the subject of dispute, either in philosophy or common life. (p. 82)

4. See p. 62.

Chapter Nine

1. See here chap. 4, pp. 78–79.

Chapter Ten

1. From *Phaedrus:*

> The story is that once upon a time these creatures were men—men of an age before there were any Muses—and that when the latter came into the

world, and music made its appearance, some of the people of those days were so thrilled with pleasure that they went on singing, and quite forgot to eat and drink until they actually died without noticing. From them in due course sprang the race of cicadas, to which the Muses have granted the boon of needing no sustenance right from their birth, but of singing from the very first, without food or drink, until the day of their death, after which they go and report to the Muses how they severally are paid honor among mankind, and by whom. (Plato, *Phaedrus*, 259c)

Chapter Eleven

1. See here chap. 1, p. 15.

2. This is a reference to my *Plenishment in the Earth,* and to Kristeva, "Stabat Mater."

3. More explicitly:

> Man is a rope, tied between beast and overman—a rope over an abyss. A dangerous across, a dangerous on-the-way, a dangerous looking-back, a dangerous shuddering and stopping. (Nietzsche, *Z,* 126)

> What is great in man is that he is a bridge and not an end: what can be loved in man is that he is an *overture* and a *going under.* (p. 127)

Chapter Twelve

1. These words are taken from a somewhat longer passage, in the original:

> « En quoi » ce *est* pour qu'il opère, antérieurement à tout savoir . . . ? Avant leur position possible en « choses » séparées. En quoi ce « est » pour avoir un tel pouvoir de fonder l'être et la présence, tout en disparaissant dans l'acte de fondation même ? Pour qu'il ait déjà été « utilisé » — et utilisant ? — sans qu'aucune naissance puisse lui être attribuée. Pour qu'il ait déjà donné lieu à l'être sans qu'aucun commencement de l'être soit. . . .
> En quoi ce *est* ? Diaphane, translucide, transparent. Transcendant ? Médiation, médium fluide mettant en rapport sans obstacle le tout avec lui-même, et certaines de ses parties entre elles suivant leurs propriétés : réelles ou décrétées « vraies ».
> En quoi ce *est* ? En air.

2. See here chap. 1, p. 16.

3. I do not need to remind you of the meanings of "rest *(reste),* " not least the ashes of mortal bodies. I discuss some of them throughout my *PE.* What gift comes from the good that does not hope for us that we will rest in peace?
A thought that may have everything to do with truth. Perhaps.

4. Discussed in my *PE*, chap. 5, and at much greater length in my *GB*, chap. 7, where abundance touches the profusion of capitalism, the blasphemy of the curse. See especially *GB*, p. 380.

5. For Plato it is the indefiniteness of the dyad, of the definite something.

Chapter Thirteen

1. See my *RR*, chaps. 9 and 10.

2. See the Introduction here, pp. 10–12.

3. I recall my *RR* in whose sonance we may hear the general economy of representation and judgment joined with its restrictions and exclusions. I also recall my *PE* and the indefiniteness of every dyad and measure.

4. See my *PE*, pp. 318–22.

Bibliography

Adams, Carol J. *The Sexual Politics of Meat [SPM]*. New York: Continuum, 1992.

Agamben, Giorgio. *Language and Death: The Place of Negativity [LD]*. Minneapolis: University of Minnesota Press, 1991.

Addelson, Kathryn Pyne. *Impure Thoughts [IT]*. Philadelphia: Temple University Press, 1991.

———. "The Man of Professional Wisdom" *[MPW]*. In *Impure Thoughts*.

Andolsen, Barbara Hilkert, Christine E. Gudorf, and Mary D. Pellauer, eds. *Women's Consciousness, Women's Conscience [WCWC]*. New York: Winston, 1985.

Aquinas, Thomas. *Basic Writings of St. Thomas Aquinas [BWTA]*. Ed. Anton C. Pegis. 2 vols. New York: Random House, 1945.

———. *Summa Theologica [ST]*. Trans. Fathers of the English Dominican Province. London: Burns, Oates & Washbourne, 1912–36.

Arendt, Hannah. *Eichmann in Jerusalem: A Report on the Banality of Evil [EJ]*. Rev. and enl. ed. New York: Viking, 1964.

———. *The Human Condition [HC]*. Chicago: University of Chicago Press, 1958.

Arens, W., and I. Karp, eds. *Creativity of Power [CP]*. Washington and London: Smithsonian Press, 1989.

Aristotle. Ed. Richard McKeon. *The Basic Works of Aristotle*. New York: Random House, 1941.

———. *The Complete Works of Aristotle*. Ed. Jonathan Barnes. 2 vols. Princeton: Princeton University Press, 1984. All quotations from Aristotle are from this edition unless otherwise indicated.

———. *Poetics [P]*. Reprinted in part in Ross, *Art and Its Significance*. From *Basic Works of Aristotle*.

Augustine. *Basic Writings of Saint Augustine [BWA]*. Ed. and int. Whitney J. Oates. New York: Random House, 1948.

———. *City of God [CG]*. In *Basic Writings of Saint Augustine*.

Bakhtin, Mikhail Mikhailovich. *Discourse in the Novel [DN]*. Reprinted in part in Ross, *Art and Its Significance*. From *The Dialogic Imagination*. Ed. Michael Holquist. Trans. Caryl Emerson and Michael Holquist. Austin: University of Texas Press, 1981.

Bataille, Georges. *The Accursed Share: An Essay on General Economy [AS]*. Trans. Richard Hurley. 2 vols. New York: Zone Books, 1988 and 1993. Translation of *La Part maudite, L'Histoire de l'érotisme*, and *La Souveraineté (Consumption [1]; The History of Eroticism [2]; Sovereignty [3])*. In Georges Bataille, *Oeuvres Complètes*. Paris: Gallimard, 1976.

———. *L'Expérience intérieure*. Paris: Gallimard, 1954.

———. *Méthode de Méditation [MM]*. In *L'Expérience intérieure*. Quoted in Derrida, "From Restricted to General Economy."

Baudrillard, Jean. *Forget Foucault [FF]*. New York: Semiotext(e), 1987.

Benjamin, Walter. *Erfahrung und Armut [EA]*. Passages quoted in Derrida, "Letter to Peter Eisenman."

———. "The Work of Art in the Age of Its Technical Reproducibility" *[WAATR]*. Reprinted in part in Ross, *Art and Its Significance*. Selections from "The Work of Art in the Age of Mechanical Reproduction." Trans. Harry Zohn. In *Illuminations*. New York: Harcourt Brace & World, 1968.

Bernal, Martin. *Black Athena: The Afroasiatic Roots of Classical Civilization, Volume 1: The Fabrication of Ancient Greece 1785–1985 [BA]*. New Brunswick: Rutgers University Press, 1987.

Blake, William. *The Book of Urizen [BU]*. Ed. and comm. Kay Parkhurst Easson and Roger R. Easson. Boulder: Shambhala and New York: Random House, 1987.

Bowden, Ross. "Sorcery, Illness and Social Control in Kwoma Society" *[SISC]*. In Stephen, *Sorcerer and Witch*.

Bullough, Edward. "'Psychical Distance' as a Factor in Art and as an Aesthetic Principle" *[PD]*. Reprinted in Ross, *Art and Its Significance*. Originally published in *British Journal of Psychology* (1912): 87–98.

Burtt, Edwin A., ed. *The English Philosophers from Bacon to Mill [EPBM]*. New York: Modern Library, 1959.

Butler, Judith. *Gender Trouble: Feminism and the Subversion of Identity [GT]*. New York: Routledge, 1990.

Caputo, John D. *Against Ethics: Contributions to a Poetics of Obligation with Constant Reference to Deconstruction [AE]*. Bloomington: Indiana University Press, 1993.

Card, Claudia ed. *Feminist Ethics [FE]*. Lawrence: University Press of Kansas, 1991.

Cheal, David. *The Gift Economy [GE]*. New York: Routledge, 1988.

Cheney, Jim. "Eco-feminism and Deep Ecology" *[EDE]*. In *Environmental Ethics* 9 (1987).

Christ, Carol P. "Reverence for Life: The Need for a Sense of Finitude" *[RL]*. In Cooey, Farmer, and Ross, *Embodied Love*.

———. "Spiritual Quest and Women's Experience" *[SQWE]*. In Christ and Plaskow, *WomenSpirit Rising*.

Christ, Carol P., and Judith Plaskow. *WomanSpirit Rising [WR]*. New York: Harper & Row, 1979.

Cixous, Hélène, and Catherine Clément. *The Newly Born Woman [NBW]*. Trans. Betsy Wing. Int. Sandra M. Gilbert. Minneapolis: University of Minnesota Press, 1975.

Clark, Cedric X. "Some Implications of Nkrumah's Consciencism for Alternative Coordinates in NonEuropean Causality" *[SINC]*. In Ruch and Anyanwu, *African Philosophy*.

Clément, Catherine. "The Guilty Ones" *[GO]*. In Cixous and Clément, *The Newly Born Woman*.

Clifford, James. "On Collecting Art and Culture" *[CAC]*. Reprinted in Ross, *Art and Its Significance*. From *Out There: Marginalization and Contemporary Cultures*. New York: New Museum of Contemporary Art and Cambridge: MIT Press, 1990, 141–46, 151–65.

Cole, Eve Browning and Susan Coultrap-McQuin, eds. *Explorations in Feminist Ethics: Theory and Practice [EFE]*. Bloomington: Indiana University Press, 1992.

Coleridge, Samuel Taylor. *Biographia Literaria [BL]*. Ed. J. Shawcross. London: Oxford University Press, 1949.

Cooey, Paula M. "The Word Become Flesh: Woman's Body, Language, and Value" *[WF]*. In Cooey, Farmer, and Ross, *Embodied Love*.

Cooey, Paula M., Sharon A. Farmer, and Mary Ellen Ross, eds. *Embodied Love: Sensuality and Relationship as Feminist Values [EL]*. San Francisco: Harper & Row, 1987.

Cornell, Drucilla, Michel Rosenfeld, and David Gray Carlson, eds. *Deconstruction and the Possibility of Justice [DPJ]*. New York: Routledge, Chapman and Hall, 1992.

Cose, Ellis. *A Nation of Strangers [NS]*. New York: William Morrow and Co., 1992.

Curtin, Deane. "Toward an Ecological Ethic of Care" *[TEEC]*. In Warren, *Hypatia* 6.

Curtiss, Susan. *Genie: A Psycholinguistic Study of a Modern-Day "Wild Child" [G]*. New York: Academic Press, 1977.

Daly, Mary. "After the Death of God the Father: Women's Liberation and the Transformation of Christian Consciousness" *[ADGF]*. In Christ and Plaskow, *WomenSpirit Rising*.

———. *Gyn/Ecology: The Metaethics of Radical Feminism [G/E]*. Boston: Beacon Press, 1990.

Danto, Arthur C. "Approaching the End of Art." In *State of the Art*, 202–18.

———. *The State of the Art [SA]*. New York: Prentice Hall, 1987.

———. *Transfiguration of the Commonplace: A Philosophy of Art [TC]*. Cambridge: Harvard University Press, 1981.

Deleuze, Gilles. *Différence et répétition [DR]*. Paris: P.U.F., 1969.

———. *Logique du sens [LS]*. Paris: Minuit, 1969.

Deleuze, Gilles, and Félix Guattari. *Anti-Oedipus: Capitalism and Schizophrenia [A-O]*. Trans. Robert Hurley, Mark Seem, and Helen R. Lane. Minneapolis: University of Minnesota Press, 1983.

———. *A Thousand Plateaus: Capitalism and Schizophrenia [TP]*. Trans. Brian Massumi. Minneapolis: University of Minnesota Press, 1987.

Derrida, Jacques. "Cogito and the History of Madness" *[CHM]*. In *Writing and Difference*.

———. *Dissemination [D]*. Trans. and int. Barbara Johnson. Chicago: University of Chicago Press, 1981.

———. "Economimesis" *[E]*. *Diacritics* 11 (June 1981).

———. "Force of Law: The 'Mystical Foundation of Authority'" *[FL]*. In Cornell, Rosenfeld, and Carlson, *Deconstruction and the Possibility of Justice*. Reprinted from *Cardozo Law Review* 11 (1991).

———. "From Restricted to General Economy: A Hegelianism Without Reserve" *[FRGE]*. In *Writing and Difference*.

———. "Geschlecht: Sexual Difference, Ontological Difference" *[G1]*. *Research in Phenomenology* 13 (1983).

———. "Geschlecht II: Heidegger's Hand" *[G2]*. Trans. John P. Leavey, Jr. In Sallis, *Deconstruction in Philosophy: The Texts of Jacques Derrida*.

———. *The Gift of Death [DT]*. Trans. David Wills. Chicago: University of Chicago Press, 1994.

———. *Given Time [GT]*. Trans. Peggy Kamuf. Chicago: University of Chicago Press, 1992.

———. "Heidegger's Ear: Philopolemology *(Geschlecht IV)*" *[G4]*. In Sallis, *Reading Heidegger*. Bloomington: Indiana University Press, 1993.

————. "Letter to Peter Eisenman" *[LPE]*. Reprinted in Ross, *Art and Its Significance*. From *Assemblage* 12: 7–13.

————. *Of Spirit: Heidegger and the Question [OS]*. Trans. Geoffrey Bennington and Rachel Bowlby. Chicago: University of Chicago Press, 1989.

————. "Parergon" *[P]*. Reprinted in part in Ross, *Art and Its Significance*.

————. "Passe-Partout" *[P-P]*. Reprinted in Ross, *Art and Its Significance*. Introduction to *Truth in Painting*.

————. "Plato's Pharmacy" *[PP]*. From *Dissemination*.

————. "The Politics of Friendship" *[PF]*. In *The Journal of Philosophy* 85 (November 1988).

————. "Restitutions" *[R]*. Reprinted in part in Ross, *Art and Its Significance*. From *Truth in Painting*.

————. *The Truth in Painting [TP]*. Trans. G. Bennington and I. McLeod. Chicago: University of Chicago Press, 1987.

————. "Violence and Metaphysics: An Essay on the Thought of Emmanuel Levinas" *[VM]*. In *Writing and Difference*.

————. *Writing and Difference [WD]*. Trans. Alan Bass. Chicago: University of Chicago Press, 1978.

Descartes, René. *Discourse on the Method of Rightly Conducting the Reason and Seeking Truth in the Sciences [DM]*. In *Philosophical Writings of Descartes*, Vol. 1.

————. *Early Writings [EW]*. In *Philosophical Writings of Descartes*, Vol. 1.

————. *Meditations [M]*. In *Philosophical Writings of Descartes*, Vol. 2.

————. *Objections and Replies [OR]*. In *Philosophical Writings of Descartes*, Vol. 2.

————. *Optics [O]*. In *Philosophical Writings of Descartes*, Vol. 1.

————. *The Passions of the Soul [PS]*. In *Philosophical Writings of Descartes*, Vol. 1.

————. *The Philosophical Writings of Descartes [PWD]*. Trans. John Cottingham, Robert Stoothoff, and Dugald Murdoch. 2 vols. Cambridge: Cambridge University Press, 1985.

————. *Principles of Philosophy [PP]*. In *Philosophical Writings of Descartes*, Vol. 1.

————. *Rules for the Direction of the Mind [RDM]*. In *Philosophical Writings of Descartes*, Vol. 1.

————. *Treatise on Man [TM]*. In *Philosophical Writings of Descartes*, Vol. 1

————. *The World [W]*. In *Philosophical Writings of Descartes*, Vol. 1.

Dewey, John. *Art and Experience [AE]*. New York: Putnam, 1934. Reprinted in part in Ross, *Art and Its Significance.*

———. "Body and Mind" *[BM]*. In *Philosophy and Civilization.*

———. "Context and Thought" *[CT]*. In *Experience, Nature, and Freedom.*

———. *Experience and Nature [EN]*. 2nd ed. New York: Dover, 1958.

———. *Experience, Nature, and Freedom [ENF]*. Ed. and int. Richard J. Bernstein. Indianapolis: Library of Liberal Arts, 1960.

———. *Human Nature and Conduct [HNC]*. New York: Holt, 1922.

———. "The Need for a Recovery of Philosophy" *[NRP]*. In *Experience, Nature, and Freedom.*

———. *Logic: The Theory of Inquiry [L]*. New York: Henry Holt & Co., 1938.

———. "Nature in Experience" *[NE]*. In *Experience, Nature, and Freedom.*

———. *Philosophy and Civilization [PC]*. New York: Minton, Balch, 1931.

———. *Quest for Certainty [QC]*. New York: Minton, Balch, 1929.

———. *Theory of Valuation [TV]*. Chicago: University of Chicago, 1939.

Dixon, Vernon J. "World Views and Research Methodology" *[WVRM]*. In King, Dixon, and Nobles, *African Philosophy.*

duBois, Page. *Torture and Truth [TT]*. New York: Routledge, 1991.

Dworkin, Andrea. *Intercourse [I]*. New York: Free Press, 1987.

Dworkin, Ronald. "Feminists and Abortion" *[FA]*. In *The New York Review of Books* 40, no. 11 (June 10, 1993).

———. Review of MacKinnon, *Only Words [OW]*. In *The New York Review of Books* 40, no. 17 (October 21, 1993).

Ecker, Gisela, ed. *Feminist Aesthetics [FA]*. Trans. Harriet Anderson. Boston: Beacon Press, 1985.

Euripides, *Hecuba*. Trans. E. P. Coleridge. In Oates and O'Neill, *Complete Greek Drama.*

Feyerabend, Paul. *Against Method: Outline of an Anarchistic Theory of Knowledge [AM]*. Atlantic Highlands: Humanities Press, 1975.

Foucault, Michel. *Archaeology of Knowledge [AK]*. Trans. A. M. Sheridan-Smith. New York: Pantheon, 1981.

———. *The Care of the Self [CS]*. Trans. Robert Hurley. New York: Pantheon, 1986.

———. *Discipline and Punish: The Birth of the Prison [DP]*. Trans. Alan Sheridan, New York: Vintage, 1979.

———. *Folie et déraison: Histoire de la folie à la l'âge classique [FD]*. Paris: Plon, 1961.

———. *History of Sexuality, Vol. 1 [HS]*. Trans. R. Hurley. New York: Vintage, 1980.

———. *Language, Counter-memory, Practice [LCP]*. Trans. Donald F. Bouchard and Sherry Simon. Ed. and int. Donald F. Bouchard. Ithaca, N.Y.: Cornell University Press, 1977.

———. *Madness and Civilization: A History of Insanity in the Age of Reason [MC]*. Trans. Richard Howard. New York: Random House, 1965. Translation and abridgment of *Folie et déraison*.

———. "Nietzsche, Genealogy, History" *[NGH]*. In *Language, Counter-memory, Practice*.

———. *The Order of Things: An Archaeology of the Human Sciences [OT]*. New York: Vintage, 1973.

———. *Power/Knowledge [P/K]*. Ed. and trans. C. Gordon. New York: Pantheon, 1980.

———. "A Preface to Transgression" *[PT]*. In *Language Counter-memory, Practice*.

———. "Theatrum Philosophicum" *[TP]*. In *Language, Counter-memory, Practice*.

———. "Truth and Power" *[TrP]*. In *Power/Knowledge*.

———. "Two Lectures" *[2L]*. In *Power/Knowledge*.

Freud, Sigmund. "Femininity" *[F]*. In *New Introductory Lectures on Psychoanalysis*. Vol. 22. From *The Standard Edition of the Complete Psychological Works of Sigmund Freud*. Ed. James Strachey. 24 vols. London: Hogarth Press, 1953–74.

———. "The Relation of the Poet to Day-dreaming" *[RPD]*. Reprinted in Ross, *Art and Its Significance*. From Sigmund Freud, *Collected Papers*. Vol. 4. Article trans. I. F. Grant Duff. New York: Basic Books, 1959.

Fry, Tony, and Anne-Marie Willis. "Aboriginal Art: Symptom or Success?" *[AA]*. Reprinted in part in Ross, *Art and Its Significance*. From *Art in America* (July 1989): 111–16, 159–61.

Fuller, Steve. *Social Epistemology [SE]*. Bloomington and Indianapolis: Indiana University Press, 1988.

Gadamer, Hans-Georg. *Truth and Method [TM]*. New York: Seabury, 1975.

Gilbert, Bil. "Crows By Far and Wide, But There's No Place Like Home" *[C]*. *Smithsonian* 25, no. 5 (August 1992).

Gilligan, Carol. *In a Different Voice: Psychological Theory and Women's Development [IDV]*. Cambridge: Harvard University Press, 1982.

Goodman, Nelson. *Languages of Art: An Approach to a Theory of Symbols [LA]*. 2nd ed. Indianapolis: Hackett, 1976.

———. *Ways of Worldmaking [WW]*. Indianapolis: Hackett, 1978.

Gottlieb, Alma. "Witches, Kings, and the Sacrifice of Identity or The Power of Paradox and the Paradox of Power among the Beng of Ivory Coast" *[WKS]*. In Arens and Karp, *Creativity of Power*.

Göttner-Abendroth, Heide. "Nine Principles of a Matriarchal Aesthetics" *[MA]*. Trans. Harriet Anderson. Reprinted in Ross, *Art and Its Significance*. From Ecker, *Feminist Aesthetics*.

Graves, Robert. *The Greek Myths [GM]*. Baltimore: Penguin, 1955.

Griffin, Susan. *A Chorus of Stones [CS]*. New York: Doubleday, 1992.

Guidieri, R. "Les sociétés primitives aujourd'hui" *[SPA]*. In *Philosopher: les interrogations contemporarines*. Ed. Ch. Delacampagne and R. Maggiori. Paris: Fayard, 1980.

Habermas, Jürgen. *Communication and the Evolution of Society [CES]*. Trans. T. McCarthy. Boston: Beacon Press, 1979.

Hallen, Barry. "Phenomenology and the Exposition of African Traditional Thought" *[PEATT]*. In *Proceedings of the Seminar on African Philosophy/La Philosophie Africaine*. Ed. Claude Sumner. Addis Ababa: Chamber Printing House, 1980.

Hallen, B., and J. O. Sodipo. *Knowledge, Belief and Witchcraft: Analytic Experiments in African Philosophy [KBW]*. London: Ethnographica, 1986.

Harding, Sandra. "The Curious Coincidence of Feminine and African Moralities: Challenges for Feminist Theory" *[CCFAM]*. In Kittay and Meyers, *Women and Moral Theory*.

———. "The Instability of the Analytical Categories of Feminist Theory" *[IACFT]*. *Signs*, 11, no. 4 (1986).

———. *The Science Question in Feminism [SQF]*. Ithaca, N.Y.: Cornell University Press, 1986.

———. *Whose Science? Whose Knowledge?: Thinking from Women's Lives [WSWK]*. Ithaca, N.Y.: Cornell University Press, 1991.

Hegel, G. W. F. *Aesthetics: Lectures on Fine Art [A]*. Trans. T. M. Knox. London: Oxford University Press, 1975. Introduction reprinted in part in Ross, *Art and Its Significance* as "Philosophy of Fine Art" *[PFA]*.

———. *Jenenser Realphilosophie I, Der Vorlesungen von 1803–1804 [JR1]*. Ed. J. Hoffmeister. Leibzig: 1932. Quoted and translated in Agamben, *Language and Death*.

———. *Jenenser Realphilosophie II, Die Vorlesungen von 1803–1804 [JR2].* Ed. J. Hoffmeister. Leipzig: 1932. Quoted and translated in Agamben, *Language and Death.*

———. *The Logic of Hegel, translated from the Encyclopaedia of the Philosophical Sciences [EL].* Trans. William Wallace. Oxford: Oxford University Press, 1892.

———. *Phenomenology of Mind [PM].* Trans. and int. James Baillie. London: George Allen & Unwin, 1910.

Heidegger, Martin. "The Anaximander Fragment" *[AF].* In *Early Greek Thinking.*

———. *Basic Writings [BW].* Ed. David Farrell Krell. New York: Harper & Row, 1977.

———. *Being and Time [BT].* Trans. John Macquarrie and Edward Robinson. Translation of *Sein und Zeit [SZ].* New York: Harper & Row, 1962.

———. *Discourse on Thinking: A Translation of* Gelassenheit *[DT].* Trans. John M. Anderson and E. Hans Freund. New York: Harper & Row, 1966.

———. *Early Greek Thinking [EGT].* Trans. D. F. Krell and F. A. Capuzzi. New York: Haprer & Row, 1969.

———. *Identity and Difference [ID].* Trans. and int. Joan Stambaugh. New York: Harper & Row, 1969.

———. *Introduction to Metaphysics [IM].* Trans. Ralph Manheim. Garden City, N.Y.: Doubleday, 1961.

———. "Language" *[L].* In *Poetry, Language, Thought.*

———. "Language in the Poem" *[LP].* In *On the Way to Language.*

———. "Letter on Humanism" *[LH].* In *Basic Writings.*

———. "Martin Heidegger interrogé par *Der Spiegel.* Réponses et questions sur l'histoire et la politique" (Martin Heidegger interviewed by *Der Spiegel:* Responses and questions on history and politics.) Trans. William J. Richardson S. J. as " 'Only a God Can Save us': The *Spiegel* Interview." In Sheehan, *Heidegger, the Man and the Thinker.*

———. "The Nature of Language *[NL].* In *On the Way to Language.*

———. "On the Being and Conception of *Physis* in Aristotle's *Physics* B. 1" *[OBCP].* Trans. T. J. Sheehan. *Man and World* 9, no. 3 (August 1976).

———. "On the Essence of Truth" *[OET].* In *Basic Writings.*

———. *On the Way to Language [OWL].* Trans. Peter D. Hertz. New York: Harper & Row, 1971.

———. *On Time and Being [OTB].* Trans. Joan Stambaugh. New York: Harper & Row, 1972.

———. "The Onto-theo-logical Constitution of Metaphysics" *[OTLCM]*. In *Identity and Difference.*

———. "The Origin of the Work of Art" *[OWA]*. Reprinted in part in Ross, *Art and Its Significance.* From *Poetry, Language, Thought.*

———. *Poetry, Language, Thought [PLT].* Trans. Albert Hofstadter. New York: Harper & Row, 1971.

———. "The Question Concerning Technology" *[QT]*. In *Basic Writings.*

———. "Time and Being" *[TB]*. In *On Time and Being.*

———. *Was ist das—die Philosophie [WP]*, 1955. Quoted in Derrida, "Heidegger's Ear."

———. "The Way to Language" *[WL]*. In *On the Way to Language.*

———. "What Calls for Thinking?" *[WCT]*. In *Basic Writings.*

Hobbes, Thomas. *Complete Works.* Ed. William Molesworth. English Works, 11 vols., 1839. Latin Works, 5 vols., 1845.

———. *Elements of Philosophy [EOP].* In *Complete Works,* Vol 4.

———. *Leviathan [L].* In *Complete Works,* Vol 1.

Hölderlin, Friedrich. *Friedrich Hölderlin Poems and Fragments.* Trans. Michael Hamburger. Ann Arbor: University of Michigan Press, 1966.

———. "Patmos." In *Friedrich Hölderlin Poems and Fragments.*

Hume, David. *An Enquiry Concerning Human Understanding [EHU].* New York: Prometheus, 1988.

———. "Of the Standard of Taste" *[OST]*. Reprinted in Ross, *Art and Its Significance.*

———. *A Treatise of Human Nature [T].* London: Oxford University Press, 1888.

Hyde, Lewis. *The Gift: Imagination and the Erotic Life of Property [G].* New York: Random House, 1979.

Irigaray, Luce. "Any Theory of the 'Subject' Has Always Been Appropriated by the 'Masculine'" [ATS]. In *Speculum of the Other Woman.*

———. "The Culture of Difference" *[CD]*. In *Je, tu, nous.*

———. *An Ethics of Sexual Difference [ESD].* Trans. Carolyn Burke and Gillian C. Gill. Ithaca, N.Y.: Cornell University Press, 1993. Translation of *Éthique de la Différence sexuelle [ÉDS].* Paris: Minuit, 1984.

———. "He Risks Who Risks Life Itself" *[HR]*. In *Irigaray Reader.*

———. *The Irigaray Reader [IR].* Trans. Seán Hand. Ed. and int. Margaret Whitford. Oxford: Blackwell, 1991.

———. *Je, tu, nous: Toward a Culture of Difference [JTN]*. Trans. Alison Martin. New York: Routledge, 1993.

———. *Marine Lover of Friedrich Nietzsche [ML]*. Trans. Gillian C. Gill. New York: Columbia University Press, 1991.

———. "The 'Mechanics' of Fluids" *[MF]*. In *This Sex Which Is Not One*.

———. "La Mystérique" *[M]*. In *Speculum of the Other Woman*.

———. *L'oubli de l'air: Chez Martin Heidegger [OA]*. Paris: Minuit, 1983.

———. "The Power of Discourse and the Subordination of the Feminine" *[PDSF]*. In *This Sex Which Is Not One*.

———. "Questions" *[Q]*. In Irigaray Reader.

———. "Questions to Emmanuel Levinas" *[QEL]*. In *Irigaray Reader*.

———. "Sexual Difference" *[SD]*. In *Irigaray Reader*.

———. *Speculum of the Other Woman [SOW]*. Trans. Gillian C. Gill. Ithaca, N.Y.: Cornell University Press, 1985. Translation of *Speculum de l'autre femme*. Paris: Minuit, 1974.

———. *This Sex Which Is Not One [SWNO]*. Trans. Catherine Porter. Ithaca, N.Y.: Cornell University Press, 1985.

———. "Volume-Fluidity" *[VF]*. Translation of "L'incontourable volume" *(Volume without contours)*." In *Speculum of the Other Woman*.

———. "When Our Lips Speak Together" *[WOLST]*. In *This Sex Which Is Not One*.

———. "Why Define Sexed Rights?" *[WSDR]*. In *Je, tu, nous*.

———. "Women on the Market" *[WM]*. In *This Sex Which Is Not One*.

James, William. *Essays in Radical Empiricism [ERE]*. New York: Longman's Green, 1912.

Johnson, Mark. *The Body in the Mind: The Bodily Basis of Meaning, Imagination, and Reason [BM]*. Chicago: University of Chicago Press, 1987.

Jung, Carl Gustav. *Modern Man in Search of a Soul [MMSS]*. Trans. W. S. Dell and Cary F. Baynes. New York: Harcourt Brace Jovanovich, 1955.

———. *"Psychology and Literature" [PL]*. Reprinted in Ross, *Art and Its Significance*. From *Modern Man in Search of a Soul*.

Kafka, Franz. *The Complete Stories [CS]*. Ed. Nahum N. Glatzer. New York: Schocken, 1971.

Kant, Immanuel. *The Conflict of the Faculties; Der Streit der Fakultäten [CF]*. Trans. Mary J. Gregor. New York: Abaris, 1979.

——. *Critique of Judgment [CJ]*. Trans. J. H. Bernard. New York: Hafner, 1951. Translation of *Kritik der Urteilskraft*. In *Kritik der Urteilskraft und Schriften zur Naturphilosophie*. Wiesbaden: Insel-Verlag Zweigstelle, 1957.

——. *Critique of Practical Reason [CPrR]*. From *Kant's Critique of Practical Reason and Other Works on the Theory of Ethics*. Trans. T. K. Abbott. London: Longman's Green, 1954.

——. *Critique of Pure Reason [CPR]*. Trans. J. M. D. Meiklejohn. Buffalo: Prometheus, 1990. Trans. Norman Kemp Smith *[CPR (NKS)]*. New York: St. Martin's, 1956. Translation of *Kritik der reinen Vernunft [KRV]*. 2 Band. Berlin: Deutsche Bibliothek, 1936.

——. *Fundamental Principles of the Metaphysics of Morals [FPMM]*. In *Kant's Critique of Practical Reason and Other Works on the Theory of Ethics*.

——. *Lectures on Ethics [LE]*. Trans. L. Infield. New York: Harper & Row, 1963.

——. *The Metaphysical Principles of Virtue [MPV]*. Indianapolis: Bobbs-Merrill, 1968.

Kheel, Marti. "The Liberation of Nature: A Circular Affair" *[LN]*. In Environmental Ethics 6, no. 4 (1985).

Kierkegaard, Søren. *Either/Or [E/O]*. Trans. David F. Swenson and Lillian Marvin Swenson. Rev. Howard A. Johnson. 2 vols. Garden City, N.Y.: Doubleday, 1959.

——. *Fear and Trembling/The Sickness Unto Death [FT]*. Trans. W. Lowrie. Garden City, N.Y.: Doubleday, 1954.

King, Lewis M. "On the Nature of a Creative World" *[ONCW]*. In Ruch and Anyanwu, *African Philosophy*.

King, Lewis M., Vernon J. Dixon, and Wade W. Nobles, eds. *African Philosophy: Assumption and Paradigms for Research on Black Persons [AP]*. Los Angeles: Charles R. Drew Postgraduate Medical School, 1976. Fanon Research and Development Center Publication, Area 8, #2.

King, Roger J. H. "Caring About Nature: Feminist Ethics and the Environment" *[CN]*. In Warren, *Hypatia* 6.

King, Ynestra. "The Ecology of Feminism and the Feminism of Ecology" *[EFFE]*. In Plant, *Healing the Wounds*.

Kirkham, Richard L. *Theories of Truth: A Critical Introduction [TT]*. Cambridge, Mass.: MIT Press, 1992.

Kittay, Eva Feder and Diana T. Meyers, eds. *Women and Moral Theory [WMT]*. Totowa, N.J.: Rowman & Littlefield, 1987.

Krell, David Farrell. *Daimon Life: Heidegger and Life-Philosophy [DL]*. Bloomington: Indiana University Press, 1992.

———. *Intimations of Mortality [IM]*. University Park: Pennsylvania State University Press, 1986.

Kristeva, Julia. *The Kristeva Reader [KR]*. Ed. Toril Moi. Trans. Alice Jardine and Harry Blake. New York: Columbia University Press, 1986.

———. "Stabat Mater" *[SM]*. In *Kristeva Reader*.

———. *Strangers to Ourselves [SO]*. Trans. Leon S. Roudiez. New York: Columbia University Press, 1991.

———. "Women's Time" *[WT]*. In *Kristeva Reader*. Published as "Le temps des femmes." In *Cahiers de recherche de sciences des textes et documents* 5 (Winter 1979).

Lacan, Jacques. *Feminine Sexuality [FS]*. Ed. Juliet Mitchell and Jacqueline Rose. Trans. Jacqueline Rose. New York: Norton, 1985.

———. "God and the *Jouissance* of The Woman" *[GJW]*. In *Feminine Sexuality*.

Lacoue-Labarthe, Philippe. *The Subject of Philosophy [SP]*. Trans. Thomas Trezise, Hugh J. Silverman, Gary M. Cole, Timothy D. Bent, Karen McPherson, and Claudette Sartiliot. Ed. Thomas Trezise. Minneapolis: University of Minnesota Press, 1993. Translation of *Le Sujet de la philosophie [Sp]*. Paris: Aubier-Flammarion, 1979.

Lahar, Stephanie. "Ecofeminist Theory and Grassroots Politics" *[ETGP]*. In Warren, *Hypatia* 6.

Langer, Susanne K. *Feeling and Form: A Theory of Art [FF]*. New York: Scribner's, 1953.

Leibniz, G. W. F. "The Exigency to Exist in Essences: Principle of Plenitude" *[EEE]*. In *Leibniz Selections*.

———. *Leibniz Selections*. Ed. P. Wiener. New York: Scribner's, 1951. All references to Leibniz are from this edition.

———. "The Monadology" *[M]*. In *Leibniz Selections*.

Levinas, Emmanuel. *The Levinas Reader [LR]*. Ed. Seán Hand. Oxford: Blackwell, 1989.

———. "Martin Buber and the Theory of Knowledge" *[MBTK]*. In *Levinas Reader*.

———. *Otherwise Than Being or Beyond Essence [OB]*. Trans. Alfonso Lingis. The Hague: Martinus Nijhoff, 1978. Translation of *Autrement qu'être ou au-delà de l'essence [AÊ]*. The Hague: Martinus Nijhoff, 1974.

———. "Reality and Its Shadow *[RS]*. Trans. Alphonso Lingis. In *Levinas Reader*.

———. *Totality and Infinity [TI]*. Trans. Alfonso Lingis. Pittsburgh: Duquesne University Press, 1969.

———. "The Transcendence of Words" *[TW]*. Trans. Seán Hand. In *Levinas Reader*.

Lévi-Strauss, Claude. *The Elementary Structure of Kinship [ESK]*. Trans. James Harle Bell, John Richard von Sturmer, and Rodney Needham. Boston: Beacon, 1969.

Linsky, Leonard, ed. *Semantics and the Philosophy of Language [SPL]*. Urbana: University of Illinois Press, 1952.

Locke, John. *An Essay Concerning Human Understanding [E]*. Ed. Alexander Campbell Fraser. New York: Dover, 1959.

Lugones, Marìa C. "On the Logic of Pluralist Feminism" *[OLPF]*. In Card, *Feminist Ethics*.

———. "Playfulness, 'World'-Travelling, and Loving Perception" *[PWTLP]*. In *Hypatia* 2, no. 2 (Summer 1987).

Lyotard, Jean-François. *Le Différend [D]*. Paris: Minuit, 1983.

———. *The Differend: Phrases in Dispute [DPD]*. Trans. Georges Van Den Abbeele. Minneapolis: University of Minnesota Press, 1988.

———. "Europe, the Jew, and the Book" *[EJB]*. In *Political Writings*.

———. "German Guilt" *[GG]*. In *Political Writings*.

———. "The Grip *(Mainmise)*" *[G]*. In *Political Writings*.

———. *Heidegger and "the jews" [HJ]*. Trans. A. Michel and M. Roberts. Minneapolis: University of Minnesota Press, 1990.

———. "Heidegger and 'the jews': A Conference in Vienna and Freiburg" *["HJ"]*. In *Political Writings*.

———. *The Inhuman: Reflections on Time [I]*. Trans. Geoffrey Bennington and Rachel Bowlby. Stanford: Stanford University Press, 1991.

———. *The Lyotard Reader [LR]*. Ed. Andrew Benjamin. Oxford: Blackwell, 1989.

———. *"Oikos" [O]*. In *Political Writings*.

———. *Peregrinations [P]*. New York: Columbia University Press, 1988.

———. *Political Writings [PW]*. Trans. Bill Readings and Kevin Paul Geiman. Minneapolis: University of Minneosta Press, 1993.

———. "The Sign of History" *[SH]*. In *Lyotard Reader*.

———. *"What Is Postmodernism?" [WPM?]*. Reprinted in part in Ross, *Art and Its Significance*. From *Postmodern Condition*.

MacKinnon, Catharine A. "Feminism, Marxism, Method, and the State: An Agenda for Theory" *[FMMS1]*. In *Signs* 7, no. 3 (1982).

———. "Feminism, Marxism, Method, and the State: Toward Feminist Jurisprudence" *[FMMS2]*. In *Signs* 8, no. 4 (1982).

———. *Feminism Unmodified: Discourses on Life and Law [FU]*. Cambridge: Harvard University Press, 1987.

———. *Only Words [OW]*. Cambridge: Harvard University Press, 1993.

———. *Toward a Feminist Theory of the State [TFTS]*. Cambridge: Harvard University Press, 1989.

Mauss, Marcel. *The Gift: Forms and Functions of Exchange in Archaic Societies [G]*. Trans. Ian Cunnison. Glenco: Free Press, 1954. Also *The Gift: The Form and Reason for Exchange in Archaic Societies*. Trans. W. D. Halls. London: Routledge, 1990.

Mbiti, John S. *African Religions and Philosophy [ARP]*. London: Heinemann Educational Books, Ltd., 1969.

Merleau-Ponty, Maurice. *Eye and Mind [EM]*. Trans. Carleton Dallery. Reprinted in part in Ross, *Art and Its Significance*. From *Primacy of Perception*, 282–98.

———. *Phenomenology of Perception [PhP]*. Trans. Colin Smith. London: Routledge & Kegan Paul, 1962.

———. *Primacy of Perception [PrP]*. Ed. James M. Edie. Chicago: Northwestern University Press, 1964.

Meyer, Christine, and Faith Moosang, eds. *Living with the Land: Communities Restoring the Earth [LL]*. Gabriola Island, BC: New Society Publishers, 1992.

Mill, John Stuart. *On Liberty with The Subjection of Women [L]*. New York: Cambridge University Press, 1989.

———. *Utilitarianism and Other Essays [U]*. New York: Penguin, 1987.

Mudimbe, V. Y. *The Invention of Africa [IA]*. Reprinted in part in Ross, *Art and Its Significance*. From *The Invention of Africa: Gnosis, Philosophy, and the Order of Knowledge*. Bloomington: Indiana University Press, 1988.

Nancy, Jean-Luc. *The Inoperative Community [IC]*. Trans. P. Connor, L. Garbus, M. Holland, and S. Sawhney. Minneapolis: University of Minnesota Press, 1991.

Nietzsche, Friedrich. "Attempt at a Self-Criticism" *[ASC]*. In *Basic Writings*. Reprinted in Ross, *Art and Its Significance*.

———. *Basic Writings of Nietzsche*. Trans. Walter Kaufmann. New York: Random House, Modern Library Giant, 1968.

———. *Birth of Tragedy [BT]*. In *Basic Writings*. Reprinted in part in Ross, *Art and Its Significance*.

——. *Beyond Good and Evil [BGE]*. In *Basic Writings*.

——. *Ecce Homo [EH]*. In *Basic Writings*.

——. *The Gay Science [GS]*. Trans. with comm. Walter Kaufman. New York: Vintage, 1974.

——. *Seventy-Five Aphorisms from Five Volumes [75A]*. In *Basic Writings*. From *Dawn [D]; Gay Science [GS]; Human, All-Too-Human [H]; Mixed Opinions and Maxims [MOM]; The Wanderer and His Shadow [WS]*.

——. *The Portable Nietzsche [PN]*. Ed. and trans. Walter Kaufmann. New York: Viking Press, 1954.

——. *Thus Spake Zarathustra [Z]*. In *Basic Writings*.

——. *Twilight of the Idols [TI]*. In *Portable Nietzsche*.

——. *The Will to Power [WP]*. Ed. Walter Kaufmann. Trans. Robert Hollingdale and Walter Kaufmann. New York: Vintage, 1968.

Nodding, Nel. *Caring: A Feminine Approach to Ethics and Moral Education [C]*. Berkeley: University of California Press, 1984.

Nussbaum, Martha. *The Fragility of Goodness [FG]*. Cambridge: Cambridge University Press, 1986.

Oates, W. J., and E. O'Neill, eds. *The Complete Greek Drama [CGD]*. New York: Random House, 1938.

Owens, Craig. "The Discourse of Others: Feminists and Postmodernism" *[DO]*. Reprinted in Ross, *Art and Its Significance*.

Pagels, Elaine H. "What Became of God the Mother? Conflicting Images of God in Early Christianity" *[WBGM]*. In Christ and Plaskow, *WomenSpirit Rising*.

Parrinder, Geoffrey. *Witchcraft: European and African [WEA]*. London: Faber and Faber, 1970.

Peirce, Charles Sanders. *The Collected Papers of Charles Sanders Peirce [CP]*. 6 vols. Ed. Charles Hartshorne and Paul Weiss. Cambridge, Mass.: Harvard University Press, 1931–35.

——. *The Philosophical Writings of Peirce [PP]*. Ed. Justus Buchler. New York: Dover, 1955.

Plant, Christopher, and Judith Plant, eds. *Green Business: Hope or Hoax? [GB]*. Gabriola Island, BC: New Society Publishers, 1991.

Plant, Judith, ed. *Healing the Wounds: The Power of Ecological Feminism [HW]*. Philadelphia: New Society Publishers, 1989.

Plato. *The Collected Dialogues of Plato [CDP]*. Ed. Edith Hamilton and Huntington Cairns. Princeton: Princeton University Press, 1961. All quotations from Plato are from this edition unless otherwise indicated.

———. *Phaedrus*. Trans. Harold North Fowler. Loeb Classical Library. Cambridge: Harvard University Press, 1914. All Greek passages from *Phaedrus* are from this edition.

———. *Symposium*. Reprinted in part in Ross, *Art and Its Significance*. From *The Dialogues of Plato*. Trans. Benjamin Jowett. 3rd ed. London: Oxford University Press, 1982. All quotations in English from *Symposium* are from this edition.

———. *Symposium*. Trans. W. R. M. Lamb. Loeb Classical Library. Cambridge: Harvard University Press, 1925. All Greek passages from *Symposium* are from this edition.

Rachels, James. "Why Animals Have a Right to Liberty" *[WARL]*. In Regan and Singer, *Animal Rights and Human Obligations*.

Randall, Jr., John Herman. *Aristotle [A]*. New York: Columbia University Press, 1960.

———. *Plato: Dramatist of the Life of Reason [P]*. New York: Columbia University Press, 1970.

Reed, A. W. *Myths and Legends of Australia [MLA]*. Sydney: A. H. and A. W. Reed, 1971.

Regan, Tom. *The Case for Animal Rights [CAR]*. Berkeley: University of California Press, 1983.

Regan, Tom, and Peter Singer. *Animal Rights and Human Obligations [ARHO]*. 2nd ed. Englewood Cliffs: Prentice-Hall, 1989.

Rigterink, Roger J. "Warning: The Surgeon Moralist Has Determined That Claims of Rights Can Be Detrimental to Everyone's Interests" *[W]*. In Cole and Coultrap-McQuin, *Explorations in Feminist Ethics*.

Roach, Catherine. "Loving Your Mother: On the Woman-Nature Relationship" *[LM]*. In Warren, *Hypatia* 6.

Robinson, John Manley. *An Introduction to Early Greek Philosophy [EGP]*. Boston: Houghton Mifflin, 1968. All Greek fragments are quoted from this edition unless otherwise indicated.

Rorty, Richard. *Consequences of Pragmatism [CP]*. Minneapolis: University of Minnesota Press, 1982.

———. "Philosophy in America Today" *[PAT]*. In *Consequences of Pragmatism*.

Ross, Stephen David. *The Gift of Beauty: The Good as Art. [GB]*. Albany: State University of New York Press, 1996.

―――. *Injustice and Restitution: The Ordinance of Time [IR]*. Albany: State University of New York Press, 1993.

―――. *The Limits of Language [LL]*. New York: Fordham University Press, 1993.

―――. *Plenishment in the Earth: An Ethic of Inclusion [PE]*. Albany: State University of New York, 1995.

―――. *The Ring of Representation [RR]*. Albany: State University of New York Press, 1992.

―――. *A Theory of Art: Inexhaustibility by Contrast [TA]*. Albany: State University of New York Press, 1983.

―――. "Translation as Transgression" *[TT] Translation Perspectives* 5. Ed. D. J. Schmidt. Binghamton: Binghamton University, 1990.

Ross, Stephen David, ed. *Art and Its Significance: An Anthology of Aesthetic Theory [AIS]*. 3rd ed. Albany: State University of New York Press, 1994.

Ruch, E. A., and K. C. Anyanwu. *African Philosophy: An Introduction to the Main Philosophical Trends in Contemporary Africa [AP]*. Rome: Catholic Book Agency, 1984.

Sacks, Oliver. *The Man Who Mistook His Wife for a Hat and Other Clinical Tales,* published in four volumes as *Awakenings [A]; A Leg to Stand On [LSO]; The Man Who Mistook His Wife for a Hat and Other Clinical Tales [MMWH];* and *Seeing Voices [SV]*. New York: Quality Paperback Book Club, 1990.

Sallis, John, ed. *Deconstruction in Philosophy: The Texts of Jacques Derrida [DP]*. Chicago: University of Chicago Press, 1987.

Salomon, Charlotte. *Charlotte: Life or Theater?: An Autobiographical Play by Charlotte Salomon [CLT]*. Trans. Leila Vennewitz. Int. Judith Herzberg. New York: Viking Press, 1981.

―――. *Leven? of Theater? Life? or Theatre? [L?T?]*. Int. Judith C. E. Belinfante, Christine Fisher-Defoy, and Ad Petersen. Amsterdam: Joods Historisch Museum, 1992.

Schapiro, Meyer. "The Still Life as a Personal Object" *[SLPO]*. In Marianne H. Simmel, ed., *The Reach of the Mind: Essays in Memory of Kurt Goldstein*. New York: Springer Publishing Company, 1968. Discussed in Derrida, "Restitutions," in *Truth in Painting*.

Scott, Charles E. *The Question of Ethics: Nietzsche, Foucault, Heidegger [QE]*. Bloomington: Indiana University Press, 1990.

Selfe, Lorna. *Nadia: A Case Study of Extraordinary Drawing Ability in an Autistic Child [N]*. New York and London: Harcourt, Brace Jovanovich, 1977.

Sen, Amartya. *"More Than 100 Million Women Are Missing" [MMWM]*. New York *Review of Books* (December 20, 1990).

Sessions, Robert. "Deep Ecology versus Ecofeminism: Healthy Differences or Incompatible Philosophies?" *[DEE]*. In Warren, *Hypatia* 6.

Sheehan, Thomas, ed. *Heidegger, the Man and the Thinker [HMT]*. Chicago: Precedent Publishing, 1981.

Singer, Peter. *Animal Liberation: A New Ethics for Our Treatment of Animals [AL]*. New York: Avon, 1975.

Sini, Carlo. *Images of Truth: From Sign to Symbol [IT]*. Trans. Massimo Verdicchio. New Jersey: Humanities Press, 1993.

Slicer, Deborah. "Your Daughter or Your Dog" *[DD]*. In Warren, *Hypatia* 6.

Sophocles. *Oedipus the King [OK], Antigone [A],* and *Oedipus at Colonus [OC]*. All trans. R. C. Jebb. In Oates and O'Neill, *The Complete Greek Drama*.

Spelman, Elizabeth V. *Inessential Woman: Problems of Exclusion in Feminist Thought [IW]*. Boston: Beacon, 1988.

Spinoza, Benedictus de. *The Collected Works of Spinuza*. Ed. and Trans. Edwin Curley. Corr. ed. Princeton: Princeton University Press, 1988, All quotations from Spinoza are from this edition unless otherwise indicated.

———. *A Political Treatise [PT]*. Trans. and int. R. H. M. Elwes. New York: Dover, 1951.

Stephen, Michele. "Contrasting Images of Power" *[CIP]*. In *Sorcerer and Witch*.

———. "Master of Souls: The Mekeo Sorcerer" *[MS]*. In *Sorcerer and Witch*.

Stephen, Michele, ed. *Sorcerer and Witch in Melanesia [SWM]*. New Brunswick, N.J.: Rutgers University Press, 1987.

Strawson, Peter F. *Individuals: An Essay in Descriptive Metaphysics [I]*. Garden City, N.Y.: Doubleday & Co., 1959.

Sumner, Claude. *The Source of African Philosophy: The Ethiopian Philosophy of Man [SAP]*. Stuttgart: Franz Steiner Verlag Wiesbaden GMBH, 1986.

Swift, Jonathan. *Gulliver's Travels and Other Writings [GT]*. Int. Louis A. Landa. Cambridge: Riverside, 1960.

Tannen, Deborah. *You Just Don't Understand: Women and Men in Conversation [YJDU]*. New York: Ballantine, 1990.

Tarski, Alfred. "The Semantic Conception of Truth" *[SCT]*. *Philosophy and Phenomenological Research*, 4: 341–76 (1944). Reprinted in Linsky, *Semantics and the Philosophy of Language*. All page references to Linsky.

Taylor, Paul. *Respect for Nature: A Theory of Environmental Ethics [RN]*. Princeton: Princeton University Press, 1986.

Theroux, Paul. "Self-Propelled" *[SP]*. In *The New York Times Magazine* (April 25, 1993).

Thomas, Elizabeth Marshall. "Reflections (Lions)" *[L]*. In *The New Yorker* (October 15, 1990).

Tolstoy, Leo. *What Is Art? [WA]*. Reprinted in part in Ross, *Art and Its Significance*.

Trinh, T. Minh-ha *Woman, Native, Other: Writing Postcoloniality and Feminism [WNO]*. Indianapolis: Indiana University Press, 1989.

Valiente, Doreen. *Witchcraft for Tomorrow [WT]*. Custer, Wash.: Phoenix, 1987.

Vattimo, Gianni. *The End of Modernity [EM]*. Trans. J. R. Snyder. Cambridge: Polity Press, 1988.

Warren, Karen J. "Feminism and Ecology: Making Connections" *[FEMC]*. In *Environmental Ethics* 9 (1987).

———. "The Promise and Power of Ecological Feminism" *[PPEF]*. In *Environmental Ethics*, 12 (1990).

Warren, Karen J., ed. *Hypatia* 6, no. 1 (Spring 1991). Special Issue on Ecological Feminism.

Warren, Karen J., and Jim Cheney. "Ecological Feminism and Ecosystem Ecology" *[EFEE]*. In Warren, *Hypatia* 6.

Wenders, William. *Wings of Desire [WD]*. Screenplay by Wenders and Peter Handke. 1988.

Whitehead, Alfred North. *Adventures of Ideas [AI]*. New York: Macmillan, 1933.

———. *Process and Reality [PR]*. Corrected edition. Ed. D. R. Griffin and D. W. Sherburne. New York: Free Press, 1978.

———. *Science in the Modern World [SMW]*. New York: Macmillan, 1925.

Wittgenstein, Ludwig. *The Blue and Brown Books [BB]*. New York: Harper & Row, 1958.

———. *Philosophical Investigations [PI]*. Trans. G. E. M. Anscombe. Oxford: Blackwell, 1963.

———. *Tractatus Logico-Philosophicus [TLP]*. Trans. D. F. Pears and B. F. McGuinnes. London: Routledge & Kegan Paul, 1961.

Wittig, Monique. "The Category of Sex" *[CS]*. In *Straight Mind*.

———. *The Lesbian Body [LB]*. Trans. David Le Vay. Boston: Beacon, 1973. Translation of *Le Corps Lesbien [CL]*. Paris: Minuit, 1973.

———. "The Mark of Gender" *[MG]*. In *Straight Mind*.

———. "One Is Not Born a Woman" *[OBW]*. In *Straight Mind*.

———. "The Straight Mind" *[SM]*. In *Straight Mind*.

———. *The Straight Mind and Other Essays [SME]*. Boston: Beacon, 1992.

Index